**Public Land Ownership:
Frameworks for Evaluation**

Public Land Ownership Conference
York University, Toronto
13-15 November 1976

Conference Committee

Neal A. Roberts, conference chairman
Osgoode Hall Law School

Ann Montgomery, conference coordinator

Dalton Kehoe
Urban Studies Program

H. Ian Macdonald
President, York University

David Morley
Faculty of Environmental Studies

Stuart B. Proudfoot
Faculty of Administrative Studies

For this volume:

Lydia Burton, manuscript editor
Ann Montgomery, administrative coordinator

Public Land Ownership:

Frameworks for Evaluation

A Record of Idea and Debate

Edited by

Dalton Kehoe
David Morley
Stuart B. Proudfoot
Neal A. Roberts
York University
Toronto

Lexington Books
D.C. Heath and Company
Lexington, Massachusetts
Toronto   London

Article 1.1 *Politics, Planning and Land Use* by Enrique Peñalosa is reprinted here with the permission of the author and the United Nations.

Library of Congress Cataloging in Publication Data

Main entry under title:
  Public land ownership.

  Based on a conference held at York University, Toronto, Ont., in Nov. 1975.
  Includes index.
  1. Public lands—Congresses. 2. Land—Congresses. I. Kehoe, Dalton.
HD105.P8   333.1   75-41925
ISBN 0-669-00486-3

Published simultaneously in Canada.

Printed in the United States of America.

International Standard Book Number: 0-669-00486-3

Library of Congress Catalog Card Number: 75-41925

Contents

Acknowledgments / ix

General Introduction / xi

Part One: Principles and Policies

Chapter 1: The Objectives of Public Land Ownership

  Values and Goals / 3

  1.1 *Politics, Planning and Land Use* Enrique Penalosa / 8

  1.2 *Prerequisites for Innovation in Land Management*
       Michel Chevalier and Thomas Burns / 13

  1.3 *The Origins of Urban Land Ownership in Sweden*
       Ants Nuder / 19

  1.4 *Citizen Participation* Chester Hartman / 24

  1.5 *Land as a Life Support System* John Page / 27

  1.6 *A Question of Scale* Jane Jacobs / 30

Chapter 2: Public Land Ownership and Planning

  Policy, Objectives, and Strategy / 35

  2.1 *Implementation Systems in Urban Land Development*
       Edward Logue / 41

  2.2 *A Review of Policy Alternatives* Peter Hall / 46

  2.3 *Critical Perspectives on Public Land Ownership*
       Stanley W. Hamilton / 57

  2.4 *Planning, Development, and Site Value Taxation*
       Hans Blumenfeld / 62

  2.5 *A Legal Perspective on Land Banking in the United States*
       Fred P. Bosselman / 66

  2.6 *Problems of Implementation: An Overview*
       R.W.G. Bryant / 68

Chapter 3: Public Land Ownership and the Management of Resources

Approaches to Land as a Natural Resource
Paul Wilkinson / 83

3.1 *The Urban Natural Environment* Kenneth Hare / 87

3.2 *The Management of Urban Vegetation* John Andresen / 89

3.3 *Agricultural Land Use in Metropolitan Regions*
William Found / 91

3.4 *Recreational Land in Metropolitan Regions*
Paul Wilkinson / 94

3.5 *Land Claims, Energy, and Northern Development*
Grahame Beakhust and Peter Cumming / 97

Part Two: Case Studies

Chapter 4: The Canadian Experience

The Political Institutionalization of Public Land Ownership
/ 105

The Federal Perspective

4.1 *The Federal Management of Land Development* / 112

4.2 *The Central Mortgage and Housing Corporation: Public Land
Ownership Objectives* J.P. Ryan / 114

Provincial Views

4.3 *Ontario's Experience with Public Land Ownership*
John White / 116

4.4 *Evaluating Ontario's Land Storage Program* Neal Roberts /
Neal Roberts / 120

4.5 *The Implementation of Land Policy in British Columbia*
Mary Rawson / 122

Municipal Experience

4.6 *Land Ownership and the Development of a City*
Michael Goldrick / 126

4.7 *The City of Toronto's Use of Public Land Ownership*
Michael Dennis / 129

4.8 *A Township Perspective* William Leathem / 137

4.9 *A Developer's View* Sommer Rumm / 139

A Special Case: The National Capital Region

4.10 *The Origins of the National Capital Commission* Edgar Gallant / 142

4.11 *A Review of NCC Policy* Kevin Garland / 144

Chapter 5: Experience in Developing Countries

Public Land Use Issues in the Third World Patricia Stamp / 149

5.1 *Social Cost Recovery in Housing Programs Using Public Land* Orville F. Grimes, Jr / 153

5.2 *Land Policy and Agricultural Development in Kenya* J. Tait Davis / 157

5.3 *Political Implications of Low-Cost Housing in Kenya* Patricia Stamp / 161

5.4 *Land Reform and Public Land Ownership in Senegal* Francis G. Synder / 166

5.5 *Land Policy in Sri Lanka* Fred W.H. Dawes / 171

5.6 *A Discussion of Public Land in the Third World* Patricia Stamp / 174

5.7 *The Chartwell Notebooks: Two Cautionary Tales on Public Land Ownership in Developing Countries* William A. Doebele / 177

Conclusion

A Review of Idea and Debate: The Social Implications of Public Land Ownership / 195

Index / 203

About the Editors / 213

Acknowledgments

This book is the result of the interest, advice, and direct contribution of many people. The editors sincerely thank all those who, through assistance with the York University Public Land Ownership Conference, and through contributions to the book, helped in its production under the intensive deadline pressure that the schedule demanded. Certain people and organizations must, however, be singled out for their contribution to the production of the book.

The editors are deeply grateful to Ian Macdonald, President of York University, for his continuing encouragement and advice as a member of the planning team for the conference, and for his support in the production of this volume.

We acknowledge with thanks the support provided to the conference by York University, the Canadian Participation Secretariat for the United Nations Conference on Human Settlements (Habitat), the Ontario Secretariat for Habitat, the Canada Council, the City of Toronto, and the Municipality of Metropolitan Toronto. Our thanks also go to the Community Planning Association of Canada (Ontario Division) for their contribution towards the preparation of this volume.

We especially thank Tim Cartwright of the Faculty of Environmental Studies at York University for his incisive criticism and constructive proposals.

We are indebted to Lydia Burton who, by her careful and conscientious editing of the many versions of the manuscript, has integrated the diverse contributions into the final form of this book. Our appreciation and thanks go also to Ann Montgomery, whose efforts as coordinator of the Public Land Ownership Conference contributed greatly to its success.

Finally to our authors, who expressed themselves so forthrightly at the conference and so made the book possible, our grateful thanks. As always, the editors assume complete responsibility for the final result.

York University
Toronto
February 1976

General Introduction

This book explores the current debate on public land ownership from the standpoint of the main actors involved in making decisions with regard to land: politicians, public planners and land managers, civil servants at federal, provincial, and municipal levels, developers and users. Since the statements emerged from a conference forum, they are a presentation of idea and a generation of debate. They are backed by examples, but usually not by detailed empirical analysis. They are a record of the current state of discussion, and reflect the pragmatism of the practitioner as well as the expectations of the theorist or ideologue. Many of the questions raised remain to be answered; in this sense, the book can be viewed as a source for future political arguments, policy analysis, and research projects. The words are those of a unique group of people brought together to define positions and evaluate possibilities.

In more specific terms, the purpose of this book is to provide the reader with a framework with which to examine public land ownership as a means to accomplish social objectives that are related to the use of land. At a time when cities in North America are in a severe financial plight, and when the countryside is facing intense pressure from continued urban growth, existing governmental mechanisms, such as zoning and regulatory schemes, are inadequate to deal with these problems. This volume explores the analytical basis for, and means of achieving, certain land use objectives through government ownership and development, in contrast to government regulation of private ownership and development.

The idea that the government might actually own the land and make the decision as to what is to be developed and what is to be protected from development is one which seems to be gaining currency in a widely dispersed series of settings. It surfaces in a variety of ways; the development of new towns, for instance, is posited on the premise that the government in one form or another would own the land and make the major development decisions. Similarly there is the idea that the government should purchase amenity lands, wetlands, or tidelands in order to protect them from development. It is proposed that the government should assemble and service land in order to augment programs aimed at generating low-income housing. Finally there is the possibility that the government purchase and hold a large supply of development land which can then be serviced and released from these "land banks" at the right time. At the heart of these various schemes is a common set of assumptions: that public ownership would eliminate the delays inherent in the present regulatory systems, would reduce the inequities between landowners who do or do not receive development permission under current systems, and would greatly enhance the ability of central and local governments to coordinate and plan urban and suburban development.

Over the last decade the idea of public ownership as a technique for government activity has, in fact, become accepted in a variety of settings. A number of major western democratic governments have adopted housing or planning policies that have such a concept at their core. Similarly, a number of developing countries have embarked on urbanization programs that use public ownership extensively. What seems to have been missing, however, was a concomitant interest on the part of intellectuals and academics in the urban field to explore this concept. While a large number of books, articles, and conferences have centred on various new regulatory and development control techniques, comparatively little work has been done on the idea of public ownership. This lack of interest has been merely unfortunate for those academics interested in the topic, but it has presented severe problems for government administrators and policy makers who are developing programs based to some extent on the idea that the government should be owning and developing land. For those charged with carrying out such programs, this lack of analysis has meant that they often have had to develop evaluation criteria and variations in a relative vacuum, without the insights available from the analysis of experiences elsewhere.

With this in mind, a group of academics at York University decided, in 1974, that the topic deserved a thorough re-thinking. They set out to commission a series of papers on the topic and then provided a forum at which the various concepts and their relationships might be discussed. It was fortuitous that this development coincided with the preparations for a far larger enterprise concerned with the world's urban built environments— the United Nations Conference on Human Settlements (Habitat), which is to be held in the summer of 1976. Thus, the York University enterprise, which developed into a Public Land Ownership Conference held in November 1975, served as a prototype for the analysis of one topic of many that will be discussed at the Habitat Conference. Indeed, under the auspices of the Canadian Government's Habitat Secretariat, it played a dual role as one of a series of national Habitat Symposia held to generate a Canadian position at the Habitat Conference.

The York Conference attracted over 300 professionals from across Canada and the United States. A better understanding of the new techniques and organizations, and of the changing social and planning philosophies that they encompass, was achieved at the conference. This book consists of some papers prepared for the conference, and the transcribed and reworked informal commentaries that resulted from that event, together with a series of synthesizing essays digesting some of the more important discussions that took place.

The structure of this volume is based on an attempt to establish the major boundaries for discussion and the frameworks for evaluating public land ownership and the application of these frameworks to both the advanced industrial countries and the Third World. Part One consists of three chapters that explore the principles and policies inherent in the idea itself. The first chapter is concerned with the social values and goals underlying any use of ownership to solve various social and land use objectives. The inquiry into objectives is approached by our authors from a number of vantage points. Enrique Penalosa looks at the world view; Chevalier and Burns explore the basis for initiating innovative land systems; and Ants Nuder looks at the development of the idea in one country, Sweden, where perhaps the highest integration of the tool with other forms of land use control has taken place. Following that, both Chester Hartman and Jane Jacobs make convincing pleas to incorporate citizen participation and mechanisms for small, human-scale development into any discussion of public land ownership. Page challenges those who advocate public land ownership to use such power to control the ecological, as well as the social impact of land use.

Chapter two moves to the level of policy making and implementation strategies, and in particular concentrates on how the technique might be used, both to augment urban planning, and to deal more fairly with the creation and division of value in land. The papers here review the state of the art and take tentative "middle-range" positions, representative of most decision making regarding land ownership and land use in North America. Ed Logue begins with a pragmatic discussion concerning when ownership might be a viable alternative. He is followed by Peter Hall's thorough elaboration of various management alternatives, ranging from mere regulation to mixed taxation and ownership, and towards total government ownership. His view concentrates on the advantages and disadvantages of various techniques. Juxtaposed against this is a critique of the same set of alternatives by Stanley Hamilton. Hans Blumenfeld then concentrates on site value taxation in combination with public ownership schemes. Fred Bosselman provides a legal perspective and deals with how such a technique might be developed in the United States. Finally, Ron Bryant deals with the success of public ownership in a variety of urban settings.

The third chapter, organized by Paul Wilkinson, considers public land ownership from a distinctly different viewpoint—the management of land as a natural resource. There is an analysis of the relationship between ownership and the physical support systems in any given land area, followed by a series of essays dealing with ownership and urban ecosystems, agricultural land, recreational land, and finally, the relationship between ownership and Arctic resource development.

After developing this basic framework for evaluation based on objectives, planning, land value, and resource management, the second part of the book considers public land ownership in two specific settings: Canada and the Third World. Chapter four deals with the unique Canadian evolution of the concept where there is a decidedly North American entrepreneurial land development system, but a political climate that encourages a measure of public land ownership. This account is useful not only for the Canadian audience, but also for Canada's neighbour to the south, who has much in common with Canada in terms of land use problems and approach. The chapter is approached from the federal, provincial, and local vantage points, with a series of essays from politicians, administrators, and developers who have actually developed or worked with programs. Finally, the chapter ends with a discussion of the unique use of public ownership to deal with a problem of inter-jurisdictional rivalry in the Canadian national capital region.

The fifth chapter, organized by Patricia Stamp, brings together seven papers associated with public land use and ownership in developing countries. The focus of the discussion is on a number of actual experiences from Kenya, Senegal, and Sri Lanka, and it concludes with a not-so-mythical discussion of two different, possible scenarios of public land ownership by William Doebele. What is most interesting about this chapter is that the framework developed in the first part of the book and demonstrated in action in a developed country in chapter four, is contrasted here with the different nature of ownership and communal public action in non-industrialized countries. Pervading the discussion are the problems of administering such policies, the political tension surrounding land, the social disruption associated with new land policies, and the impact of the international economic system in determining the success of such efforts. In particular, the tension between the efficacy of the economic system and the distribution of land benefits is shown in this setting and appears not substantially different from the same tension between cost and distribution in Canadian cities. In addition, the acceptance of the idea of communally owned land in the Third World is a reminder that private ownership is a relatively recent phenomenon, and that the public alternative has both historic and contemporary precedents.

Finally, the volume concludes with an assessment of public land ownership in theory and practice. Based on the framework developed in the first part of the work and illustrated in the second, we draw some conclusions concerning the social and planning impact of this type of technique, and discuss the means of evaluation that can be brought to bear on programs as they are developed, tested, and reshaped. In the papers, there is little concentration on evaluation methods and criteria that might allow governments to understand whether their new tools are accomplishing the objectives they have set for them. It is disconcerting to observe this lack of clearly articulated evaluatory criteria at this point in the development of the idea of public land ownership.

We hope that this work will provide the reader with a framework for considering an approach that may come to be increasingly important for politicians, planners, and administrators. The ideas should be as useful to highly placed administrators as to citizens in the local community who will see government taking a much more active role in owning and developing land, not merely in regulating and controlling that development.

Part One:
Principles and Policies

1

The Objectives of Public Land Ownership

Values and Goals

The ownership and use of land is the central concern of this book. In many parts of the world, land is owned privately and is treated as a commodity or private good. It is packaged, priced, and exchanged for personal profit. However, this approach to land is linked to problems that are undermining human communities in many countries. Community ownership of land would result in a radical alteration of the basis of current urban social and economic order. Thus, the consideration of revisions in ownership, and of government intervention into the land market is a recurrent theme in this volume.

Concern with private land ownership goes right to the heart of the value system of western societies. The right to own land is seen as the cornerstone of economic life and personal freedom. In fact, until relatively recently, it was land ownership that conferred the political rights of citizenship upon an individual. Land ownership has been and still is the mainstay of individual wealth, social worth, and political influence in a community.

Individual pursuit of these highly valued goals through the ownership and improvement of the value of land has produced both intended benefits and many unintended costs for society as a whole. In recent years, these larger costs have become overwhelmingly apparent in highly urbanized and industrialized societies. Unlike most private goods, the possession and use of land has a unique public or community aspect. The use of one piece of land can vitally affect the value and use of surrounding pieces. Public support for government regulation of the private use of land, chiefly through zoning, is based on this principle. Governmental specification of land use is aimed at maintaining or improving the exchange values of the lands affected. The landowner is expected to accept regulations in exchange for the knowledge that he and his fellow landowners can avoid ill-planned, privately initiated development. Also, the scarcity of land, and thus its market value, often has little to do with the absolute amount of undeveloped land. The accessibility of a given parcel in relation to the land use structure of an urban region, and particularly its location in relation to a city centre, or major subcentres, is critical. Any community effort to improve access immediately increases the value of land that is adjacent,

3

whether the owner has improved it or not. The increase in value accrues to the individual owner. The justice of private gain (and, indeed, private loss) because of public action is central to the analysis of governmental intervention into the land market that is discussed throughout this text.

The strongest statement about the relationship between public and private ownership comes from Penalosa (1.1), who argues for the abolishment of private ownership in urban areas or, at least, for massive public intervention into the market in urban and peri-urban land. Since the private control of land has produced such effects as urban sprawl, segregation by economic class, chaotic urban administration, and the continuing impoverishment of the poor, he sees the need to alter the situation, even though "there is no issue more politically charged and complicated than changes in law and practice governing land use." The issue of land ownership is the fundamental dividing line between private rights and community needs.

Penalosa calls for making a public trust of all urban land (particularly undeveloped land); an end to land speculation; tighter governmental control of land use; and the recognition of the right of every community to acquire control of its land at a reasonable price. These programmatic objectives will support the larger goals of effective planning and social justice that are necessary to ensure that every society provides sufficient land to meet the needs of individual citizens. This right is denied in almost all countries, and the principle of public land ownership can become the basis for governments to act firmly to rectify this situation.

Practical examples of effective large-scale intervention by public authorities into the private land market are available from several countries. Bryant (2.6) provides a number of these in outlining how some cities have been able to develop in a controlled, efficient, and humanely effective way by owning most of their development land and leasing it out to private developers for improvement.

Most conference speakers, however, took a much more restricted view of the problems of private land ownership. For them the concepts of private land ownership and the supporting market system are fundamentally correct, although flawed in their current expression. They assert that public land ownership should be used simply as a tool to manage a land market that is disorderly, but not destructive.

Many speakers emphasized the use of public land ownership to achieve middle-range program objectives like preserving agricultural lands and natural resources, creating new communities, preventing urban sprawl, and controlling housing costs. There was little emphasis on large-scale intervention into the private market and little or no real confrontation of the problems of conflicting social values, of unintended effects, and of hard political choices. This analytical difficulty was side-stepped by defining public land ownership as simply one among many tools for land management that can be applied in a rational exercise of planning. In following this approach in private or public organizations, Chevalier and Burns (1.2) feel that professional planners and managers will be incapable of making any more than marginal changes in whatever situations they are attempting to improve. Substantial innovation in any area, including alteration of the pattern of land ownership, requires radically new perspectives on the part of the various vested interests within a community. Chevalier and Burns say they are not talking of a new perspective opposed to private property as such, but are concerned about the abuse of the rights of private property that may cause hardship and an unjust distribution of resources (or values) in the society.

The difficulty of maintaining such a carefully balanced position is illustrated in Nuder's paper (1.3), where he discusses the communal ownership of land in Swedish towns during the early 19th century. There was a similar early period of communal ownership in the United States. In Sweden, there had been no conflict between public and private interests; the public held all the rights inherent in ownership and returned these to individuals only upon request and negotiation. Moreover, the right to receive unearned increment from the improvement of land was returned to the community through ground rents. Nuder argues that with the transfer of the rights and powers of ownership to the individual, particularly the right to the unearned increment, the case for private ownership is immediately lost. Undesirable social and economic effects on the community were so widespread as to prompt successive attempts by Swedish government in the past 100 years to correct the allocation of ownership rights. Nuder asserts that all these attempts have produced very little change because the value of private ownership itself has never been questioned. If the rights to alter the land, dispose of it, and accrue any value from it are all based on owning the land, then the nature of that ownership cannot be ignored. Private ownership cannot be a "taken-for-granted" good if real improvements in the community are to be made; and yet it has been, Nuder asserts, by every party in power and each commission that has studied the problems of land. The result has been a highly complicated system of regulations wherein discussion of larger social benefits is overshadowed by concern for resolving the technical problems of the control system.

The problem of growing legislative complexity accompanying attempts to solve the difficulties of private land ownership, without alteration of the principle itself, has also been addressed by Hall (2.2) who describes a spectrum of policies relating to the land market that move from right to left in a political sense. Generally speaking, the simplest policies are at each end of the spectrum. That is, policies of non-intervention and North

American-style zoning at the right, and nationalization of land at the left. The simplicity of these policies lies in their complete acceptance of the value of private land ownership or their complete rejection of that value and the rights attached to it. The policies in between these extremes alleviate elements of the land control and use problem but produce complex administrative, legal, and fiscal problems that occupy most contributors to this volume. It is clear that the differences in fundamental values and associated political ideologies inherent in the choice between zoning and full nationalization are largely implicit. They tend not to be addressed, even by those directly concerned with the choice and implementation of such contrasting policies.

Dealing with these more basic issues, Hartman (1.4) explores the possibility that a redistribution of political power and influence in communities might occur if the nature of ownership were changed. A central dilemma in western countries is the imbalance between the ideals of a popularly based, representative democracy and the reality of extraordinary influence on political decision making by the wealthy. This problem has been particularly obvious at the level of local government, where the pressure to protect the right to earn private profit from land is most strong. Hartman asserts that a restructuring of political power and decision making in a community would not necessarily follow from a major shift to public ownership. However, under the conditions he outlines, such a restructuring could be hastened to the benefit of all.

The essential conflict between our private commodity approach to land and the organization of the ecological basis of all life is made clear in the paper by Page (1.5). The act of dividing the land into saleable packages, with accompanying individual rights of usage, is in conflict with the fact that the elements in the natural ecosystem respect no boundaries. In a system of individual ownership rights, how can land be cared for as a complete life support system? Page argues for more than just public ownership, since the concept of ownership itself still reflects the principle of subjugating nature rather than living with it. This assertion is supported by Beakhust's argument (3.5) that our interlocking beliefs in dominance over nature and land as a profitable commodity make it almost impossible for us to deal justly with the land claims of native peoples, even though the land in question is already under public ownership.

Finally, Jane Jacobs, renowned for her critical book, *The Death and Life of Great American Cities*, reacted very negatively to the description of costly complexity characterizing many types of government legislation that endeavour to control city development processes. She felt laws were too complex to be understood even by the well-educated public. "When anything gets as complicated as that, you know it's falling apart. It's been stuck together with baling wire and tape, and that's chaos. The more the attempt is made under these chaotic, jerry-built, ever-more complicated arrangements to save real values for the community, the less financial value there is for the community" (1.6).

Nuder argues that such "chaos" is an almost inevitable result of government efforts to deal with the symptoms of a basic problem without confronting the problem itself. His message is that we cannot have it both ways. Since the work of trying to correct the results of private land ownership has been going on for over 100 years in Sweden, with limited positive results, it is time to reconsider the principle itself. This is essentially what Penalosa is asserting for the rest of the world in his remarks. Most efforts to resolve the problems of land ownership, particularly in urban areas, have tried to protect the principle of private control while trying to cure the problems it produces.

We must look objectively at the value of private ownership in assessing the problems of our communities and our efforts to solve them. If the principle itself is the problem, we must study those cases where it has been set aside in the public interest and the results have been positive. Outright public ownership has the advantage of solving two of the most basic problems in one stroke. It allows government to restrict undesirable development through negative control, and to initiate development that is socially desirable. Further, it solves the perennial land use dilemma of the recapture of the unearned increment attributable to the actions of government rather than to the landowner's productivity. Only through stepping outside our current perspective on land and its ownership will we really be able to re-examine the basis of many of the problems that have plagued modern urban society for so long, and evaluate the role of public land ownership in dealing with them.

1.1 Politics, Planning, and Land Use*

Enrique Penalosa
Secretary General for the United Nations Conference on Human Settlements (Habitat)

A global perspective of the implications of public and private land ownership.

In June of 1976, the Habitat Conference in Vancouver will convene to consider the future of the built environment and the steps that must be taken to deal with its chaotic and unsatisfactory development over the last quarter century. For those of us who have studied and worked in fields relating to these problems, this will be a very special opportunity and should be a source of new hope.

It is my very strong belief that of all the issues before the Habitat Conference the most fundamental will be the use of land, which is the basic resource not only of human settlements, but indeed of life itself. It is on land that we grow our food, build our homes, and declare our nationhood. It is in the use of land that we reflect our cultures and build our prosperity. Yet, because of population growth, we are using up this vital natural resource at an astonishing rate. Every year hundreds of millions of acres are "taken over," by our ever expanding need for homes and other urban uses, and are thereby lost, probably forever, to the production of food and the preservation of open space.

Indeed, the convening of a conference like Habitat amounts to a recognition by the world's governments of a common crisis. And if there is global recognition of a crisis of human settlements—and an urgent need for changes in policies and systems—it must follow that there is a need for change in the way we use our land resources.

Planners have understood the key role of land in human settlements for many years. I think there is a widely held consensus among professionals on how we are misusing our land and even on the direction of required change. I read recently, for example, the final report of a seminar on land use held under United Nations auspices in Madrid just four years ago. The experts at that meeting (and the mountain of documentation supporting them) clearly made every point that I could hope to present. Yet I think we also know that practical steps to implement the recommendations of that meeting have been limited. In the main, and particularly in free market or mixed economies, misguided and even destructive patterns of the past have been continued and often accelerated. The nearly universal agreement of expert opinion has had relatively little effect. The reason, as

*Text of a speech presented to the conference. Edited.

you know, is more than the time lag between planning consensus and political implementation. It is also because in few countries is there an issue more politically charged and complicated than changes in law and practice governing land use.

In our efforts to deal with this problem we must accept that we are confronting a fundamental issue that divides private rights and community need. We must accept that we are dealing with an issue that involves tremendous private economic advantages. And we must recognize that, in Western societies at least, we are trespassing in an area in which private rights have powerful traditional and even constitutional support.

Historically, community need has won out over private greed only slowly, and most often where private interests have been able to gain supplementary economic advantages. For example, public construction of roads has been accepted by community and private developer as useful to both, as has subsurface development for public services; by general agreement, a certain proportion of land is set aside for parks, schools, hospitals, and public buildings.

The nature of the issue today is quite different. Now the issue is control of land for residential use and for open spaces in conditions of rapid population growth and the global process of urbanization. It is not so much a question of control over land already fully in use, but over land needed for the future. Traditionally, in most countries, development of new urban land has been in the hands of the private sector as a commodity of the marketplace, its use either completely uncontrolled or subject to such minor restrictions as to be meaningless. It is equally clear that the use and development of such land has been a major source of private profit.

Let me cite the obvious example of zoning. The value of land, even unserviced land, can be increased five, ten, or even twenty times by a change of zoning from agricultural to industrial or residential use. This is a kind of modern alchemy, in which huge sources of profit and wealth are created at the stroke of a pen. This new wealth, let it be said, can accrue not only to private interests but also to local governments through higher taxes and use charges.

However, it is increasingly evident that the results of this alchemy are not always, or even usually, in the best interests of the community. In the face of such an extraordinary opportunity to create wealth without effort, it is almost inevitable that such considerations as environment, hidden social costs, and future community need will be swept aside.

The consequences of private control are seen everywhere: in wasteful urban sprawl, segregation by economic class, chaotic municipal administration, pollution, and huge public outlays for transportation and other public services. But I would especially like to point to still another consequence of the private ownership of land, and that is the systematic impoverishment of the poor.

In a time of rapid population growth and urban migration, the law of supply and demand applied to land produces an inevitable cost inflation. Rising land value is the greatest device for concentration of wealth in the world today. Uncontrolled pricing is therefore the greatest impediment to the more equal distribution of wealth, which is the pious promise of every society and its economic system.

A further consequence, which every planner is familiar with, is the progressively greater inability of the poor to buy or rent at fair prices the land they need for housing and small industry. The poor are pushed onto land which is the most difficult to service and furthest from opportunity, and which is often physically dangerous.

One has only to visit any city, in a developed or developing country, to see the residential areas of the poor built on easily flooded river banks, on barren hillsides without water, or in smoke filled areas adjacent to industrial activity. These are symbols of injustice that most nations do not even bother to hide. And these conditions are a direct consequence of the treatment of land as a commercial commodity. Without a change of approach, such distortions will increase in the future in direct proportion to population growth.

Now, let me go back to the report of the seminar on land use controls in Madrid four years ago, and the recommendations of the experts assembled there. I think they will not be very far from the views expressed today. For the fact is that all the basic research is complete and the necessary conclusions are already drawn. We know the problems and we know what must be done to solve them. They are no different today than they were in 1971 when the Madrid seminar laid down four central points.

First: all urban land, and particularly land not yet developed, must be viewed as a public trust, and its use must embody principles of social need, environmental safeguards, and the requirements of future generations. I think this is self-evident. That it needs to be said at all is an indictment of our present system.

Second: land speculation is the most serious impediment to optimal development of urban areas and is particularly injurious to the most deprived strata of society. To this I would add an ethical and social consideration. There is *no* justification for enrichment without effort. Since all profit must, in some way, come from effort, unearned profit must come from the efforts of others who are not protected from this exploitation.

Third: control of land use is a prerequisite to effective urban planning; so government should differentiate between land ownership and land use. This is of course at the very heart of planning as a practical science. It is evidenced not only in the benefits of integrated and planned land use, but also in the tremendous social and human costs of the unregulated or largely unregulated systems prevailing today. Among obvious social costs I would mention the laissez faire systems of industrial location, without regard for the responsibility of the community to supply water and electric power, the polluting effects of industrial effluents, and the social cost of housing and transporting the workers involved.

Fourth: public acquisition of private land holdings is a fundamental right of the community. In my view, this does not go far enough. The public right to acquire private land is already widely recognized and accepted. The real issue is the price to be paid. Immediate payment for land in full and at inflated prices is not a reform but a commercial transaction and an onerous one. A speculator cannot be allowed to dictate to a community the price at which he is willing to stop his abuse of that community! Moreover, inflated prices often make purchase impossible because municipal governments are already straining financial resources to provide social services. Thus, municipalities must have the legal right to take over land, now and in the future, at prices within their means.

The debate over forms of payment has already been won in the struggle for agrarian reform in most countries, where compensation has been partial, or in long-term bonds at low interest, or by other devices. A very useful expedient for the protection of future land needs is a land price-freeze; private holders will see no further benefit in speculation, so that the price of land becomes progressively lower due to inflation in other sectors of the economy. This is, of course, a complicated problem, because not all land required by the community will be held by speculators and the small property owner cannot be wilfully deprived of his security. It will be up to each community or nation to differentiate between proper and improper holdings.

The central point is this. The community's theoretical right to expropriate land is useless unless legal and financial tools exist to make it practical. This is the principle of enabling legislation in all areas of government, but it is almost always inadequate for the purpose of land management.

The four considerations emerging from the Madrid seminar are neither new nor revolutionary and, in principle at least, it is difficult to disagree with them. The same points were covered more recently in a paper prepared for the Habitat Secretariat by the International Union of Local Authorities. Yet none of them, to my knowledge, is fully embodied in the laws and practices of any country of the world outside the centrally planned economies. Nor can they be as long as the status of land as a commercial commodity continues.

To these four basic points of land use control and rationalization, I would like to add two others which I think are also basic—one to effective planning and the second to social justice.

The first of these points is the need for planning to be active rather than passive, both at the national and local levels. Because of the operational difficulties of land management, many of which I have touched on, planning for human settlements until now has been too narrow both in terms of space and scope.

At the national level, we must introduce territorial macroplanning based on future needs, especially of population growth and distribution. To create an orderly continuum of village, town, and city; to foster balanced regional development; to coordinate policies among levels of government; and to meet social needs—we must have national policies. Land use guidelines are the first point on the Habitat agenda under recommendations for national action.

At the local level, and in particular in the case of land use, government must stop waiting for the initiative to come from the private developer, for example for rezoning or subdivision. This occurs because governments do not have active and long-term plans for urban growth which stipulate guidelines for the spatial dimensions of land use, which are known and understood far in advance of actual development, and which are supported by public opinion and even public legislation.

I appear to criticize private enterprise, but on the contrary, I believe it can be a tremendous force for good. Throughout the world, it has been shown again and again that government cannot do everything. The built environment today is largely the result of private initiative. What I am saying is that this force must be channeled and regulated, and that this will not happen until government takes the initiative.

The second point is that a societal obligation exists to ensure sufficient land to meet the minimum needs of every citizen, especially for living space. In my view this is a human right which is now almost everywhere denied. A nation is essentially land, or at least land is the most fundamental part of the national patrimony. A citizen, regardless of wealth or station, must have the right to use a tiny portion of the national territory to establish a home for his family. This does not promise where that portion of land shall be located, but it also seems self-evident to me that any land for ordinary residential use must be reasonably close to community services and employment opportunities.

Yet, in most countries, this is not the case, either in practice or in theory. Rural areas in developing countries are full of landless and "superfluous" people. When these people drift to the city, they are called squatters. They are again landless, beginning their new urban lives in insecurity and even illegality.

To a lesser extent the same is true in the industrialized world. In some countries, for example, a man without money or property and no reason to be where he is can be arrested on a charge of vagrancy. The tie between land and citizenship is as old as history. In the early years of most countries, and still today in many, the right to vote is linked to property. Not only does citizenship fail to imply the right to land, but lack of land denies the basic rights of citizenship. This is unjust. With population growth in the years ahead, it will be seen to be unjust by the landless majorities. May I point out to you that the most important single issue in Latin America over the past 300 years has been agrarian reform. In the years ahead, when four out of every five Latin Americans will live in urban surroundings, the issue of *urban* land reform is inevitable. I believe that we must begin to weigh the ramifications of this principle: that some form of urban land ownership or access to shelter is a human right.

These are the kinds of considerations that will be studied at the Habitat Conference. In every country that I have visited in the past year and a half, I have said again and again that solutions to the problems of human settlements are not technical, but political. It will be the response of governments to these challenges—the political will to implement change—that will be the measure of our success or failure in Vancouver and in the years that follow.

This is why I said in my opening words today that this will be a great opportunity. At Habitat, the demands of planning will be weighed in a global forum, at the highest political level. The need for greater control over land use will be a prominent part of that global review. It is for this reason that meetings like this one and all others that take place in the months leading to the conference are so important. In every country, through our personal contacts, our professional associations, through the media, and through political action, we must debate these issues and seek public support. We must make the case that a better environment for all people is not only possible but within our grasp.

1.2 Prerequisites for Innovation in Land Management*

Michel Chevalier
Professor, Faculty of Environmental Studies, York University, and Faculté D'Aménagement, Université de Montréal

Thomas Burns
Research Associate, Faculty of Environmental Studies, York University, and doctoral student, Social Systems Sciences, University of Pennsylvania

A discussion of "marginal" and "substantial" innovation in land management policies in Canada and the role of "network organizations" in achieving substantial innovation.

*Paper submitted by the authors, based on Chevalier's remarks to the conference. Edited.

A significant move toward public land ownership cannot be approached simply as a technical land management problem. Adjustment in established land management techniques and the professions responsible for their administration must be secondary to other more basic technical, professional, and institutional changes. This broader arena of change must be the critical focus of planning concern if we are to consider seriously the prospect and merits of a new pattern of land ownership.

Public land ownership goes beyond mere public ownership for established public purposes. The spectrum with which we are concerned falls roughly between two poles: the complete elimination of private land ownership; and temporary or permanent public ownership (as distinct from regulation) for uses now considered to be in the private domain.[1] Free enterprise in the development and use of land, and in the ownership of improvements, is not at issue in the present discussion, either in an ideological or operational sense. That is to say, free enterprise could be stimulated or constrained regardless of whether land is publicly owned or privately owned. It depends on how the land is managed, not on who owns it. However, the whole question of land ownership (and regulation) is set within an encompassing, ideological perspective[2] of the rights of private property. It is this well-established perspective that handicaps and largely prohibits the exploration and testing of new ways of managing land. And when the established societal perspective of the primacy of private ownership is reinforced by the established structures and processes of decision making in government, then the possibility of change is very slim indeed.

The Canadian Perspective

The national, provincial, and local governments in Canada are virtually locked into a multitude of established patterns of regulation for taxation, planning, development, and use. Compare this frozen state of affairs in land management with rising evidence in Canada of the misuse, distorted use, and spiralling costs of land. Examples are growing speculation (further compounded by massive injections of foreign capital); large-scale manipulation of land markets; rising foreign control of land markets; growing absentee Canadian and foreign ownership of rural and recreational land; increasing concentration of corporate power in the real estate industry; steady loss of prime agricultural land to speculation and development; higher costs, and growing housing shortages; and wasteful patterns of urban development with high long-term as well as immediate price tags. There is increased allocation of government funds to try to patch things up.

Governments have not been wholly unresponsive in other ways. Big Ontario clamps on a land speculation tax. Tiny Prince Edward Island restricts the sale of private land to aliens or non-residents; that legislation is tested in the Supreme Court and is upheld. Provinces in-between take corresponding action of various kinds, or discuss doing so. The federal government, through its Central Mortgage and Housing Corporation, Ministry of State for Urban Affairs, and other agencies points in many directions with many (small) studies and programs. But the dysfunctional pattern of land use spreads and deepens for future generations to live in and pay for. Fortunes are made in land. The clicking, ratchet effect of rising land costs goes on.

This is Canada, with just about as much land and as varied a landscape as any nation on earth. And its land management is among the worst in the western world—scarcely better (and worse in many respects) than its great profligate neighbour to the south, the United States.

The above points highlight some of the weaknesses of the present system of governmental and private management of land in Canada in either foreseeing or adjusting to the multiplicity of forces affecting land development. How, then, to go about transforming the existing land management "system," which rests upon and reinforces an existing perspective of land use in the best interests of the individual, to one reflecting a new land management perspective based on the best interests of the community? How to break through the well-established norms and practices, institutional and legal frameworks and processes which work together to support the status quo? One way is through a transformation in perspective. It must extend across the full range of interests which contribute, through established ways of doing things, to the existing land management perspective we have identified. It must touch on professional practice, politics, public and private land management, and of course on landowners of all kinds.

A New Perspective

The new perspective must replace, first of all, the unquestioned ideological view that private property ownership is in itself "good." Rather, private ownership must come to be seen primarily as useful in achieving other "goods"—for the individual and the community. We are not talking of a new perspective opposed to private property per se, but rather one opposed to the abuse of the rights of private property which causes hardship and an unjust distribution of resources (or values) in the society. This implies more public ownership of land in cases where such abuses are evident, and may be clearly alleviated by means of changes in land ownership and control.

The ideological factor, though significant, is certainly not the only constraint in moving toward a larger share of public land ownership. There are other (not unrelated) changes of equal importance. Among them three particular kinds can be noted:

1) a major restructuring of public organizations which in turn would mean a redistribution of roles in the private sector;
2) a profound reorientation of assumptions and techniques in planning and design, land economics, law, engineering, consulting, and public management generally; and
3) a new form of public information and communication which extends through and integrates policy making and implementation at all levels of government.

It is all three factors—government structure, professional knowledge, and public information processes—which together contribute to the maintenance of a perspective supporting private ownership. Likewise, it is only through a programmed attempt to alter all three factors that a particular community or society is permitted to gain a more open and objective view of the ownership problem. This is a prerequisite to any shift toward a new perspective as a basis for policy intervention.

An attempted shift of this magnitude requires a distinctly different, open-ended planning strategy. The conscious search for new perspectives and the design of policies and programs based on them is a process of *substantial innovation*. It is distinguished from the process of *marginal innovation*, which is characterized by the kind of policy design and implementation done implicitly or explicitly within an established perspective of, say, the public management of privately owned lands.[3]

The distinction between these two classes of innovation has strategic implications. *Marginal innovations*, because they occur within established perspectives, do not require significant realignment of existing institutional relationships (i.e., patterns of activity among interests in a community or society). Marginal innovations can be realized by working through the various planning and decision-making mechanisms now present within and among public and private organizations. In the case of land management, such innovations are achievable within existing patterns of regulation, taxation, planning, and development. The innovation process is thus more focused on technical than institutional planning. It can most often proceed according to a logical, sequential process of selecting and applying means to achieve relatively well-defined ends.

Substantial innovation, on the contrary, does require a realignment of existing institutional relationships into a new pattern based on a shift in perspective which, if it becomes established, results in substantial change in trend. This kind of innovation implies a transformation beyond the adaptive capabilities of any single organization. It is a process of seeking and creating an entirely different perspective around which a new institutional pattern takes form. The substantial innovation process is thus focused on institutional or "constituency-based" planning from which a new perspective emerges. It is based on a strategy which seeks consensus through negotiated design of new problem responses. It cannot be mapped out in advance with the same degree of clarity, because in the beginning at least, ends are not well defined. It requires continual learning and a much higher degree of integration and feedback between planning and implementation.

Because these two kinds of innovation are fundamentally different, they require different planning or policy development strategies. This distinction must become an explicit part of public management, so that it can influence the design of programs concerned with land ownership and management.

Organizing for Substantial Innovation

We have argued that if more widespread public land ownership involves a perspective change of some magnitude, then a substantial rather than marginal innovation process is appropriate. This kind of constituency-based innovation process is one for which existing public (or private) organizations are not well suited. Not only must new functions be created, but quite different institutions are needed to carry out these functions. In particular, a new kind of organization must be formed which specializes in managing this kind of innovation process.

Such an organization belongs to a new class of *network organization*, "concerned with integrating the activities of the networks of organizations in which they are located."[4] Network organizations are beginning to be understood and to be designed with this special integrative, information-processing function in mind. An example of this kind of organization is the National Economic Development Organization in Britain. Certain of its characteristics are apparent in the early "grass roots" style of the planning of government, labour, and management in the Tennessee Valley Authority in the US, and in the joint labour-management Norwegian hydro industrial democracy project. Other examples of network organization are increasingly becoming a focus of social science research.[5] Such organizations are designed to operate in a highly flexible, non-bureaucratic style; they do not have "programs" in the normal sense. Rather they bring together information and interests around common problem concerns, and help in designing complementary activities aimed at resolving aspects of those problems. Sometimes they are temporary organizations, with a lifespan of no more than 3-5 years. They are capable of redesigning themselves and devising new roles according to the integrative needs of the network of organizations in which they operate.

It is organizations of this type which are needed to test and implement new forms of land ownership, and new patterns of land management which support them. Network organizations could be an effective means of designing and experimenting with such things as large-scale land assembly by government for redistribution to private developers—as was done, for example, in post-war Rotterdam by means of land bonds coupled with speculative controls. They could be an equally effective way of managing the development of new information systems, to foster public attention and debate on the potential advantages of alternative forms of land ownership. And they could be employed within and across the land-related professions, to help in reorienting both education and practice in support of broader public ownership. This new kind of organization deserves more careful study, if we are to implement any new forms of land ownership.

It is essential to recognize 1) the depth and scale of the "perspective-shift" transformation needed in this regard, 2) the particular implications this has for the kind of innovation strategy employed, and 3) the unique organizational requirements of a strategy of substantial innovation. If we are unclear or uncertain about any of these points, then we are unlikely to achieve more than a familiar (though perhaps louder) plea for public land ownership, based either on further utopian design or more extensive technical detail. Neither will result in any significant change in the established land ownership perspective nor in the reality it reflects.

Notes

1. A question closely related to the question of public or private ownership is the nature and extent of public regulation which apply to private land holdings. Ownership is not absolute; some rights in respect of that ownership are vested in the Crown. In this sense, ownership is "shared."

2. We use the term perspective to denote a view or "image" (Boulding) of a policy problem or situation. Such a perspective may be "established," that is widely held in a community or society and connected with institutionalized patterns of activity and interest. Or it may be "new," that is not yet widely held or well defined, and not yet reflected in an institutionalized pattern of activity and interest. The notion of perspective, as we employ it, is similar to Kuhn's use of the term "paradigm" in

relation to the advancement of scientific knowledge. See Kenneth Boulding, *The Image: Knowledge in Life and Society* (Ann Arbor, Mich.: University of Michigan Press, Ann Arbor Paperback, 1961) and Thomas Kuhn, *The Structure of Scientific Revolutions*, International Encyclopedia of Unified Science, Vol. 2, no. 2 (Chicago: University of Chicago Press, 1970).

3. The distinction between marginal and substantial innovation has been elaborated in M. Chevalier and T. Burns, "Learning to Manage the Environment," Research Paper for the Environmental Systems Branch, Office of the Science Advisor, Environment Canada, 1974 and *idem*, "A Field Concept of Public Management," paper prepared for the Advanced Concepts Centre, Office of the Science Advisor, Environment Canada, 1975. Similar distinctions between incremental systems change or transformation have been made by J.L. Metcalfe in "Systems Models, Economic Models and the Causal Texture of Organizational Environments: An Approach to Macro-Organizational Management Theory" (*Human Relations* 27 [September 1974]: 639-63) and Edgar Dunn, *Economic and Social Development: A Process of Social Learning* (Baltimore: Johns Hopkins, 1971).

4. J.L. Metcalfe and W.F. McQuillan, "Managing Turbulence: A Design for Economic Development," paper presented at a Conference on Inter-Organizational Networks and Public Policy, International Institute of Management, Berlin, June 1975 (London: London Graduate School of Business Studies, 1975).

5. We recently proposed a form of network organization as the mainstay of a research design strategy for the Institute for Research on Public Policy. This is described in a research report to that Institute, "A Proposed Strategy for Action-Oriented Policy Research" (Chevalier and Burns), September 1975.

1.3 The Origins of Urban Land Ownership in Sweden*

Ants Nuder
Special Advisor to the Minister of Housing and Physical Planning, Stockholm, Sweden

A discussion of the role of allocation policy in the evolution of land ownership in Swedish towns from public to private hands.

Land ownership as a basis for the allocation of the right to build is a relatively novel phenomenon in Sweden, dating from the first half of the

*Extracted and edited from a paper prepared for the conference.

19th century. Before then, private land ownership was unknown in Swedish towns and cities, where land belonged to the individual town or city or to the state. The right to build was accorded by the town or city in keeping with the status of the individual inhabitant. Only those who acquired the freedom of the town in the established manner, thereby becoming burghers and members of the corporation by which the town was governed, could be granted building rights. Persons acquiring building rights had to exercise them within three years, failing which their rights would revert to the town. Mining once used to be connected with land ownership in Sweden, but is now divided according to the share of the individual in the actual discovery of the deposits (the claim-staking system) or else on other grounds established by the state (the concession system).

Until the beginning of the 19th century, urban expansion in Sweden did not involve any conflict of interest between landowners and society, because practically all land in towns and cities belonged to the community, except for the very rare instances where land was conveyed in freehold, above all to the church and the nobility. Thus the question of an urban land policy simply did not arise.

Expansion must have been preceded by the determination of the scope and content of building rights awarded (the land was *planned*) and of the more detailed *design* of the building in question. Since the right to carry out these measures was not apportioned according to land ownership, the question must have arisen as to who was best suited to carry them out. The same applied to the right to exercise building rights, i.e. to *produce* and to *administer* the finished building. Thus the urban regime was confronted with a problem of planning and building policy, namely that of devising a basis on which to allocate the right to plan, to design, to produce, and to administer. The solution adopted in any particular case would of course depend on the values subscribed to by the leaders of a particular town at a particular time.

The value of the building resulting from the exercise of the rights referred to above came to depend on people's willingness to pay to live in a town. How much they were prepared to pay would depend primarily on the general attractiveness of the town, particularly for purposes of trade and the practice of crafts. This level was not the same for all settlements. Thus buildings that were favourably positioned for purposes of trade and handicraft came to be more valuable than other, identical buildings in less favourable locations. An annual payment called ground rent, which was expressed as a percentage of the assessed value of the property, was retained by the town.

Because the attractiveness of a town and areas within the town was subject to constant change, both positive and negative, people's willingness to pay also varied. The town adjusted ground rents to these changes by revising assessed property values every three years. In this way the prospects of an individual property owner reaping annual gains from a rise in the willingness of other people to pay for their living when the attractiveness of the town increased were greatly reduced. The scope available for capitalizing on a future rise in willingness to pay when selling the property was also greatly circumscribed. Thus there was no need for capital gains taxation in the present sense of the term, because that portion of any future increase in people's willingness to pay which was connected with the actions taken by the town constantly reverted to those responsible for the changes, i.e. the town. Negative changes also affected the town, through the medium of falling revenues. However, this liability, expressed in revised ground rents, did not always exclusively affect the town. Particularly in the early middle ages, falling revenues could be shared between the town and the state. It is worth mentioning in passing that the town also had something of a right of first refusal and pre-emption when properties came up for sale, and also that there were regulations forbidding a burgher to own more houses than he personally had use for.

Freehold purchase of communal land in towns and cities was already gaining acceptance in Sweden by the end of the 18th century, under the influence of the liberal doctrine of the virtues of full and free ownership. This doctrine was inspired by Roman law, in which land ownership is characterized by individual and absolute title. To begin with, however, freehold purchase was restricted to burghers, but beginning in 1810, the right to acquire buildings and land was extended to practically any citizen. The freehold purchase price came to be fixed by means of an advance payment (a capitalization) of the estimated future ground rent. The right of pre-emption previously enjoyed by the town was gradually eliminated during the middle and the second half of the 19th century.

Freehold purchase was considered to confer upon the proprietor the perpetual right to avail himself of future changes in people's willingness to pay occurring in response to public action. At the same time, the proprietor also became entitled to determine the scope and content of the building right to be exercised on the land he had purchased freehold. It also became his right to determine the more detailed design of the building, to erect the building, and to administer it after it had been completed. These rights (planning, product determination, production and product administration, and benefits from changes in people's willingness to pay for living in the town) could also be sold together with the actual land.

As a result of these changes, land in towns was placed on a level with land elsewhere, in terms of ownership. The powers of the community were

·reduced, while the powers of a limited number of citizens (the urban proprietors) were considerably increased. At the same time as the community relinquished its former powers of controlling social construction, it also transferred to these proprietors the right to that portion of people's increased willingness to pay (accrued value) which was connected with the action by the community. An allocation of wealth occurred in favour of the proprietors and they became entitled to trade (speculate) freely in this accrued value. Almost immediately, the allocation thus established on the basis of a philosophy of absolute ownership proved to have undesirable social and economic effects on social construction. Society was thereby prompted to make successive attempts to correct the allocation structure.

There are basically two ways of looking at these corrections, depending on one's values. *One way*, which for example is still the main approach adopted by Swedish law, is based on the fundamental conviction of the sovereign right of the proprietor to plan the use of his land, determine the product, produce and administer, and also to pocket the accrued value in its entirety. Seen in these terms, corrections will of course invariably be interpreted as reduction of the rights of land ownership. *The other way* of looking at the corrections is to see them as a reaction against an allocation principle which has been detrimental to the interests of a majority of the population. Corrections are then to be regarded as an attempt to revert to a system conferring greater influence on the community, the aim being to improve the prospects of rational and responsible social construction without leaving any scope for speculative reallocations resulting, among other things, in unjust accumulations of individual wealth. Seen in these terms, the corrections that proprietors regard as reductions of their rights appear as expansions of the rights of non-propertied urban populations.

The development of the allocation of mining rights presents an instructive example of a more goal-oriented discussion of this kind. The values enshrined in current Swedish legislation preclude the acquisition of mining rights through the acquisition of land, because mining rights are not allocated according to proprietary title. As has already been explained, mining rights were once geared to land ownership. However, the abolition of this basis of allocation was not achieved by means of land acquisition or land nationalization. Instead it was founded on a discussion of allocation which led to a reallocation of mining rights from landowners to prospectors and the state.

None of the myriad of commissions set up in Sweden during the past 100 years to study these matters has ever queried the assumption that land ownership is the foundation on which the rights of planning, product determination, production, administration, and accrued value are to be allocated. This is remarkable in a way, since the commissions were set up—at different times and under different regimes—to rectify the consequences of this very principle. These repeated corrections have resulted in a highly complicated system. The system itself has come to incorporate so many technical problems that the analysis of the reallocation effect of corrective measures has been increasingly overshadowed by more or less separate discussions of marginal technical problems.

Corrective efforts concerning allocation of the rights associated with land ownership are made through legislation for planning, building and restrictive practices, and allocation of accrued values. Certain measures of correction will quite naturally affect more than one field of legislation. For instance, site leasehold includes elements referring both to the allocation of planning rights and to the allocation of the right to accrued value. Different terms of ownership cause administration to comprise an administrative service of a productive character and also a basis on which accrued value can be apportioned, for instance, between landlord and tenant.

In those countries subscribing to the fundamental principle that the rights of planning, product determination, production, and administration, as well as the right to accrued value, should primarily be allocated in terms of land ownership, discussions of allocation centre around the general concept of land policy. Because this policy is to be regarded as the result of a series of constant corrections to the original basis of land ownership allocation, the term land policy has come to denote a combination, unique to every country, of a series of technical solutions.

These repeated corrections of the status of land ownership have led to the creation of systems which, after each new correction, have tended to become more and more complicated. Thus, the effects of new corrective measures have become increasingly difficult, not to say impossible, to predict. A great deal of public investigation has had to be devoted to various adjustments of technical detail, often occasioned by previous corrections, while considerations of a more long-term nature have had to take second place. In Sweden, for example, this work of correction has been going on more or less continuously ever since land ownership in our towns and cities began to be de-collectivized in the 19th century. It is therefore only natural to wonder whether more objectively chosen premises—involving for example detaching from all forms of ownership, the rights of planning, product determination, production, and administration, and the right to accrued value—may not have to be adopted in discussing the complex laws now governing legal relationships in connection with land use.

1.4 Citizen Participation*

Chester Hartman
Author and urbanologist, San Francisco, California

A plea for incorporating the issue of citizen access to the planning process into any discussion of public land ownership.

Citizen access to and participation in the planning process are major issues in the US, as well as in Canada. But they are generally not seen as issues central to discussions of public land ownership and control.

Let me state at the outset that I strongly favour far greater public ownership and control of land than we now have in the US or in Canada. But at the same time I see the possible and dangerous illusion that by itself public ownership/control is *the* answer. It is by no means certain that this development would result in greater public access to and participation in the land use planning process, something I consider absolutely essential to a good society. Frankly, planners worry me: their values, their notion of professionalism, their view of their clientele, their frequent arrogance. More planning, even by government officials rather than the corporate power elite, does not necessarily mean better planning, in terms of either results or process. The scale question raised by Jane Jacobs is crucial. Wherever possible, we must bring these planning and control decisions down to the level of those whose lives are most intimately affected by such decisions. And that means widespread and meaningful participation by plan-ees—something not very many planners I know of feel comfortable with. Participation and democratic planning of this type are an essential element of human dignity and community.

A general discussion of the principles of more widespread public participation in and control of land use planning can best be structured using the following four categories of land suggested by Logue [see 2.1].

1 *Undeveloped land that is to remain undeveloped.* In order to carry out public policy with regard to this category of land, the maximum degree of public control and/or ownership will be required. Widespread public participation in the planning process will, however, be minimal, since the set of interests affected by such decisions is diffuse and poorly organized. The primary participatory role, beyond official planners and decision makers, should be played by conservation and recreation organizations, many of which have a large membership and support basis, although the degree of direct "passionate" involvement by most members is small. Other participants may be "no growth" advocates and their opposite number, developers' and builders' organizations.

*Paper submitted by author, based on his remarks to the conference. Edited.

2 *Undeveloped land that is to be developed.* This will almost always be in areas adjacent to existing uses, most often residential, since one of the primary purposes of sound development planning is to avoid uneconomic "leapfrogging." It is in this type of planning that the "planner-knows-best" syndrome is most likely to be found. Although there obviously are important regional considerations to such planning decisions, central representation must also be given to those in adjacent areas whose lives will be directly affected by these development projects. Only in this way can a proper balance be achieved between broader development needs and the rights, needs, and desires of abutting communities. This must be seen not as merely a review or advisory role, which all too often turns out to be window dressing or a meaningless stamp of approval. (In an increasing number of cases this has become a stamp of disapproval, often in the form of litigation. While this oppositional tool is frequently necessary and advisable, it can also have ancillary effects that are destructive to the overall public interest and even to the litigants themselves. Establishing a proper and timely planning role for all affected parties will reduce the need for and likelihood of litigation.) A wide range of representative groups from adjacent and affected areas should be brought into the development planning process from the outset, as full participants. To enable these groups to perform their role properly, it will be necessary to provide them with adequate staff and resources to hire consultants and advisors in planning and other disciplines, and in some cases to provide funds to reimburse participants for the time they devote to this process and incidental expenses (such as childcare). Input by these groups can only result in a better development plan, responsive to legitimate interests, and one which produces a development pattern more integrated with and organically related to the existing environment.

3 *Land to be redeveloped.* This and the next land category, unlike the first two categories, involve existing uses, usually residential, and thus present a more compelling case for participation. But US experience in this area demonstrates irrefutably that public ownership does not necessarily lead to more and better public participation in the planning process. Under our urban renewal program, a local public agency acquires land and then disposes of it for redevelopment according to the agency's plan (which has been approved by the local governing body). It is a program that has been widely and justly criticized for ignoring citizen participation in deciding which areas are to be redeveloped and what the reuse plan will be. Rather, such agencies have been largely representative of and responsive to a very narrow segment of local interest groups, primarily the downtown business community and its drive for commercial revitalization (which has often meant kicking poor people out of potentially valuable land and using eminent domain powers and public subsidies for the benefit of those least

in need of such aids). The program has not concentrated on meeting the cities' most pressing social needs; nor has it endeavoured to bring about the most efficient use of land; it has not been concerned with minimizing or eliminating the negative effects of the redevelopment process on those displaced and otherwise adversely affected by planning decisions and their implementation. These biases and directions have not been inadvertent, due merely to oversight in failing to include a wider set of interests in the redevelopment planning process. They stem from the uses to which the program and its government apparatus have been put by a coalition of powerful urban interests, with the redevelopment agencies as their allies. So broadening the planning process is intimately tied to the political question of who redevelopment is for and what its goals are. Participatory planning, structured in from the outset, then would be a means of bringing about change in redevelopment priorities. But if it is to be allowed and encouraged, it also presupposes a willingness to change these priorities, and that will usually involve political struggle. The result of such a change may be a vastly different agenda regarding what parts of the urban area will be redeveloped, what the reuse plans will be, and the treatment of those displaced by redevelopment. As with category 2, it will be necessary to furnish adequate resources to citizen groups so that they can participate as equals with public planners in the redevelopment planning process, with their own professional advisors and staff.

4 *Land on which nothing is to be done except possible rehabilitation.* For this category of land it is necessary to develop participation mechanisms that can insure that public control and/or ownership results in a set of improvements and incremental change that meets the needs of existing occupants and permits change and growth in an acceptable and satisfactory fashion. Such actions as removal or improvement of blighted conditions, provision of municipal services and construction/renovation of community facilities, as well as the overall responsiveness of public officials, are best facilitated through local representative planning bodies. Various neighbourhood government proposals, put forth by local planning councils, neighbourhood corporations, and so forth, would seem the ideal vehicle for decentralizing many areas of urban decision making. It is in already built-up areas that local needs and desires, as expressed through democratically selected representatives of the neighbourhood community, most need to be seen as a central (and at present missing) element in the planning process. Outside planners—with no direct knowledge of or commitment to the area they are planning for—simply must not dominate in such situations. Those with a stake in the area should be calling the shots, within whatever legitimate financing and other constraints must be imposed by broader public policy.

More generally, the relationship between participation and power must be acknowledged. Public ownership and control of land is one means of redistributing political and economic power and the patterns of who benefits and who loses from the development process. Structuring in a real participation process of the type outlined can help hasten this redistribution, which in my view ought to be the central goal of the planning process. Within the framework of this over-riding goal we should be as concerned with the process by which the goal is reached. Real participatory planning is itself empowerment, and without it the end of redistributive justice will come about more slowly, with greater (although often hidden) conflict, and perhaps not at all.

1.5 Land as a Life Support System*

John Page
Professor, Faculty of Environmental Studies, York University

A challenge to regard land as the "framework" for a life support system of almost infinite variety and complexity, rather than as a commodity to be exploited.

If "life support system" replaces the word "land" in land ownership, it results in a new way of thinking about the issue of public ownership. It has been traditional to think about ownership of land as the ownership of a "commodity" or a "resource." This way of conceptualizing "land" is inappropriate today because of increased understanding of the "life support system" of the planet upon which all life depends. It is not a matter of securing life by owning land (except in a very narrow sense), but rather of having limited rights of use over intricately related components of life organisms and their physical setting. For example, the water that falls on land in the form of rain or snow and runs off or percolates into the soil is part of the life support system. The way in which this water acts is a function of what else is happening on the land. If there is tree cover and a well-developed humus cover, the water that falls is scattered and soaks into the ground; part of it runs off slowly into streams and their tributaries, or it keeps soaking down into the underground aquifers to replenish underground water supplies. Water is not just a commodity any more than is the land; its journey onto and into the ground depends upon what is happening to the land. When we live in cities paved over with concrete, asphalt, buildings, and well-worn pathways, we tend to think of water as a

*Paper prepared for conference workshop. Edited.

nuisance. But the quality of the land depends upon what happens to the water that runs off into sewer drains. Many tons of "land" get carried off each year if the land is not held together by vegetation of some kind suited to the terrain and soil quality.

With these kinds of connections in mind, it might be more accurate for us to address the problem of "public control of life support systems," rather than public ownership of land. We are then faced with the notion of one kind of life form—human—wanting to, attempting to, or thinking it has a right to, control the activity of other forms of life. So long as we hold to the notion of land as commodity or resource this embarrassing conflict does not appear.

Considerations of land ownership have historical roots that make it very difficult for us to take account of land as a life support system. When Europeans came to settle Ontario, surveyors were brought along to lay out land plots for assignment to settlers. The methods of laying out lots were based on Euclidean geometry, convenience of doing the job in the field (setting boundary stakes, etc.), describing the parcel of land in legal terminology, and providing a convenient sized parcel to facilitate the calculation of prices and exchange values in the marketplace. But for all practical purposes, it was assumed that the surface of the ground was as homogeneous as the paper upon which the diagrams were drawn to show the plots of land, their numbering, their assignment to settlers, and allotments for church, school, or public purposes. Whether there was a stream running through a property, whether it was covered with trees or grass or water was unknown until the settler made discovery by trekking out to his "property." All trading and commerce about land since then has been in terms of lot numbers in certain concessions of certain townships or certain counties. Further dividing of land into smaller parcels always had to include reference to the legal identity of the parcel of land.

Today, we are confronted literally with a contradiction of interests when we attempt to shift our way of conceptualizing "land" in its various manifestations. If we look at a map of southern Ontario, say from the Oak Ridges Moraine south to Lake Ontario in the Toronto Centred Region, we see a strong contrast between the layout of these legal parcels of land (whether 10-acre lots or 100-acre farms) and the natural lay of the land with its clear pattern of stream and river valleys running south from the highest point of the morain down to the lake. Each set of lines, the legal boundaries and the stream courses, disregard the other. The slope of the land does not influence the shape of the land parcel. When we examine the vegetative covering of the land, we see some fitting of agricultural cropping to the legal boundaries, while the tree patterns and random greenery relate to the stream and river alignments. Two different systems of relating to the land are obvious.

Are we talking about ownership of one of these systems—the legal parcels of land? If so, then we are dealing with a package of rights that our culture has associated with land ownership. But how, then, does this package of rights relate to the other system—the implied relationship to the life of other species who also inhabit the land, who have worked out a very delicate (and yet basic to life) support system? These other life forms have worked for millenia to establish themselves in this part of the world. Do they have any place in our considerations? After all we cannot say cavalierly that they do not count when we know that our survival depends upon their survival.

I have raised this issue, not for the sake of philosophizing about land ownership, but because it is a very real problem, one which has come out of a workshop with students in the Faculty of Environmental Studies at York University dealing with the Central Ontario Lakeshore Urban Complex (COLUC) structure plan (published in 1975). In our efforts to develop alternative approaches to the plan, we discovered that a "biocentric approach" to the planning of this region was highly desirable and probably necessary if we are serious about having human and other life forms thriving in this region a hundred or more years from now. We say this with some confidence because so many indicators suggest that at the rate at which land is being exchanged, and changed in its use, the life support system presently provided by nature will have suffered much serious deterioration; the artificial life support system of relentless urban spread will have lost its natural support basis. The region is already a net importer of food; not many decades hence it will be ever more dependent on outside food sources. The "land," which offers fertility for food production, will have vanished irretrievably. Once the soil has been turned under or washed away, it is gone and only the work of soil-building organisms over centuries can restore it.

One of the elements of the COLUC structure plan was the notion of a "parkway belt"—essentially a mile-wide utility corridor with some green or open spaces provided. Public land acquisition figured largely in the development of the parkway concept which would link up with the Niagara Escarpment and Lake Ontario. In our reconsideration of the life support needs of the region, it seemed that more innovative approaches were needed to realize the potential of the parkway belt concept. A very basic element of an innovative approach turns out to be the consideration of "public ownership of land." Given the aerial extent of the parkway, a vast amount of land is involved. Even for the basic functions envisaged as a utility corridor with interspersed recreation areas, even with encouragement of continued farming operations mentioned in the Parkway Belt Act, a vast public investment would be necessary.

If land ownership becomes a misnomer when we see "land" as a life support system, then how ought we to ask questions about "public ownership of land" in relation to the Parkway Belt? If "land" is really a systemically relating array of life organisms, then "land ownership" is faced with handling the question of how landowners deal with other forms of life. The title to any parcel of land in this southern Ontario region assigns "ownership" or "control" to humans through a legal system defining land boundaries. But we now know that various life forms (varying in size from micro-organic bacteria to large mammals) do not confine their individual or collective activities to any legally defined piece of "land." Thus, the very concept of land ownership becomes ante-deluvian when we come to understand "land" as a living life support system made up of countless living creatures who have laboured for millenia to bring a cooperative enterprise to its present stage of evolution. This system survives, despite the sustained destructive efforts of so many Europeans in this area for nearly 200 years.

The notion of considering "public ownership of land" for the sake of achieving some "public interest" or goal reflects an assumed arrogance of humans over other life forms. Some fundamental reconsideration is clearly necessary beyond the concept of ownership of land as a commodity or resource.

1.6 A Question of Scale*

Jane Jacobs
Student of the city

A critique of large-scale planning for public or private ownership.

I think most people in planning and development fields hold an underlying assumption that large-scale planning and development is a good thing. In fact, that's the only real meaning behind this question of public versus private ownership and I am going to quarrel with this underlying assumption. I don't care whether large-scale planning is under public or private ownership. You can't tell the difference anyway. When you see them, they're all done the same. The same people do them, in fact.

We seem to think there is something economically inevitable or progressive or sacrosanct about large-scale planning and development. However, this sort of thinking is really a step backwards. The time has passed when this sort of thing can be done. I would like to remind you that the large-scale planning and development of company towns is an old

*Remarks to the conference. Edited.

thing. In fact, all feudal arrangements are large-scale in planning and management and always have been. However, large-scale planning and development in urban areas and in subdivisions is not very old in Canada and not much older in the United States, from which Canada has copied these things.

It took a great deal of rearrangement, new instruments, rigging of all kinds, to make large land assemblies possible and to make them preferable to finance. Or in other words, to make small-scale development difficult to finance, difficult to get approvals for, and handicapped in every possible way. The suburban subdivision, which we now call sprawl, one of the things that all these instruments made possible, only dates back to 1928. The prototype of it was built in Cleveland by the Rockefeller family, which was then headed by John D. Rockefeller, Jr. It was not a success for one reason, so *Fortune Magazine* said in describing it. There was no way to get to it except by automobile. It was a dream of what subdivisions should be, of what should be done on the edge of cities. It didn't work. The FHA and all kinds of other arrangements were set up (including ultimately great subsidization of highways) to make it feasible. There is nothing in nature that makes these sprawls, these large-scale subdivisions, feasible. Nor is there anything in nature that makes the highrise, the other form of large-scale development, feasible either. It's all done by the various "instruments." Now the instruments are apparently going to be used for something called medium-density housing. This will also, I am sure, be done on a large scale. It will be just as dull, just as unsatisfactory, and will have all kinds of problems built into it.

What is wrong with large-scale building, large-scale planning, and large-scale land assemblies? For one thing, they have an inherent low quality to them. Quality comes out of caring. You cannot get this kind of caring, a density of caring in things that are planned, managed, thought up, envisioned by the strange sub-human thing called a team or a committee. You can only get this from a great many different people, with different ideas, different thoughts, different and passionate carings. There is a lack of ingenuity that goes with large-scale land assembly and planning. It doesn't require ingenuity; the clean slate never requires ingenuity. We need difficulties to bring out ingenuity. Nothing is duller than a clean slate except what goes on the clean slate.

A strange thing has been happening to our cities since we accepted, and made easy, these large-scale arrangements. One of the glories, advantages, and deficiencies of cities and towns, even villages, in the past, has been the ease with which edifices originally erected for one purpose, could be converted to others. We call it recycling. In small-scale building, with all its quiddities and quirks, recycling is very simple—if not of every building in an area, then of many buildings in an area. Under our large-scale arrangements now, whether publicly or privately owned, publicly or privately assembled, it is very difficult to recycle buildings—and in fact, this is the whole idea. If you are going to have comprehensive, controlling, long-term, thoughtful planning, you know what you want and it's going to be fixed there so it can't be anything else. Right? So, you're stuck with it.

There are attempts to make large-scale developments diverse, interesting, and quirky. I saw one of these in New York. I was particularly interested in seeing it because someone had written that it was a Jane Jacobs kind of project, whatever that means. Well, it sure isn't. I can see what the idea was—to try and look unregimented—but, you know, you can't do that in an artificial way. It looks like a stage set. It has a phony diversity. There is no way to get real diversity without a real diversity of ideas, and that means a real diversity of separate people, not teams.

All this large-scale planning and development is expensive. Land banking in itself, whether done by a private developer or by private speculators, or by the public, is inherently very expensive and very wasteful. It means that whatever is already there, whether it's parking lots or buildings that are being used, is going to have to run down. It cannot have natural things added in the interstices that might have happened in the meantime. It's going to have to decline in real use and real value until it's ready for the new scheme, or else it's going to have to lie fallow for quite a while. This is a terribly destructive process. It was one of the most destructive things that went on in urban renewal planning and in slum clearance. I can't see how it's not going to be equally destructive in what is now to be called land banking.

A city is a living organism. You cannot just cut off a finger here and a leg there and say, "get along without that now until we're ready to supply you with a new, artificial limb." The only person who has touched on this problem, which I think is far more serious than public or private ownership, was Mr Hamilton, when he mentioned Vancouver and its 19 character areas [2.3]. He questioned whether these areas would exist now if there had been public land ownership earlier in Vancouver. No, and they would not have existed if there had been large-scale private ownership, either. It was because there was a great deal of small-scale ownership (both public and private) in Vancouver while these areas were being built up, that they exist at all today.

Large-scale ownership and arrangements for it are so unsuitable to cities that it is all coming apart nowadays. It's not the wave of the future. We have public taxation laws and others that cannot possibly be understood by the public, even the well-educated public, unless they are going to make themselves experts in these arcane things. When anything gets as complicated as that, you know it's falling apart. It's been stuck together with baling wire and tape, and that's chaos. The more the attempt is made under these chaotic, jerry-built, ever-more complicated arrangements to save real values for the community, the less financial value there is for the community. That's what's happening in Britain. It's not a question of who's getting the division of what; it's that it is disappearing.

We find in America that these projects, whether they are privately owned like the real estate investment trusts, or whether they are publicly financed and sponsored and done as a mixed private and public thing like the UDC, are not financially successful. They are all running into very bad financial trouble.

Finally, we can see from the feelings of the public that these large-scale developments are coming apart. People do not like them. Hardly a kind word is ever said nowadays for any highrise buildings, publicly or privately owned, or for urban sprawl. I would suggest that the real question we need to examine is how do we find out what are the riggings that make large-scale ownership so easy to finance and acquire, and that make small-scale ownership so difficult. What were the arrangements that made this possible? How can we begin to negate them and get things back to a more human, more diverse, and financially more sound level? What new ideas can we think of to keep ownership spread in as small packages as possible for the purposes, whether public or private? I don't have much hope that people are really going to address themselves to this. I imagine that most of you come from bureaucratic institutions of one sort or another and that their very reason for existing, in many cases, is to work out or maintain systems of large-scale power rather than to disperse power. Ownership of land, believe me—whether it's public or private—is power.

Public Land Ownership and Planning

Policy, Objectives, and Strategy

The concept of public land ownership can be considered analogous to the ubiquitous "black box" so familiar to social scientists. That is, the concept is used as a general catch-all for a myriad of approaches to problems allegedly arising from the operations of the contemporary land market. It is only by opening the black box, and by examining more closely its contents, that we can assess public land ownership as a potential solution to land use problems.

In Canada and elsewhere, public land ownership is more than a concept; it is a fact. All three levels of government and other public authorities in Canada own substantial amounts of land. However, in many instances such ownership has been a result of more or less unique circumstances with ad hoc decisions being made in each case. In the context of this volume, public land ownership means something more; it implies the acceptance of public land ownership as a legitimate weapon in the policy maker's arsenal, alongside such devices as zoning, taxation, and expropriation.

As continued debate demonstrates, the present system of land use management is inadequate. But what exactly are the criticisms of the present system that lead to proposals for public land ownership and other innovative policy initiatives? While different countries respond in different ways, the criticisms giving rise to political action (extant, proposed, or merely contemplated) appear to take two separate but related forms. First, there is the criticism that the "distribution of benefits" from current methods of urban and other growth and development are inequitable. This criticism centres around the issue of the "unearned increment," which is the appreciation in land values due primarily to various kinds of public activity rather than to improvement by owners of the land. It is argued that the wealth thus created ought to accrue to the community at large, and not to individual property owners, since it was not due to productive activity on their part. This criticism is, of course, not a new one. Henry George devoted considerable attention to the question nearly a hundred years ago in *Progress and Poverty* and other works. What is interesting is that the debate concerning the "unearned increment" remains timely. The second major criticism of current land management "practices" is based on considerations of planning. This criticism has three components: first, that current methods (in North America, basically the market plus zoning) are inadequate to ensure that lands possessing special characteristics in terms of agricultural capability, ecological fragility, unique landscape, or recreational potential, are protected. Secondly, that present practices usually result in piecemeal development when more comprehensive approaches are clearly demanded; and finally, it is argued that prevailing management routines are too time-consuming and costly.

While the papers in this chapter would appear to indicate a general recognition of the problems associated with present land use methods, there is considerably less agreement concerning what to do about it. In part this stems from ideological differences. In North America, particularly the United States, private land ownership is valued very highly. The political feasibility, for instance, of substantially greater participation by governments in the operations of the land market in the United States would appear low at this time.

Ironically, Ann Louise Strong of the University of Pennsylvania, in remarks made to the conference, noted that land ownership by the public in the United States is in fact widespread. For example, over 40% of total US land is publicly owned; this figure rises to 90% in the State of Nevada. Furthermore, the concept of public land ownership is not a new idea in the American context; as Professor Strong points out, "The pattern of settlement in many early New England towns included the village common, cultivated land which sometimes was zoned in common, sometimes zoned privately, and . . . pasture land and the woods. The only privately held land was the land on which people had their houses, their barns, and their gardens. So, [we] . . . started out with owning of most land in common." This tradition extended to urban areas as well. New York City owned over half the land in the city in 1645. Strong recounts that "they set the land out in a checkerboard fashion and [they] sold every other checker and kept the rest. The city-owned land was out on fairly short-term lease on the assumption that the land was going to rise in value fast enough that they could keep renegotiating their leases and have a handsome income for the city. For about 200 years, New York City didn't need to levy a real estate tax because they gained a sufficient income from their own leased land." What brought this advantageous situation to an end was not an ideological back-lash against public land ownership, but financial stringency. The city needed funds to complete the Croton Aqueduct and sold its property to do so.

Yet in the United States today, there is little question that public land ownership is considered an ideological issue. The papers in this section by Logue and Bosselman make reference to ideological difficulties in proposing a greater public role in land use management in the United States. Strong mentioned that in the US public land ownership is often identified with communism. In Canada, for reasons stemming mostly from the historical role played by government in the economic development of the nation, there appears to be a wider definition of what is considered an appropriate governmental role in economic activity with respect to land (but certainly not only land). Therefore, the prospects for a more aggressive government role and stronger management schemes appear to be relatively greater in Canada than in the United States. The Canadians represented in this chapter indicate that the reluctance concerning public land ownership as a solution to the problems of land use management in Canada stems primarily (not solely) from doubts about the technical feasibility of the various proposed techniques, rather than from ideology.

In order to assess public land ownership as a solution to the problems of land use management, it is necessary at the outset to define objectives. Logue (2.1) argues that stronger public powers, including ownership, are appropriate in four broad land use situations. The first instance concerns land that should be retained in its present use in agriculture or forest. We can probably assume that he would also include in this category land of special ecological fragility and the like. In this situation, there is no need for public ownership; the police powers are sufficient. Second is land to be developed, primarily that on the urban fringe; control is what matters here and ownership itself is unnecessary. Public acquisition is required in the third category—land that should be redeveloped. In this instance, Logue asserts that development to a more intensive use by the private sector does not often "put the public interest very far ahead." In such cases, he suggests that public land ownership is an appropriate policy tool. Finally, there is land that should be retained essentially in its present state, but "with the opportunity for modification." This point is not elaborated. Logue's remarks reflect the perspective of the practitioner's disdain of ideology as a factor in land use management. "Whenever you get unnecessary ideological baggage you just have to carry it along [but] it doesn't help you at all."

Hall (2.2) argues that the objectives of a revised land management system spring directly from a recognition of the inadequacies of the present system. Thus, our objectives might be a more equitable distribution of the benefits of land development and improved land use planning. What is not clear is whether public ownership is necessary to achieve these objectives. As Hall points out, if the objective is simply to recapture the "unearned increment" for the public benefit then various taxation devices including the "betterment levy" will probably suffice. This was the approach taken in the British 1967 Land Commission Act. The critics of present practices argue, however, that if planning objectives are also sought, some degree of actual public ownership seems to be required. Public land ownership, then, can be seen not as an end in itself, but a means—a strategy whose appropriateness depends upon the objectives sought.

Hall makes a major pedagogical contribution in laying out clearly and concisely the range of policy devices available to achieve either planning or equity objectives, or both. Among the alternative proposals considered are the following:

1. Laissez-faire (the "Houston model").
2. North American zoning (police powers).
3. A betterment tax.
4. Site value rating.
5. Temporary pooling and reallocation of landholdings (Lex Adickes).
6. Unification of development rights (the British 1947 scheme).
7. Widespread state or city purchase (Sweden).
8. Permanent transfer of development land: to local or central authority (the British 1967 and 1975 solutions).
9. Unification of the reversion.
10. Total nationalization.

Finally, after an evaluation of the various techniques, he draws some conclusions that will be of interest to academics and policy makers on both sides of the Atlantic.

Hamilton (2.3) is considerably less sanguine about the alleged benefits of public land ownership schemes. While agreeing that it is essential that the objectives of any public ownership program be clearly spelled out, he contends that several of the policy devices, short of full-scale land nationalization, are merely preludes to eventual public land ownership. He argues that these interim policies are proposed by public ownership advocates simply because they realize that the real goal is too costly to reach, financially and politically. Much of Hamilton's argument rests on the grounds that nothing further can be derived from the conditions written into a leasehold contract that cannot be achieved through existing police powers. While he agrees that the unearned increment does in fact exist and should accrue to the community at large, he cautions that the measurement of such value is a very difficult problem. The unearned increment issue is not solved by public land ownership; it is merely shifted to the "micro" level. The tenant on Crown-owned land would still seek (and equity would demand) recompense for that portion of the increase in rent resulting from his private decisions and capital commitment.

As for the planning claims made on behalf of public land ownership, Hamilton counters that the critical assembly problem would not be overcome, but merely altered. Tenants would have leases of different terms; consequently the process of putting together "properties" of different tenants (while no doubt within the powers of the landlord) would involve substantial administrative and probably political costs. Finally, Hamilton asks if planning benefits of public land ownership are to be realized through positive covenants in a Crown lease, couldn't the same objectives be achieved at less cost by purchasing the covenants rather than by taking ownership outright?

Blumenfeld (2.4) argues that land planning and land control are self-defeating under a system of private ownership. Like Hall, he contends that planning benefits, in terms of the ability to develop in a comprehensive fashion, accrue from public ownership schemes. In addition, he notes that the powers of expropriation at the hands of public authorities make it easier to deal with "holdouts." The public as developer has certain advantages over the private developer in terms of economic efficiency. For instance, Blumenfeld suggests that public authorities can borrow money more cheaply, thus incurring lower carrying charges in the financing of a project. He takes strong issue with existing methods of real estate taxation, arguing that the tax on improvements has the effect of discouraging this worthwhile activity. Instead, he proposes a greatly increased level of site value taxation balanced against a lowered (or eliminated) tax on improvements. As well as encouraging the "full" development of land, he suggests that a high site value tax would make it impossible for a private developer to buy land long in advance, and hold it. This would make public land assembly virtually a necessity.

Bosselman (2.5) discusses the evolution of the American Law Institute's Model Land Development Code, which proposed a method for state governments to engage in public land banking. The recommendation came as somewhat of a surprise, for the Institute is generally regarded as a conservative body. However, the endorsement of an idea by an expert body is a long way from political acceptability and implementation; and there is little evidence that public land ownership in the United States is at that stage. The main interest thus far in land banking appears to derive from the desire to preserve prime agricultural land. While the Institute recognizes that land banking can provide other planning advantages such as large-scale development, there is no mention of "equity" considerations. Constitutional obstacles, not present in parliamentary democracies, are also formidable. In addition, the extreme fragmentation of governmental units in American metropolitan areas raises the possibility that land banking could be used as a technique to exclude poor people or other "undesirables" from the community. This concern led the Institute to recommend that state governments rather than local governments be the agencies in charge. But, Bosselman correctly points out that exclusionary practices are currently carried out by local governments in the United States under the zoning powers; land banking would perhaps simply make it easier. In contrast, the greater centralization of decision-making power in Canadian urban areas probably precludes or severely limits this problem.

Bryant (2.6) deals with the experiences of several cities in Europe and Australia that have public land ownership programs. He also examines the operations of the Saskatoon land management program, which interestingly does not yet appear to have had much effect on policy making in Canada. One thrust of Bryant's paper is that there are many examples of successful public land ownership schemes in operation, and some aspects of these programs are relevant in the Canadian context. He uses the operation of the Amsterdam leasehold system to define the results of a successful public land management program: 1) speculation in land can hardly exist; 2) the citizens and the building industry have confidence that land will be available without profiteering, and that leases are not going to be terminated capriciously, or without good and over-riding reasons of public interest; and 3) the city has far better control over its development than could be afforded by any amount of zoning or other statutory land use control.

Bryant's second major point is that the legal basis for public land ownership schemes is well-founded in Canada. Both English and French law recognize property rights as a "bundle," composed of separate components. This notion, of course, formed the basis of the Uthwatt Report in the UK wherein it was proposed that development rights in land be separated from the right to enjoy its use in its present state. The concept is also at the heart of the transfer of development rights proposals gaining currency in the United States. Bryant argues in favour of leasehold over freehold systems because the public authority involved retains ultimate control of the land.

One major conclusion emerges from the various discussions in this chapter. The problems associated with current methods of land use management are widely recognized. The techniques for dealing with those problems are available, and there is considerable experience with their implementation in actual situations. In most countries there is a legal basis for public ownership. What appears to be missing is the political will to implement this tool.

2.1 Implementation Systems in Urban Land Development*

Edward Logue
Commission on Critical Choices for Americans, New York; former President, New York State Urban Development Corporation

A discussion of the role of public land ownership as a means of helping implement programs of urban development, with special reference to four broad categories of land.

This conference is being held because there is a sense, among many people, that neither the ordinary operations of private enterprise nor of public enterprise are doing what is needed to assure the proper development of Canada, and more particularly its significant urban areas. Nevertheless, I believe it's a mistake to be overly ideological about public land ownership or for that matter, about almost any other aspect of housing, community development, urban growth, or national land use policies.

For 30 years in the United States we had an ideological commitment to low-rent public housing—despite the clear and overwhelming evidence that it was an unsuccessful program which was unpopular, which was not meeting needs, and increasingly could not win local acceptance except in the hearts of ghettos. Yet an ideological commitment kept that program alive 10 years after it had seriously started to fail the people it was intended to serve. Similarly, the Soviet Union has boasted of its ability to have effective state planning. But 50 years ago Moscow flatly determined to have 3 million people; right after the war it was 5 million. Now they will tell you with equal certitude that it's going to be 8 million. What will it be 10 years from now?

Another example of ideology concerns Japan, which has perhaps the worst urban sprawl problem anywhere in the world, certainly in the developed world. The urban sprawl problem is more intractable there than anywhere. I suspect it goes back to Douglas MacArthur and the creation of the most effective rural land reform program I know about anywhere in the world. It put ownership and control of land in very small landholdings and abolished any kind of large-scale landholding. It thus gave an immediate political base to any kind of opposition toward efforts at undertaking public ownership of land on a large scale. I doubt that this conference could take place in Japan.

Another example of ideology comes from the UK where there is a commitment to the idea that new towns are a very important part of the solution to the urban growth problem. To the extent that they've been built, I think new towns have been helpful. But after 30 years, one has to

*Remarks to the conference. Edited.

say that the actual population increment that has been taken care of in the United Kingdom by new towns is very small and relatively insignificant. Similarly, going over to the other extreme, many people have long held the view in the United States that unfettered private enterprise, the right of private people to make private decisions about private property is the only proper thing. Yet the strip development that one can see outside any American city proves the hazards of holding to that kind of principle.

These matters of urban growth and community development are far too complicated and too varied to have simple doctrinal solutions. Public ownership of land can be a very effective lever in achieving goals, but to set it up as an objective in itself is silly and in North America, fruitless. First, we need to try to establish a process for defining objectives, a continuing and flexible but effective process. For example, if one labours to substitute human-scale housing for out-of-place highrise housing in a neighbourhood, then there should be a continuing interest in, and responsibility for, some kind of a follow-through system. The systems for implementation, and this is the thrust of what I have to say, are terribly important, but there is no one true path. Conditions vary from community to community and from time to time, and so do circumstances. In the matter of land there are objectives on which it is possible to get a consensus without too much difficulty. Perhaps because of the relative absence of an equivalent race problem, it is easier to get a consensus in Canada than in the United States.

I think we could all agree that we want to protect good agricultural land, watersheds, and land that has visual significance; thus, the concept of maintaining open space has considerable value and support. I think we also want to try to renew or assist in the rehabilitation of blighted land. Since we have not achieved an effective zero growth policy or practice, we need also to try to calculate how much land we are going to need for the growth that we cannot avoid, and the price that we can afford to pay for it. A lot of people do not want to face the reality that in the United States for instance, there will be 50 million more people in the next 25 years; that's a good deal more than twice Canada's present population. Such growth has to be accommodated; there is no way of preventing that population from being there. This means that for guidance and as a kind of baseline, we need a comprehensive plan of land use and a program for management of land use changes—not just old-fashioned land use plans or social policy planning (which has become fashionable in the United States as a lazy alternative to serious physical planning). There is a role here for all of the various levels of government: an overseer role at the national level, a financial role at the provincial level, and an implementation role at the metropolitan and perhaps municipal level. And I believe strongly, as well, that there should be a significant role for private enterprise.

I have long admired the British "planning permission" system. I am somewhat surprised that this idea does not have more support in the United States, particularly from those who want to keep things as they are, stop change, or at least establish an early warning system. That's the function of the planning permission system, which basically means that nothing of any significance whatsoever can be done in England without a public say-so. However, when one looks at the actual operation of that system in London, one wonders whether it is not perhaps one of the reasons why there is less economic dynamism there than one might have otherwise expected. When we have sorted out plans and priorities, it is quite clear that public ownership will quickly emerge as a very useful tool.

I should like to focus briefly on four broad categories of land in areas with an urban core, and on problems of implementation with respect to them particularly with reference to the role of public ownership. *First, there is land which is not to be developed* or is to be retained in present low-density use, primarily say, agricultural or forest. It seems to me that this land should be controlled only as to use, or change of use, by zoning or other planning permission controls, and without compensation for the loss of freedom to change its use. That is, I would assert, constitutional in the United States, and I should think it would be in Canada as well. But, on the other hand, we would have to recognize that if we are limiting the freedom or potential freedom to change use, we must value land accordingly for property tax purposes. If that's a valid category of land, then no public ownership is required and no compensation is required. The fundamental problem created is that basically this is a denial of prospective windfall, something which is very appealing to real estate speculators of which Canada and the United States have such an abundance. Speculation is also part of your ethos and ours, going back to George Washington or even earlier in the States. Perhaps the time has come to put that notion behind us, because if we are going to use public ownership, we damned well have got to limit speculation. Public land ownership should not be used indiscriminately; it should be used only where it is most necessary— and it is clearly not necessary for basically rural land which does not need to be developed.

The *second category involves land to be developed*. We need to identify the land that's to be developed, to plan for it, and acquire or control it as soon as possible. It's my understanding that in Canada the pattern is that the land on the developing periphery tends to be held by relatively few people. Some would immediately suggest that we convert that land to public ownership. But it's also possible that if you're dealing with a relatively small number of people, you can make other kinds of arrangements to protect public interest which do not need to magnify direct public administrative responsibility. More good public ideas have fallen victim to Parkinson's Law than to any other law I can think of. We must be sure that the supply of land to be developed and available in appropriate ways and serviced appropriately is ahead of any immediate need. This is the case in Stockholm, but the pattern in Canada and the United States is exactly the reverse. That's a basic reason for price levels. We have to make sure, somehow or other, that we get ahead of that growth instead of being behind it as we are now. The problems in doing this are very serious. It means large amounts of public money and very large-scale direct public intervention. It could mean a very sharp reduction in private initiative, which from one point of view might be very desirable but from another might not. The alternative to this direct public ownership is quite strict land use planning which tends to have to overdo the controls in order to achieve the same results.

The *third category is land that should be redeveloped*. In that category belong lands which are blighted, or slums. You seem to have relatively fewer slums in Canada, but clearly if you did not have the intensity of land redevelopment in downtown Toronto as you have today, you simply would not have had the kind of vitality that this city is now world famous for. It's a by-product, whether you like it or not, of those highrise office buildings and those highrise apartments. Public acquisition is often quite the best way of assuring that redevelopment to more intensive use takes place in ways which maximize the public interest. Private acquisition for more intensive redevelopment often does not put the public interest very far forward. Competent planning can very easily establish where these lands are to be and what the priority in redeveloping them should be. The problems are the same: significant costs, very large-scale direct public intervention, and (if you do too much of that) perhaps a sharp reduction in private initiative.

I will avoid, other than to mention it, any discussion of the question of whether the land, once publicly owned, should be held permanently or whether it should be resold. In the long run this basically ideological notion, which has been put forward to me over 20 years, doesn't make a damned bit of difference in actuality. Whenever you get unnecessary ideological baggage, that's something you just have to carry along, which doesn't help you at all.

The *fourth category is land that in its present use should be retained more or less as it is*, but with the opportunity for modification. Subject to some mechanism for protecting the public interest, we're going to be a lot better off with as much private initiative and private incentive as we can maintain. We have large-scale urban problems which will yield only to large-scale solutions and we have small-scale problems which shouldn't be obscured by large-scale solutions. I can't think of anybody, for example, going into Harlem in New York City with a small-scale solution and maintaining that it was going to make a significant difference.

I am sure that this analysis will strike many of you as simplistic, but using these points as a guide, it is possible to design an implementation system to carry them out in almost any metropolitan area. Priorities have to be defined and there should be a recognition that most land does not need to pass through public ownership. But a screening process is essential, so that we concentrate on the kinds of public ownership that really may be urgently needed.

When we design systems of implementation, there are some essential ingredients that may not be universal, but which are useful guidelines for analyzing potential and existing systems. *First* is an implementation system based on a comprehensive approach, with clear goal-setting, and with an acknowledgement of the values to be served. It's fine to redistribute wealth, but trying to redistribute it through an urban development system seems to me to burden two difficult objectives with each other, again a case of unnecessary ideological baggage. *Second*, in such a comprehensive approach; it is necessary to calculate and arrange for an adequate financial system. *Third*, there has to be an integrated administrative system. This is probably more relevant in the United States than here. The administrative systems by which cities attempt to redevelop or renew themselves are very important. It should be a concentrated and integrated system, rather than a one with divided authority and responsibility. *Fourth*, there must be a competent, well-paid, non-political staff. *Fifth*, there should be administrative leadership, since it is an illusion that a coordinating committee can make it work.

An implementation system must have political leadership because without it schemes wind up on the shelf. Behind that political leadership it is necessary to have some measure of civic support and particularly citizen involvement. The evidence is that without citizen support, the political leadership doesn't stay around very long. Rather than concentrating on technical aspects of implementing comprehensive efforts to deal with urban development problems, it is first important to identify the key social and potential elements and see whether you have them or not. Most American cities—I would say about 98%—couldn't get a passing grade on this kind of analysis. How about Canadian cities?

2.2 A Review of Policy Alternatives*

Peter Hall
Professor, Department of Geography, University of Reading, England

A discussion of different techniques for public land management, ranging from zoning to full-scale nationalization, in the light of achieving both efficiency and equity in planning.

The organizers of this conference, in inviting a British academic associated with the genesis of the Community Land Act, may well have expected a contribution dealing with the "pro" rather than the "con" of public land ownership. But I wish to claim the privilege of surveying the policy field rather more widely and rather more dispassionately. I want to base this paper on the theme of What, then How? What aims exactly does a community want to achieve in its land policy? And how does it best achieve these aims?

The Objectives of Land Policy

A voluminous literature on the subject seems to agree that there are two quite different aims, or groups of aims. The first is concerned with better planning of land use and urban development. The second is concerned with the enjoyment of the added value that comes from development. The two should be considered separately; then, any connections between them may be traced.

Planning. There are very few communities in the advanced industrial world today that allow complete laissez-faire in the use of land. All of them must control dangerous or noxious land uses, and all must regulate standards of building, including maintenance of public health and safety. Most go further: they entrust to local authorities the making of plans for the development of land, and the enforcement of controls over the type and the intensity of land use, generally (but not invariably) in conformity with the plans. In Great Britain, these controls are exercised by local authorities under the powers conveyed to them by the Town and Country Planning Acts from 1947 onwards, which in effect nationalize the right to develop land. In North America they take the general form of zoning under police powers, which needs no specific intervention by central government and consequently entails no compensation for refusal of a permission to develop; but by the same token, these powers are limited,

*Paper prepared for the conference.

and a number of test cases seem to have definitely established that they cannot deprive an owner of the right to develop his land in some way or another. Thus green belt policies to restrain urban growth, which have been effectively applied in Britain since the mid-1950s, would appear to be virtually impossible under current North American zoning ordinances. Indeed, in a study of Houston (Texas), which is unusual in having no zoning, Siegen (1970)[1] has concluded that in practice private covenants achieve much the same effect. Zoning is thus a fairly minimal form of control, and in consequence has been much criticized by planners.

The first criticism is that it is simply ineffectual: as already noticed, it cannot reserve land that is potentially or actually valuable—whether for agriculture or recreation or ecological protection, or simply as landscape—against development. One might argue that the market should be able to achieve such protection, if the community sufficiently desired the end to will the means. But as economists well know, this begs important questions of externalities and changing time preferences. Similarly, market forces plus zoning frequently seem incapable of ensuring adequate comprehensive redevelopment of central and inner city locations; the exceptions, Toronto and Montréal notable among them, merely prove the general rule. Associated with this is a general argument: that for what they do manage to achieve, zoning and similar controls are extremely costly both in monetary resources and in time. And lastly, these controls lead to potential conflicts within the local authority, which may be tempted to support a development that is bad on planning grounds simply because it yields valuable local tax revenue, even though it may destroy an historic neighbourhood, valuable buildings, and a well-knit community.

The aims of land policy in the interests of good planning are by definition obverses of the present deficiencies. First, land policy should achieve positive planning; it should make it possible for local authorities to achieve the aims of good land use planning without the need to compromise because of the high cost of land. It should make comprehensive redevelopment easier, where such development is thought right on planning grounds, through the possibility of easier site assembly. It should simplify and expedite planning processes. And it should ensure that planning is not compromised by notions of enhancing the local tax base.

Enjoyment of value. The most important deficiency in the present system from a fiscal viewpoint, as is only too well-known, is its failure to collect betterment except in very special cases. Betterment is here defined in its widest sense to include not merely increases in land value arising from positive communal action (through public works such as sewerage schemes, highway schemes, or rapid transit lines), which are occasionally collectable by the community under existing legislation, but more germanely from the exercise of negative restrictions on development. Thus, if a local community prohibits development on one area of land, but allows development on another (as in Britain it may), it creates substantial gains for the owner of the second plot, which appear legitimately to belong in large measure (if not entirely) to the community. And the same argument applies, though, of course, on a more limited scale, to the more restricted powers available to local communities under North American zoning ordinances.

The failure to collect betterment is the principal defect alleged against existing arrangements; but three further consequences follow. The first is that there is inequity between individual landowners, since one may gain a great deal and another nothing; and this may create intolerable moral pressure on those officials responsible for decisions. The second is that the cost of land is raised for essential public services (for instance roads, sewerage, or schools), often for those very public authorities whose actions have created the enhanced values. The third is that the very process may encourage unhealthy speculation in land. On this point there is much dissension, since rapid rises in land values have occurred during the last 30 years alike in countries with strict land use control systems (such as Britain) and in those with weaker controls (such as Japan).

The aims of land policy in the interest of fiscal equity are again the obverse of the presently observed deficiencies. First, land policy should include arrangements for the collection of betterment for the public authorities whose actions have created (or helped to create) it. Secondly, and relatedly, it should reduce the costs of public purchase (whether voluntarily or compulsorily) of land required for communal purposes. Thirdly, it should establish equity between individuals, in that all landowners should be treated alike when they sell or develop land. Fourthly, insofar as this is possible through fiscal measures of this kind, it should try to eliminate or at least reduce inflation in land and property costs. Of these objectives, it would appear that for most commentators the first and second appear to be the most important; indeed, in most countries a wide spectrum of political opinion now seems to accept them as proper objects of policy.

The outstanding general point that emerges from this analysis is that the planning arguments and the fiscal equity arguments are to a considerable degree independent. In particular, it is possible to achieve the fiscal objectives by various means which, however, do not meet the planning objectives, so that these latter would be ignored, or alternatively would need to be assured in other ways. This is important to keep in mind in considering a systematic analysis of alternative solutions.

Alternative Solutions: (A) Mainly Fiscal

Betterment Levy. Essentially, in whatever form, this is a special form of capital gains tax, which may be charged either as an alternative to such a tax, or as a special supplement to it. It is usually at a higher rate than general capital gains tax, reflecting the notion that betterment is created by the community and should be returned to it. It can be charged on actually realized gains, either at sale or the point of development, or both. It may also be charged on unrealized gains, so long as they are realizable, as the British Uthwatt Committee recommended in 1942. Though there is a perfect case in equity for this, it presents great political difficulties in implementation. Any betterment levy requires accurate sales records which distinguish the value of the site alone from the value of any building on it; similarly it requires a revaluation at the point of development. A tax on unrealized gains, as the Uthwatt Committee recognized, would demand regular total revaluation of all sites in the country, which could be coupled with general revaluation for local property tax or rates.

Britain offers particularly interesting case studies here, since it has introduced such a levy three times in the last 30 years and is just (1976) about to do so again. One important question is the rate that is charged. In the regulations made under the 1947 Town and Country Planning Act, the so-called Development Charge was fixed at 100 per cent of the increase in value; the justification for this was that it was part of a general nationalization of development rights and development values, for which compensation was payable. The 1967 Land Commission Act introduced a betterment levy of 40 per cent rising to 45 and then to 50 per cent; in the long run it might have risen even higher, but the Act was repealed in 1970. The Development Gains Tax introduced in 1974 is based on income tax rates and thus varies from 35 to 83 per cent, depending on the marginal tax bracket of the landowner. The Development Land Tax, which is proposed to replace it in 1976, will be charged at a flat rate of 80 per cent, but this is coupled with a scheme which in effect again transfers the responsibility of land development to the community. Closely associated with the rate is the question of when the levy is charged. Generally it is levied whenever land changes hands, and also at the point of development.

Many such schemes provide for specific exemptions, often for admittedly political purposes. Owner-occupiers of single houses are frequently exempt, as are public authorities and charities (including universities and similar bodies). Most schemes do not provide for "worsement"—the rare case (at least in modern society) where land values may decline due to public action, as with a decision to build a noisy or noxious piece of infrastructure near an existing community. Some countries have independent legislation to deal with such cases, e.g. the British provisions in the Land Compensation Act 1973. Most do not provide for taxation of unrealized gains, even though owners may enjoy indirect benefit from these (for instance in their power to raise mortgages).

The advocates of betterment levies argue that they will deal perfectly well with the financial equity problem without the need for more elaborate measures, such as public land ownership. Certainly they can recoup much of the development gain for the community and also reduce the cost of land purchases by public authorities through the simple device of exempting these bodies from the levy. But, unaccompanied by other supportive measures, such as public land ownership, they may present problems. The British evidence is that at least in the short run, they may cause sales resistance among landowners, which dries up the land market in expectation of early repeal—as was certainly the case in Britain between 1947 and 1951 and again between 1967 and 1970. At least, this seems to be the effect in times when the land market is sluggish. In more buoyant times, the risk is that the levy may be paid twice—first to the developer, then to the public authority. To guard against these dangers, widespread compulsory purchase may be necessary, and this is equivalent to public ownership at least on a partial scale.

Site Value Rating. This can be seen in essence as a variant on betterment levy, since it places an annual property tax on all land based on the value of the land alone. As the price of land rises in anticipation of development, so does the rate or tax—not on a once-for-all basis, but annually. Over a long period, there is no reason why site value rating should not yield precisely the same revenue as a betterment levy; but the pattern over time is somewhat different, since by definition site value rating yields more slowly over a longer period of time. As illustration:

Year	Value of land per hectare	Betterment Levy (50 percent of increase)	Site Value Rate (20 percent of value annually)
1	$ 5,000	–	$ 1,000
2	$ 10,000	$ 2,500	$ 2,000
3	$ 50,000	$20,000	$10,000
4	$100,000	$25,000	$20,000
5	$100,000	–	$20,000
	Total Yield (5 years)	$47,500	$53,000

Like a betterment levy on unrealized gains, site value rating requires regular revaluation of all sites; it may, therefore, be expensive administratively. Because by definition it is charged on value whether realized or not, it presses constantly on the owner and consequently acts as a permanent incentive to develop up to the highest and best use of the land. (In this regard, it has almost the opposite effect to the betterment levy, which may actually inhibit development.) It can be argued that site value rating could encourage development contrary to good planning, and indeed it seems to find a natural home in areas of the world having a free attitude to development (as, traditionally, in Australia). But against this, it is claimed that it is useful in persuading developers not to hoard land.

At any rate, site value rating "cuts the Gordian knot," in the words the 1942 Uthwatt Committee applied to betterment levy; it collects increments in land value of all kinds, whether they arise from planning controls or public works or general urban growth. And it does specifically allow for "worsement." The difficulty is to know how it can work in a system where the site values are basically fixed by the action of planners or zoners. For the existence of site value rating could easily cause local authorities to try to zone as much land as possible for development, in the hope of collecting extra revenue. In this sense, though site value rating may be an effective if arbitrary fiscal device, it is difficult to see that it could ever serve planning objectives.

Alternative Solutions: (B) Mainly Planning

Temporary Pooling. This in essence is a purely administrative device to secure comprehensive redevelopment, or at least comprehensive reorganization. The eighteenth-century Parliamentary Enclosure Acts, which fenced the medieval open fields and created a whole new landscape of separate farms, are perhaps the best example. The German Lex Adickes, named for the Burgermeister of Frankfurt-am-Main, is another. In all such schemes, owners pool their rights of ownership, which are then added and redistributed according to some law of equity. It achieves no other purpose in itself, though it may readily be coupled with some form of taxation of betterment levied at the point of pooling, or even with acquisition by a public authority of a stake in the equity. Unless something like this is done, it will still lead to public authorities losing the betterment they have helped create, and even to their having to pay inflated values for public acquisitions of land.

Nationalization of Development Rights. This was the essence of the ingenious solution embodied in Britain's 1947 Town and Country Planning

Act. Instead of nationalizing land itself, which would have been quite politically unacceptable, this Act nationalized merely that part of the title to land which consisted in the right to develop it. Thus the owner could remain in complete possession of the land in its existing use. But the right to develop was transferred to the community, and for this compensation was payable. (Originally all these claims were to be paid simultaneously from a global fund, representing the assessed value of all development rights in the country scaled down to eliminate duplicate claims; but this was replaced by a piecemeal approach.) After compensation was paid (or payable), all interest in development value, logically, reverted to the state.

The state then in effect transferred the development rights to local planning authorities, to whom application must be made for any proposed development or redevelopment outside fairly narrowly defined limits of tolerance. These authorities could refuse permission on the ground that the proposed development did not conform to their development plan, or for a great variety of other reasons. Though appeals against a refusal were allowed (to an appeal tribunal, not a court) this was an administrative, not a judicial process, and the relevant central government minister had the last word. This, of course, is the vital difference between the British and North American systems of land use control, which allows British authorities to prohibit urban development and thus to contain urban areas by green belts or other devices; and it has survived unchanged for over a quarter-century.

There was, however, another important element in the 1947 Act. Since all development value reverted to the state, the state would collect it. If permission to develop were granted, this would be on condition that the developer paid a development charge equal to a proportion of the resultant change in value. Under regulations made subsequently this charge was fixed at 100 per cent of the increase, though it could in theory have been any proportion. This was thus a betterment levy tied to the nationalization of development rights, and as we have already noted it had the effect of drying up the land market. The original expectation seems to have been that the market was not required to work; compulsory purchase on a wide scale (at existing use value) would be the usual rule. But the incoming Conservative government repealed this part of the Act in 1963-4. Later (in 1969), to rectify a resulting anomaly, they specified that compulsory purchase by public authorities should be at market value, not existing use value. This has broadly been the situation ever since, with the complication of forms of betterment levy between 1967 and 1970 and from 1973.

In fact, the situation in Britain after the introduction of the 1973 levy is similar to that which many experts advocated in 1947: a levy at less than 100 per cent, giving some incentive to develop. The fact that it was introduced by a Conservative government, and that a Labour government have now introduced a more radical measure, is a good indicator of the shift in the political spectrum that has occurred in Britain since 1947. Because of this incentive, Conservative spokesmen can now argue that it achieves fiscal and (most) planning objectives without the need for widespread public ownership.

Widespread State or City Purchase. This is the solution adopted in a number of places in the world, of which the most notable is the city of Stockholm since the early years of this century. The city builds up a land bank at agricultural or forest value in the free market, in advance of need. Ebenezer Howard advocated this solution for his garden cities, and London used it for purchase of green belt land in the 1930s before introduction of the 1947 Act allowed the green belt to be implemented in other ways. This solution demands that the land is bought a very long time in advance (50 years in the case of Stockholm), or alternatively a long way from the city, to avoid paying speculative values. This latter can be coupled with deliberate development of new communications. to the parent city, which increases the land values after purchase. Stockholm did this in the construction of its Tunnelbana (Metro) after 1945. The solution involves a considerable injection of public money, which may take a long time to fructify. If it takes place on a sufficiently wide scale, it may become indistinguishable in practice from "creeping nationalization."

Public Purchase of all Development Land. Under this scheme (or variants of it) all land needed for development in any defined time period is defined by plans and must then be bought by public agencies, either central or local, which then dispose of it either by lease (hence the use of the term "creeping nationalization") or by sale (in which case the term is inappropriate). Purchase is at existing use value (agricultural or forest value) in the case of new development; sale or lease is at market value (perhaps with special exceptions for classes of development thought worthy of support, e.g. local authority developments). This scheme differs from the last one in that it is supposed to be universal and compulsory; it replaces the normal workings of the land market.

Such a scheme can readily be coupled with a betterment levy, since the public agency may be enabled or required to buy land net of the levy, leaving some incentive for the developer. (This is true of the intermediate stage in the British 1975 Community Land Act.) It deals both with fiscal equity and planning objectives: by definition it collects betterment (in whole or in part) for the public purse; it allows land for communal purposes to be bought at or near existing use value (or net of betterment); and by putting all land at the point of development into public hands, it should encourage a much higher level of positive planning. By definition however it involves a very great initial cost in building up a public land bank; this eventually will be returned to the public coffers and the whole scheme should become self-supporting.

The British 1975 Community Land Act is of course a model for public purchase of this kind. It provides that local authorities be given powers but later also duties (to prevent backsliding) to acquire land, through five-year rolling programs called Land Acquisition and Management Schemes. In a transitional stage, to commence in April 1976, they will buy net of a betterment levy, called Development Land Tax, which will be charged initially at 80 per cent, rising to 100 per cent. In the later stage, when DLT rises to 100 per cent, logically they buy at current use value. Some categories of land are however DLT-exempt; they include owner-occupied sites up to one acre, builders' existing stocks just before the Act was passed and land owned by charities. The money needed for these purchases will all be borrowed; no government money will be available. The land will then be sold (in most cases of land for residential development) or leased (in the case of most other kinds of development) to the actual developer, who may have been the owner in the first instance. The proceeds of the sale will go 30 per cent to the local authority concerned, 30 per cent to a pool of local authorities (since some authorities will benefit much more than others), and 40 per cent to the central government treasury.[2]

The Community Land Act is a scheme that ingeniously satisfies both criteria. By definition it collects betterment for the community, eventually at 100 per cent. The market is not required to work as it was under the 1947 Act, since local authorities will progressively be required to buy land. Thus there can be no question of the supply of land drying up at any rate, once authorities have the duty to acquire it. And, since these are also the planning authorities, it should be possible for them to draw up much more positive plans (or development briefs) for the prospective developer, releasing the land to developers they are assured can fulfil these briefs. The scheme however does have the disadvantage that it would seem to need a large new bureaucracy, with new skills which combine planning expertise and an understanding of land management and development—though these will presumably be paid for by local authority borrowings. And the scheme does not collect betterment on any land that remains in the same hands and is not developed; in other words, Development Land Tax is strictly on realized gains.

Unification of the Reversion. This is a more radical alternative to the last variety of scheme. It was most fully spelt out in a pamphlet published in Britain in 1971 by the British magazine *Socialist Commentary*; it was in fact considered and rejected by the British Labour Party when developing the scheme that led to the Community Land Act. Its essence is that all freehold rights are abolished and replaced by Crown Leases—a step that is said to be legally quite in order, since all rights in land derive from the Crown anyway. All leases would be based on the assumed life of the building or buildings that happened to be on the site. They would incorporate rent revision clauses so that the rent, at first nominal, would rise sharply towards the end of the term of the lease. Thus, when the land was required for development or redevelopment, it would be acquired by a public authority at the value of the land alone, which would be assumed to be nil.

Unification of the reversion deals neatly with both equity and planning considerations, and it involves no expenditure of money whatsoever. It is alleged that owners could hardly complain since they could still enjoy the whole of the value of any building on the site subject only to an obsolescence tax. But the scheme takes a very long time to mature, while the political objections are immediate and acute. They would be compounded by the fact that it would be very difficult to place an objective life on a building (consider the Tower of London, St Paul's Cathedral and Westminster Abbey). So there seems little doubt that in practice, this is a scheme with more pure logic than political acceptability.

Total Nationalization. The same is true for this final variant, but in even greater measure. Total nationalization means what it says: the immediate acquisition of all land in the country, including not merely development land but also land that it is not proposed to develop immediately, and including not merely development rights but general title also. In fact this extreme variant is seldom advocated, for some obvious reasons. First, it is not really necessary to use this solution to gain the agreed objectives. Only the control over development land, which also happens to be the land that is appreciating most rapidly, is really necessary either on fiscal equity or planning grounds. Secondly, if any compensation is to be paid (and in a democratic property-owning country it could hardly be otherwise), it would be almost ruinously expensive and inflationary, unless a way can be found of postponing payout. And thirdly, it is almost certainly a political non-starter in any country where more than 50 per cent of households are homeowners on their own land—for instance in Canada, the United States, Great Britain, or Australia. So it is not surprising that most so-called public land acquisition schemes fall under the categories earlier considered: widespread state or city purchase, public purchase of all development land, or unification of the reversion. The first two of these shade into each other according to how widespread, uniform, and compulsory the scheme is; the third stands somewhat apart, and appears decidedly less politically practical.

Some Criteria for Evaluation

Discussing this same subject in a conference in London 10 years ago, Nathaniel Lichfield drew up a checklist of criteria.[3] These were so comprehensively, and so succinctly stated, that I cannot do better than draw on them here.

Lichfield starts from the assumption that an economic evaluation should be based on two general criteria: *allocative efficiency* and *distributional equity*. Under allocation, he asks: does the scheme, introduced into a mixed economy, stultify the forces of "development"? Does it make it possible to carry out planning objectives? Is it economical of time and skilled manpower? And does it involve a transfer of assets from the private to the public sector that is so rare as to disturb the economy? Under distribution, he asks: does it establish clear and uniform principles in denying development permission and accordingly offering compensation? Does it fix a "fair" price for compulsory purchase of land, bearing in mind that any owner hopes for far more than in practice he might get in a free market? Does it collect betterment for the community? And more broadly does it collect "unearned increment" from the ownership of land, which is perhaps not the creation of a public authority but which represents no effort or service on the part of the owner?

These questions help to establish some conclusions. If one's main concern is with distributional equity, a scheme based on a purely fiscal solution should prove sufficient—particularly since it should do less to disturb the market and the forces of development (though even then, its effects may be far from negligible), and because it should involve less manpower. But if general planning objectives are uppermost, some further intervention in the land market may be desirable. The least disruptive and most politically feasible solutions seem to involve varying degrees of advance purchase of development land, either in the free market or on some uniform compulsory basis, at or near existing use value, with sale or lease at full market value. Such a scheme, as the British 1975 Community Land Act shows, could be progressively applied over a period of years until it became mandatory on all authorities. It would engender fierce initial political opposition; but this might be softened over time, as more and more local authorities came to enjoy a share of the resulting proceeds. And, if carried through on borrowed money, it could be fully self-supporting without even an initial burden on local tax or ratepayers.

Notes

1. Bernard H. Siegan, "Non-Zoning in Houston," *Journal of Law and Economics*, 13 (1970): 71-147.

2. Great Britain, Department of the Environment, *Community Land Act, Circular 1: General Introduction and Priorities*, Circular 121/75 (London: The Department, 1975).

3. N. Lichfield, "Land Nationalization" in Peter Hall (ed.), *Land Values* (London: Sweet and Maxwell, 1965).

2.3 Critical Perspectives on Public Land Ownership*

Stanley W. Hamilton
Professor of Commerce, University of British Columbia

The case against full-scale public ownership of land.

Many of the objectives that we think we can achieve through public land ownership are ones that I would support. But there may be other more feasible alternatives that will achieve the stated objectives. In order to present a case against public ownership, we must establish general agreement on three basic points: 1) what is meant by public ownership, 2) what are its objectives, and 3) what criteria can be used to evaluate this instrument as a means of achieving those objectives.

Public ownership is a fee simple interest in land, which is the most absolute form of ownership. Similarly, the term land nationalization is simply the process of building up this public ownership once the land has been alienated from the Crown. It is important that we keep in mind this fee simple notion, because immediately the Crown takes title, it should be looking for an opportunity to create a new interest or estate in land, generally thought to be a leasehold estate or ground lease. This is critical in as much as many of the advantages claimed on behalf of public ownership of land will be lost immediately after the creation of a leasehold estate. If there is a case for public ownership, it must rest on the ability of the public authorities to incorporate or control more conditions in a contract or lease than is generally the case under existing use of police powers.

Hall mentioned a spectrum of alternatives with nationalization or public ownership at one extreme. At least four of these alternatives represent nothing more than halfway measures, proposed with a long-run view of public ownership. They are proposed in part because public ownership would be financially costly and politically unpopular. These halfway measures include public land banking as it is now practised in Canada, but coupled with a lease rather than resale arrangements; the acquisition of development rights; temporary ownership for assembly purposes for redevelopment; and finally, the acquisition of a reversionary

*Remarks to the conference. Edited.

interest with the expectation that, when the reversions are realized, the public ownership of land would be accomplished. Each of these halfway measures has some advantages, inasmuch as they all provide immediate benefits towards some of the objectives, but each can be viewed as simply one step towards the process of nationalization.

In contemporary Canadian society, three major objectives are important in regard to public land ownership: 1) the price control of land, 2) a solution to the compensation-betterment question (unearned increment), and 3) improved land planning. It should be obvious that these three objectives are not totally compatible: someone must make a value judgment, and that's what it will take to determine whether price or equity or planning is to take precedence. How is public land ownership to achieve these objectives, and what are these objectives in detail?

With regard to price control, the argument is advanced that a public authority controlling the land could reduce land values or control the rate of increase in land values by providing a constant supply of land in the right place at the right time. It is further argued that public ownership of land, coupled with a very carefully drafted lease, would eliminate land speculation (the bogey man of the '70s) and make land available to worthwhile users at a rate below market values. Thus, worthy public users, such as schools, parks, hospitals, would not be deprived of land in the area of their selection; they would not be forced to use alternative and perhaps cheaper sites. The public authority would not take the same large mark-up as we sense is present here in our quasi private system, and as a result, would be in a position to sell at a lower price.

The compensation-betterment problem is perhaps one of the most perplexing. I don't think anyone can deny that some portion of unearned increment is rightfully owned by the Crown or the public. The difficulty is that we have not been able to find a viable means of measuring and separating out that portion of value belonging to society and that portion of the increment belonging to the owner or tenant because of his initiative and his decisions. We will not solve or resolve the compensation-betterment problem through public land ownership. What will happen instead is that emphasis will shift. At the present time, most gains seem to accrue to private entrepreneurs or landowners. Under a system of public land ownership, again coupled with a very carefully drafted lease, the Crown would attract the majority of the gains. The tenant would still expect some just reward for his private decisions and the committment of his capital—and the land value increment allocation problem would remain. Moreover, in order to realize any of the unearned increment, it would be absolutely necessary that the leasehold estate have provisions incorporated within it for frequent rent reviews, which re-create (in a micro scale), the compensation-betterment question all over again. Reviewing the rents and bringing them up to market values still requires determining what proportion of market values result from public-sector decisions and what proportion from actions of private enterprise.

Advocates of public land ownership perceive improved land planning "to ensure development in the best interests of the community" as a major objective. If public land ownership is achieved, the public authority would be faced with no land assembly problem, and as a result, comprehensive planning would be much easier and much more efficient—*if* we could wipe the slate clean and begin tomorrow with all the land back in the name of the Crown. It would also be true on the anniversary of every lease, when the reversionary interest goes back to the Crown (which would be in a position, without land assembly, to convert to another use). This presupposes that some subset of leases, some geographic area, will fall due simultaneously, at the time when redevelopment is desirable or in the public interest. Through the leasehold system, an authority can exercise positive, as well as negative controls, and this has to be one of the most important arguments in favour of public land ownership. Covenants can be introduced into the lease, requiring the tenant to build according to specific standards, to use the property for a constrained list of uses, and to maintain the property to an acceptable standard. Negative controls, many of which exist in present zoning systems, can be custom designed to an individual site or a small area. They are a wide open form of spot zoning. The public authority can also ensure that we have adequate lands for public purposes by transferring the land at a price that public users can afford, so that schools, hospitals, and other public uses will have choice sites. Those I think, are a fair rendition of the arguments that are advanced under each objective.

There are two criteria against which to evaluate these claims: 1) will the objective be achieved (and I don't think that is self-evident): and 2) will this process be the most effective/efficient? Will public ownership reduce land values? It will, if public authorities can maintain the necessary supply in the desired locations. This assumes that whoever is in charge of this gigantic land bank has some notion of what society requires, when they require it, and will be in a position to deliver on demand. This also assumes that planners have some insights that the rest of us do not. I suggest that planners have no more predictive capacity than any other individual. They, like you and I, cannot see much beyond the ends of their noses. The price objective can be achieved if speculation is eliminated, and if, at the same time, it can be proven that speculators were in fact price-setters under the old system, and not price-takers. I see no evidence here in Canada that speculators are establishing prices in the market. They are quite clearly taking advantage of every nickel that is there, and that's what speculation is all about. That doesn't make it good, and we ought to direct our attention toward those who are in every sense, unproductive, but it will not occur when prices are enforced. The lease that must be drafted in order to eliminate speculation will probably not be marketable in our society. In order to eliminate all opportunities for speculation, it would be necessary to have rent reviews within that lease that would guarantee there is no benefit to be gained by purchasing leasehold estates.

It is further argued that because of cost efficiencies, the public landowner agency would be in a position to sell at a profit, but well below market values. One might be cynical and observe that when a monopoly exists there is no such thing as market value, so it's a historical figure that we are dealing with. I suggest that if in fact a Crown agency is more efficient and sells at ċost plus a reasonable profit, the value of land is not reduced. The cash cost to the next user is simply reduced. Transferring a parcel of land that in a free market would be worth $100,000 to a school board for $75,000 is not in the interests of the public because it provides transferring subsidies from one department to another at less than market value. This is a hidden subsidy, concealed from the public. We also cannot isolate the land issue from the more general problem of inflation. To assume that we can control the price of land or control the price of housing without controlling all other commodities is, I think, a false hope and expectation. Public ownership may in fact achieve a reduction in land costs, but it will not reduce land values and, therefore to allocate this scarce resource according to an artificially low price is to encourage its misuse and abuse.

Public land ownership does not resolve the compensation-betterment question either. It makes it more acceptable from the public's point of view inasmuch as they reap the benefits immediately and then the tenant or former owner must come forward to ask for his just reward. The problem of unearned increment is one that our society must deal with immediately; if it could be resolved in a satisfactory manner, we would take gigantic steps towards eliminating the function of speculation. Rather than trying to attack the speculator directly, you can simply let himself opt out of the market by making his function non-profitable. But the compensation-betterment or unearned increment question is nothing more than a measurement problem at this stage.

Another aspect of this problem is that we hear very little of the compensation question in respect to other products. Public authorities do not recoup from auto manufacturing plants that element of profit that accrues to them because of the trade barriers that we have created on their behalf. There is no attempt to recoup from farmers that element of profit that arises because of public non-import policies or marketing board policies. The notion that public decisions bestow upon private individuals a windfall gain applies right across the board and it is not limited to land.

It is, however, much more evident and obvious in respect to land, which can't be taken away, so we can always come back to it.

Public ownership will also not result in improved planning; it will result simply in more planning. Once achieved, widespread public ownership, coupled with a leasing program, gives no assurances that political considerations will not take precedent over planning considerations. Planners may tell a politician that in order to get the unearned increment at rent review time, rents should be raised by 70%. If this occurs just before an election, a politician may well question the advice. There are all kinds of illustrations indicating the reluctance of government at the political level to take the stand that has been encouraged and recommended by its civil servants.

There is a further problem with respect to planning objectives, which is the carefully drafted lease providing for positive controls. These positive controls will work up to a point, but problems arise in terms of reuse of the land at some future time. Covenants restricting use of the land will encourage low bidding for the land. Eventually there will be no bidders because the objectives that are sought through the leasehold system and the types of covenants that are introduced in a particular case will be so onerous that the developer will have to be paid to take over the land. This does not mean that the covenants are wrong. It simply indicates that there is a cost to planning and the cost will be reflected in the combination of rental covenants and the rents paid.

One also ponders about who will draft the leases and who will design the covenants? We are asked to believe that civil servants and planners are more informed about the public good than any other private developer. Vancouver provides an illustration of what I have in mind. The city has this past year rezoned the downtown community. Nineteen character areas were identified and new zoning by-laws designed to preserve them were introduced—a very worthwhile undertaking. But one stops to reflect that if these same planners had been in City Hall 30 years ago, would there have been 19 character areas, or would there be a sameness that we would find difficult to live with.

The tool of public land ownership is perhaps unacceptable in Canadian context. That ought not prevent examination of its viability. But it may cause us to look elsewhere for more efficient ways to achieve objectives. The planning claim put forward by the advocates of public land ownership rests solely on the notion of positive covenants in the lease. This could be achieved more efficiently by the direct purchase of positive covenants without the acquisition of fee simple. The public simply needs to pay the private landowner to acquire these benefits. On occasion, that will be incredibly expensive. If it is too expensive, then the activity that is underway should be questioned. There is nothing to be achieved by making land cheaper simply so we can use more of it for the public. What we have to do is consciously decide whether we really believe, as members of society, that we want more expensive parks, more schools. The desire to attract more and cheaper land for appropriate public uses is commendable, but if the general public agrees, it should be prepared to vote the necessary funds. Subsidies, in the form of artificially low land prices achieve nothing except to deceive and defraud the public of their right to participate in the decision process.

Bryant has stated [*Land: Private Property Public Control*, Montreal, 1972] that public speculation and the ensuing profits are justified as legitimate returns of values created by public action. He apparently perceives all increments in land value as being caused by public decisions, an indefensible position to say the least. While it might be assumed that the public would have more commendable uses for the profits, this only serves to obscure the fact that speculation, unearned increments, and the compensation-betterment problem persist, even under a system of public ownership.

There are already many strong planning tools. What I therefore advocate is that we look closely at the price mechanism and ask how can it be used to the advantage of the community before it is thrown out. Otherwise, we are faced with today's version of "who controls the controllers?" which is "who controls the planners?"

2.4 Planning, Development, and Site Value Taxation*

Hans Blumenfeld
Professor of Urban and Regional Planning, University of Toronto

The case for higher taxes on site-values and lower taxes on improvements, along with limited public ownership of land.

There is a contradiction, which works itself out in many ways, between public planning and the private ownership of land. This is true not only of regulatory mechanisms such as zoning, subdivision control, building and housing by-laws, etc., but also of public works like roads, transit facilities, water, sewers, schools, and parks, which are undertaken and planned by the community. Anything planners do affects the value of one piece of land differently from that of another. In other words, planning actions transfer value from one piece of land to another and once this transfer has been achieved, it is very difficult to reverse for reasons of equity, which of course makes itself felt politically.

---

*Remarks to the conference. Edited.

One of society's legitimate concerns is to prevent sprawl. In a purely unregulated private market, a developer is forced to do a good deal of leapfrogging. He can't get the land he might want to develop because it's priced too high; so he goes farther out, buys some land, develops it there. This involves a good deal of public expense for roads, sewers, water, and so on. It also involves a great waste in time and increases the travelling expenses of the people who live farther out. Public authorities tend to prevent sprawl by restricting the land allowed for development to the amount which will really be needed within the next few years. But this practice creates a monopoly in which the speculator, if he's lucky enough to have a piece of that land, makes a very fat profit. The only way out of the dilemma of either accepting the wastefulness of leapfrogging and "scatteration" or inducing monopolistic land prices is by public land ownership, which can then release land at normal value.

The value of a piece of land, its "site value," is determined by its access to other people and to other activities. This value, of course, is created entirely by the people who engage in these other activities, by what we call the general growth of the whole community, and by the public investment in making these mutually accessible. There is no doubt that land value is not the same thing as the value of an investment in a factory, a mine, or a house. Economic theory, for whatever it's worth, says you have to allow a man to make a profit if he risks his money by putting it into a mine, factory, or house; otherwise there will be no mines, factories, or houses. But the land will be there whether anybody puts his money into it or not; so this argument doesn't really apply.

The conflict between public planning (which is unavoidable because nobody else builds roads) and private ownership also comes to the fore in other ways. Private land ownership restricts tremendously the flexibility of planning. Everybody says planning should be flexible. I have often said that concrete doesn't flex and this is a limitation in terms of buildings and utilities already in place. But this is not the case prior to development. However, if you don't make a plan in advance, you can't really even dimension a sewer or water pipe. You must know where the next piece will go. If you make a regional plan 10-20 years in advance and design what shall be done with the land and where everything shall go, later developments or later insights may indicate that changes in the plan need to be made. But land values have already been established by the original design and individual owners may thus stand to gain or lose accordingly, if plans are radically changed. They will resist the change as depriving them of their property rights and will usually prevail for reasons of equity. It's therefore self-defeating to try to have effective land planning and land control with private ownership.

When public ownership exists, you can make such changes. You can change the value from one piece of property to another within the same ownership because what you lose at one end you gain at the other. In principle, this is also true of large-scale private ownership and it is perfectly true that within a large-scale, privately owned estate you get just as good planning, and maybe better planning, than in publicly owned large-scale ownership. There are, however, a number of difficulties in this. First, it can be done only within a limited area, for if most of the potential development land is held by one owner, there would be a complete private monopoly. Therefore, planning is limited to a certain area and is not planning for a whole development area. Second, the private developer experiences great difficulty and considerable cost in assembling an appropriate piece of land which a public authority, armed with the power of condemnation and expropriation, will not have. This is particularly true in dealing with holdouts. Every private developer knows there are always some holdouts. Either he has to plan around them, thus disrupting his plan, or he has to buy them out at quite excessive cost. Finally, there is a further difference in that the public can borrow money at a lower rate and with lower carrying charges than the private developer.

Generally, public ownership hasn't been discussed primarily in terms of what it can do for better planning, but from two other points of view. First, the community should receive the unearned increment because a landowner can really do nothing to raise or lower the value of the land he happens to own. The value is entirely created or decreased by the community, so it is quite logical to say the community should receive profits from it. Second it is claimed that the land should be cheaper for the user who wants to be housed on it. These two arguments are, of course, somewhat contradictory. It's what game theorists call a zero-sum game. If the community gets the unearned increment, then the man who buys or rents a house can't get it and the other way around. I don't see any justification why a man who just happens to build a house on a piece of land should get it below its normal market value. I'm not referring now to the additional monopoly rent value but to the value placed on the normal differential rent which results from the growth of the community. People who can afford new houses, either as buyers or renters, are certainly not members of the lowest income group. If the land were still owned by the people, by the white men who first came here and grabbed it from the Indians, it would be perfectly legitimate just to take it, or to tax it, away from them. But land has been treated as a commodity since white men came here, and you can't just expropriate that way or have a tax of an expropriatory character. Any investor has a right to be protected against expropriation without compensation. Nobody, however, has a right to be protected against every government action which may affect the value of his investment; this happens every day. Changes in monetary policy, tariff policy, taxation policy may of course affect any investment either positively or negatively. So may the real estate tax.

The real estate tax is really two quite different taxes. We tax the site value, i.e. the capitalized differential rent together with the buildings which are on it. It would be perfectly possible and I think highly desirable to greatly increase the tax on the site and decrease the tax on the building. It's generally recognized that the tax on the building very much discourages people to improve their properties because they are afraid that their assessment will go up, but the same is actually just as true for any new building. Nothing could be more helpful for bringing more housing into the market than lowering or completely eliminating the tax on improvements. At the same time, this would make it much easier to raise the tax on the site because for the great majority of the affected people the two would balance. Many would gain; some would lose. Those who would lose are those who hold undeveloped land and this, of course, would discourage that practice and encourage them to sell it. A high site-value tax would actually make it impossible for a private developer to assemble land long in advance, thus making public land assembly virtually a necessity. It would have actually considerable advantages for the private developer because he wouldn't have to tie up his capital in buying and holding land. When he is ready to develop, he would go to the government to try to get required land on a long-term lease. My preference would be to grant these long-term leases by competitive bidding under certain conditions which we have even now in our zoning legislation, etc. We could institute a system of leasing by developers, to develop the land and sell the houses. While the houses would continue to be in private ownership, the leases would be periodically renegotiated as the value of the land actually goes up. So, while I think that a strong site-value tax could be effective only with public land ownership, I think the same is even more true the other way around. Without reducing the market price of land, the cost to the user would be the same because he would pay what he saves in his mortgage interest because the land is cheaper, but he would pay more in the site-value tax. If you reduce the market value, however, and thus put pressure on the landowner to sell, of course you make public land assembly for public ownership infinitely more easy.

I would indeed be somewhat leery of going into a very large-scale program of public land assembly at this point because land may be quite a bit overvalued now. By introducing a large-scale additional buyer, prices would be driven up even more. I think there has to be a combination of these two measures of a site-value tax and of public land ownership.

2.5 A Legal Perspective on Land Banking in the United States*

Fred P. Bosselman
Attorney, Chicago

A discussion of the land banking section of the American Law Institute's Model Land Development Code, 1975.

The American Law Institute is basically a very conservative legal, establishment institution—a voluntary organization of some of the leading lawyers and judges in the country. It proposes model state legislation in a number of different fields and for many years has been trying to formulate a model state statute for dealing with the whole spectrum of land development. Professor Allison Dunham and I were reporters of the project and were later in charge of drafting recommendations. We did not reach the question of land banking until fairly late in the project and at that point we examined the issues and concluded that it was highly unlikely that the conservative American Law Institute would ever support the idea of land banking, which many people consider basically a socialist scheme.

The Institute eventually did support the idea of land banking, though our original proposal to the Institute was something quite different. We felt that the idea of encouraging large-scale development was a very good one. The views of Jane Jacobs to the contrary, at least at that point in time (four or five years ago), there was general sentiment in the planning community in the United States that large-scale development was the solution for many urban problems. That attitude is not as strong today as it was then.

Our proposal was that large-scale developers, whether private or public, be granted the power of eminent domain so that they could condemn land for large-scale development in the same way as public utilities (which are private institutions) in the United States have always had the power to do. We recommended against land banking, but wrote a fairly extended commentary in which we described the issues pro and con. These two proposals were presented to an Annual Meeting of the American Law Institute. A number of people spoke very vehemently against the idea of granting the power of eminent domain to private developers, who (even among these conservative lawyers) have acquired a sufficiently bad name that nobody wanted to do them any favours. Everybody agreed that the problem of the holdout in the land acquisition process was a serious one and that assembling land for a new community was very difficult because of it. The Institute finally agreed that government agencies could be given the power to acquire land for private developers in holdout situations. It

*Remarks to the conference. Edited.

seemed much safer to have land acquisition go through the government agency.

On the land banking issue, however, a number of people said that our commentary recommending against land banking was so persuasive in stating the issues in favour of it that they were convinced we were wrong. It was suggested that we should draft an article on land banking, which we did, still fully convinced that when this group actually saw what a departure this was from the American tradition of free enterprise and private development, it would be rejected. There was a certain amount of opposition, but it was relatively mild and, surprisingly, on a vote of about 3 or 4 to 1, the Institute voted to adopt the land banking provisions.

We have a serious constitutional issue in the United States about land banking: whether it is constitutional for the federal or any level of government to acquire land when it is not for a specific use. In some states there is even doubt about acquiring land for long-term future use, and very little authority for the proposition that land can be acquired for just the general purpose of keeping a land reserve. However, the Institute took the position that land reserve acquisition in itself should be a valid constitutional public purpose.

One issue concerned the level cf government at which land banking ought to be done. The conclusion was that the state level was most appropriate. There is some sentiment for land banking by local governments, but there is also considerable fear that if local governments engage in land banking, there may be exclusionary motives in many cases. Our current attorney-general, Edward Levy, who is a member of the Law Institute, at that time expressed very strong suspicions of the motives of much of the proposed land banking that now exists in suburban areas in the United States. He felt that it might be abused as a technique to keep poor people or minority groups out of the community. This is, I think, a serious problem, though land banking power is not any more susceptible to abuse of this type than regulatory power. In any event, the conclusion was that a state-level agency would be less likely to abuse the power in a discriminatory fashion and, therefore, our recommendations were that the power ought to be concentrated at the state level.

There are two very different group views concerning the motivation for land banking: one, the economists, think of land banking as a means of adjusting prices and keeping land prices down; and the second, the planners, are interested in land banking as a way of controlling growth. We, as lawyers, weren't prepared to tell the states what purpose they ought to use land banking for or even to say that they must necessarily use it. Either of these purposes seemed like a legitimate and reasonable exercise of government power. We felt also that there ought to be a very strong relationship between land banking operations and overall state planning operations, so that a state planning agency would have veto power over any acquisition or disposition of land that the land reserve agency might make.

There is currently a great deal of interest in land banking in the United States. A number of states now have commissions or task forces that have recommended a series of land banking proposals. This is related to the desire to preserve prime agricultural land. There have been study commissions in Connecticut and Maryland recommending extensive proposals and there is talk about it in New Jersey. There is also a great deal of interest on the part of large suburban county governments in the Washington and New York areas. A proposal in Suffolk County, New York, which is the eastern end of Long Island, is in the later stages of implementation, and there is a good chance that the county will actually begin acquiring land next year.

2.6 Problems of Implementation: An Overview*

R.W.G. Bryant
Professor of Geography, Concordia University, Montreal

A wide-ranging discussion of land policy implementation in various parts of the world. Britain, British Columbia, Saskatoon, Canberra, and Amsterdam are case-study examples of such implementation at federal, provincial, and municipal levels.

I do not believe that land should be treated as a commodity, or that the play of the market is a proper determinant of land use. To say that is to toss a considerable amount of land economics, urban rent theory, etc., out the window. There is no aspect of our so-called free enterprise system that produces less satisfactory results than the market in urban and peri-urban land. If the market is to be regarded as highly suspect, it nevertheless has to be lived with. Hence, wisdom lies in the direction of suggesting that public authorities should act within the framework of the market, and that dollar signs should be liberally sprinkled throughout the discussion.

If the market did not exist, we would have to devise alternative means of making rational choices between different possible uses of land. Experience in communist countries suggests that this problem exists even where there is no private property in land as we know it. Power plays between different segments of an all-embracing bureaucracy may be no more efficient in determining land use than is our market mechanism. There can hardly be much dispute that organization for owning and

*Paper prepared for the conference. Edited.

managing land is a matter concerning all levels of government, acting both individually and in partnership. The best kind of organization is the simplest. One would, therefore, not normally contemplate ad hoc organizations, unless a strong case can be made.

At the most senior level, both in Canada and the United States, the respective national governments own very large areas of land, forest reserves, national parks, defence installations, etc., and this is also true of provincial and state governments.

However, it is at the municipal level that the problems of urban development seem greatest. The British White Paper on "Land" (September 1974) very sensibly made the following point:

Undoubtedly a central agency has advantages: it can respond with ease to national decisions and it can cross local boundaries to assemble land which ought to form one parcel. On the other hand, the citizen has never felt personally involved in the work of such agencies, and local authorities have generally felt, with some justice, that they were more aware of their own problems than any central organization.

Britain

In Britain, the Central Land Board established by the Town and Country Planning Act of 1947 had as its main function the administration of the financial part of the Act and concern with the nationalization of development values in land, over and above "existing use" value. The board's powers to acquire land were primarily "reserve powers." The board, if it wished, could acquire land at its "existing use" value, from sellers who ignored the fact that the development value, in theory at any rate, was no longer theirs to dispose of. There are those, including myself, who still argue that the vigorous use of these powers would in time have induced the market to adjust itself to the new regime. But it is a matter of increasingly ancient history that the whole scheme was wound up before it had a chance to prove itself. The British are still stuck with the results of that foolishness. The second attempt was the Land Commission Act of 1967, which empowered the commission to acquire by agreement any land deemed to be needed for development or redevelopment. Its powers of compulsory purchase were confined to land declared suitable for development by a planning authority, and falling in any one of the following categories: 1) land that ought to be acquired to secure early development or redevelopment; 2) land that ought to be assembled for comprehensive development or redevelopment; 3) land required by a public authority for the exercise of its functions; and 4) land to be disposed of to housing associations or other private housing. These powers of acquisition were associated with a levy or tax on development values—an attempt to recoup "betterment" for the public. In any case, the Land Commission machinery was dismantled by the succeeding Conservative Government just as the Central Land Board had been.

It should be noted that in both cases, the power of acquiring land outright was associated with attempts to settle the question of compensation and betterment. Although this is somewhat outside our theme of public ownership of land as such, it is noteworthy that this issue keeps cropping up.

The third attempt—the policy set out in the White Paper of 1974—is now law. One can only express a fervent hope that it will not suffer the fate of its predecessors.

British Columbia

The British Columbia Land Commission represents an important step in the direction of a province-wide land use control system. It,was set up by the provincial legislature in 1973 for the particular purpose of preserving agricultural land from urban encroachment. Good valley-bottom farm land represents a tiny fraction of the whole area of the province, yet it is precisely on this land, especially around Vancouver, that urban pressures are most intense. The B.C. Land Commission is empowered to acquire, but not to expropriate land, though this is basically a subsidiary part of the operation. The main thrust of the commission's task is to designate or zone land for agriculture, parks, greenbelts, and land banks. It raises important and interesting questions relating to injurious affectation, and the extent to which public authorities may properly exercise control over land use when this involves financial loss to property owners. This problem is well discussed elsewhere.[1] Interestingly, the commission's power to purchase land may be exercised either on its own or jointly with local and regional governments. It may hold, manage, lease, or sell purchased land at its discretion.

Municipal or regional bodies (referred to in the Hellyer Report) are, of course, the appropriate organizations to acquire and service land for urban purposes. There is no reason, however, why that land should lie within the boundaries of the authority concerned. Several years ago there was a problem around Halifax, Nova Scotia of scattered and highly uneconomic suburban growth in Halifax County, with single houses and subdivisions spread like buckshot over rocky terrain where utility services come expensive. Much money could have been saved by a more compact form of planned development, confined to areas with suitable subsoil. A suggestion that the city acquire land in a suitable part of the county for such development was met with the point that the city had no legal powers to do so. Closer examination of the Revised Statutes of Nova Scotia showed that the Halifax city charter did indeed empower the city to acquire land for any public purpose as it might see fit, inside or outside its boundaries. This illustrates the point that legal powers often already exist empowering authorities to do much that they might never think of doing. As for boundaries, the highly successful Saskatoon land program does not stop at the city limits.

One is bound to confess that the Canadian experience in land assembly has been somewhat disappointing. The National Housing Act was amended in 1949 to provide for a federal contribution of three-fourths of the cost of buying and servicing vacant land, on the condition that the provincial and local governments concerned would apply for it, and agree on sharing the other quarter of the cost. But although the legislative powers were there, they were not much used. Between 1949 and 1969, over 23,000 acres were assembled under these arrangements, but this represented only 5% of the land use for urban growth during the same period.

The reasons for this are well discussed in the Dennis Report.[2] The Central Mortgage and Housing Corporation was not very keen on federal participation in land assembly from the start. It passed the buck to the municipalities, but they for their part were loathe to take the initiative. Official policy was to interfere as little as possible with the private market, and to keep down the costs involved in any substantial federal activity in this field. In short, the federal-provincial land assembly suffered from the same lukewarm attitude which characterized policy on publicly aided, low-cost housing. We need not go into the whole dismal story in detail. Matters changed somewhat towards the end of the 1960s when most provinces set up provincial housing authorities. Furthermore, the climate of opinion seems to be changing. The Dennis Report of 1972[3] came flat out in favour of a large-scale land banking program, sufficient for ten years' residential requirements.

In discussing the implementation of any such policy, the important thing is to be quite clear about the purpose of the exercise. They are: 1) to hold down land costs, 2) to control the shape and form of development, 3) to cater for social needs not met by private enterprise, and 4) to produce revenue.

Canadian Municipalities

Apart from the federal-provincial partnership arrangements, interest in Canada, from an urban viewpoint, must centre on those few municipalities which have used public ownership of land—Saskatoon, Edmonton, Red Deer. The Saskatoon case is documented[4] and is an excellent "laboratory test" for appraising the results of a long-standing policy of municipal land assembly carried out by one city with a minimum of political hassles and without the complexities involved in partnership with senior levels of government.

The initial impetus in Saskatoon and elsewhere arose out of the fact that some cities found themselves in possession of considerable areas of land forfeited for non-payment of taxes during the Great Depression. Of course, this did not necessarily involve use of such land as part of a public policy. In Montreal, for.instance, such land was mostly sold off for what it would fetch (as soon as possible after World War II), without any attempt being made to meet any of the objectives mentioned above. The small city of Red Deer, Alberta, is perhaps not sufficiently quoted in the literature relating to public land assembly.[5] Both the acquisition of raw land and its servicing are undertaken by the municipality according to a planned program of expansion.

As for Saskatoon, the city in 1945 held title to 8,500 building lots; a little private building land remained within the city limits.[6] The city-owned lots were taken up by the early 1950s and the city made a momentous decision, namely, to continue in business as a retailer of serviced lots. This involved acquiring raw land. The objective was to secure orderly future growth, reduce speculation as much as possible, and keep land values low. Interestingly, to earn as much profit as possible does not figure in this list. By that time, too, the city had had nearly 35 years of experience in the land business (sale of the tax-delinquent lands) and it had received $3.5 million from this operation between 1920 and 1954. Hence it could plough this profit back into the acquisition of raw land without running into debt.

The scale of the city's dealings in land, both before and after 1956, has been such as to overshadow development on private land. Decision making by the city has been the important factor. This in itself distinguishes the Saskatoon experience from the various federal-provincial land assemblies, which have rarely been a decisive factor in shaping urban growth. The city has thus been able to set standards for all development, on private as well as on municipal land, and to maintain harmonious relations with the developers.

The Saskatoon experience in municipal land management ought to be taken as a model for other Canadian cities. Nonetheless, it may not be generally applicable, simply because other cities have "missed the bus." Saskatoon had the advantage of starting early, when land values were much lower than today. It would hardly be possible in Vancouver, for example, for the simple reason that the enormous post-war increase in land values has already occurred in that region. Any attempt at this late stage to emulate Saskatoon would be saddled from the start with enormous costs. Likewise in Canberra, Australia, for example, the whole operation was enormously facilitated by the fact that the Crown assembled the land needed for urban purposes well in advance of requirements (more than half a century ago), at prices based on what was then remote pastoral use.

The matter of disposition and management of publicly owned land inevitably raises the question of freehold as against leasehold tenure. It also involves very practical and workaday issues in the field of what the British call "estate management." Much publicly owned land will in any case be required for the rather large proportion of urban space needed for obvious public purposes: highways, schools, recreational areas, and so on. In this case, transfer to the appropriate organization within the public sector is a simple matter of book-keeping. Where development is to be carried out by private enterprise, there are highly significant options. In Canada, "disposition of public lands may take the form of leasing arrangements or resale to the private sector. To date, land assemblies have operated on the principle of resale."[7]

The whole topic seems to have been discussed rather inadequately in Canada. Hence it is worthwhile to devote some attention to it, and it ought to be possible to discuss the matter without evoking the emotional reactions that often accompany such discussions. It is not sufficient to say simply that leasehold is not the usual practice and has not been done here.

As is often the case in Canada, the legal basis exists for leasehold tenure, but the legal possibilities are not fully exploited. Both in English and in French law it is well understood that property in real estate comprises a bundle of rights, and that the components of the bundle can be separated. This familiar concept dates back to Roman law, which is the common ancestor of English and French law.

Having accepted this, the scene is set for a variety of important and interesting arrangements of the utmost significance for guiding the impact of man and his works on the environment. The separation of the right to develop land, from the right to enjoy it in its existing use, was a fundamental feature of the recommendations of the Uthwatt Committee in Britain (1942) and of the financial arrangements of the Town and Country Planning Act (1947). In America, the same concept underlies the various suggestions for the transfer of development rights (TDR), which may well be of enormous value, not only for the preservation of historic buildings and districts, but also for securing open space for recreational and other purposes.[8]

Likewise, the legal framework can well accommodate the granting of easements or servitudes. This is familiar enough, for example, in arranging rights of way for pipelines or transmission lines. Easements may also be used, as an alternative to outright acquisition, to preserve open space for recreation or greenbelt purposes. This has been much discussed for example, by Whyte,[9] as an alternative to outright acquisition of land.

As for leasehold, it is already used on a "micro scale" in relation to the "bundle of rights." Place Ville Marie in Montreal, over Central Station, is a good example of development on air rights. The freehold in the land is vested in Canadian National Railways, which is a Crown corporation. (The land, in effect, is already publicly owned, although this is not relevant at this point.) The actual occupancy of an office suite involves a whole series of leases and rental arrangements.

We are not, therefore, talking of anything novel in considering leasehold as a possibility in relation to publicly owned land. In Canada it has been a well-established feature of the management of Crown land in the national parks. There seems to be no evident reason why it should not also be applicable in an urban setting.

Amsterdam

The Netherlands present a rather well-known example of the extensive use and management of municipally owned land; this is a basic feature of the growth of Dutch cities. In some cases, the city sells land outright to developers; in others, it leases it. Amsterdam has been organizing its own growth on municipally owned land ever since the 17th century at least. There is a special local reason for this. The land on which Amsterdam is built is so soggy, in its natural state, that it has to be prepared for building by spreading sand on it. The equipment needed is such that the operation can only be done economically on a large scale. In days of yore, the municipality was the only feasible agency to undertake this work; it became an accepted and traditional practice. Nowadays, large-scale developers would be capable of doing the job, but that is not the Dutch way.

In Amsterdam, the advantages of having the built-up area extended in an organized way are well appreciated. Municipal acquisition of the land is the means, and retention of the land in municipal ownership is the key to its successful management. The city disposes of the building land it has prepared almost wholly on long leases rather than outright sale.[10]

The long-lease system now operative was introduced as early as 1896. There had been a phase of sharply rising land prices, and it was felt that future increments of value should be retained for the community, rather than by certain individuals. Here then, is yet another expression of the feeling about the "unearned increment" in land values.

A further advantage of leasehold tenure was also perceived, namely, that it would give the municipality greater control over the kind and character of the buildings that would be erected. The 1896 arrangement was that land would be let out on long lease for a maximum term of 75 years with full reversion, meaning that the land and the buildings thereon would revert to the municipality without compensation.

The difficulties with this system was that it put obstacles in the way of mortgage financing, and maintenance suffered in the later years of a lease. (These difficulties are also familiar in England where the owners of the chief interest have generally been private rather than municipal.) Hence, in 1915, Amsterdam instituted the system of "perpetual leasehold" for dwellings. Henceforth, leases would be almost automatically extended after the initial term of 75 years, for succeeding periods of 50 years. Leases are terminated normally only when the municipality wishes to change the zoning or the nature of the building, and leaseholders may claim compensation for buildings erected by them. At the end of each term, ground rents and the conditions of the lease are subject to renegotiation.

In the case of housing associations and industries, the original system of 1896 was retained in the 1915 reforms. But one of the important features of land management in Amsterdam is flexibility. An industry, for example, might well need to rebuild its plant at some point of time not in any way related to the term of the lease. In 1937, therefore, flexibility was introduced, by providing that lessees could apply for the lease to be "moved up." The full term was taken to start from the date of renegotiation. In 1966, the "perpetual leasehold" system was applied to industry in the same way as it had applied to dwellings since 1915. At the same time, ground rents have been set, subject to quinquennial adjustment, rather than at the termination of a lease. The adjustment is linked to the changing value of money.

The Amsterdam system has been operating rather satisfactorily for 80 years. This means that 1) speculation in land can hardly exist (nobody is getting a free ride at the expense of the community); 2) the citizens, and the building industry, can have confidence that land will be available without profiteering, and that leases are not going to be terminated capriciously, or without good and over-riding reasons of public interest; and 3) the city has far better control over its development than could be afforded by any amount of zoning or other statutory land use control.

Canberra

This Australian city affords a very instructive example of public ownership of land, in a free-enterprise economy, operated under a leasehold system. The origin of the leasehold system in Canberra is section 9 of the Seat of

Government (Administration) Act of 1910: "No Crown land in the (capital) territory shall be sold or disposed of for any estate of freehold." All parties in the Australian Parliament were agreed that there should be no opportunity for speculation in land in consequence of the decision to set up a National Capital in a federal territory, in a region which was at that time very sparsely populated. It was clearly recognized that the additional value in land created by this development ought in all fairness to belong to the community. The ideological component in the insistence on leasehold tenure seems to have been strong—not surprising, in view of the stormy history of the alienation of Crown land in 19th-century Australia to the big "squatters."

Much of the Federal Capital Territory (911 square miles) was in freehold ownership, but the Commonwealth purchased 213,830 acres between 1911 and 1930, and has more recently been buying the residue. The land not immediately required for urban uses was leased for rural use, under an Ordinance of 1918, but a clause enabled land needed for development to be withdrawn at any time, without compensation, except for the lessee-owned improvements.

Canberra grew with "all deliberate speed" between the two world wars. This was a stated objective of government policy, though with the wisdom of hindsight one might judge that fast initial growth might have been more economical in the long run. In the 1920s, the leasehold system was operated with maximum revenue as the chief object. This is one option, but the Canberra experience shows clearly that there are other options where the land is publicly owned, not attractive to private enterprise.

The Federal Capital Commission was established in 1924, when the city was emerging from the construction camp stage. It was required by law to manage its affairs as a business. At this period, leases were offered at auctions—bidders had to offer a capital sum representing the unimproved value at which land rent would be payable. The problem was (and still is to a certain extent) how to balance supply and demand in conditions where the supply of serviced land is strictly under monopoly control, but where the demand is not. In the 1920s, the commission was doing its best to perform the impossible, namely, to recoup costs inflated by investment in infrastructure well in advance of growth, while at the same time trying to keep the supply of serviced land in line with demand. It was forced to abandon the "business" approach.

In parenthesis, it seems fair to comment that the problems of that period were not due to the leasehold system as such, but to the deliberate policy of slow growth. In the more recent British new towns, by contrast, the policy has been to induce growth as quickly as possible, so that infrastructure costs have not been an undue burden, and after a decade or so the towns have become financially viable. Canberra, on the other hand, did not take off properly for half a century after its inception. It was only after World War II that the transfer of civil service departments to Canberra got going on a fairly massive scale; and it was not until 1957 that the National Capital Development Commission (NCDC) was set up. Now that the city has passed the threshold of self-sustaining growth, the early difficulties are of historic interest only.

The practice of auctioning leases on serviced land which had lapsed in the 1930s, was resumed in 1951 and has continued since as the normal method of disposal. The latest fundamental change was in 1970, when the government decided to reduce ground rents to a nominal or peppercorn figure. Over the years, many anomalies and inequities have arisen due to different lessees taking up leases at different periods and under widely different terms. The attempt to relate their rents to market values was therefore abandoned. It was pointed out, in criticism of this measure, that remission of land rent represented a windfall of some $100 million (Australian) to lessees, and that the government had thrown away the opportunity to make further profits out of the increasing value of land.

To sum up a rather complex situation without being dogmatic, one may state that the leasehold system in Canberra has proved its worth. The only time that it was seriously called into question was around 1930 at the time of the Great Depression. On the other hand, there has been a succession of changes in its detailed application. Basically, the Canberra situation is one in which the supply of serviced land is in the hands of a monopoly, now represented by the National Capital Development Commission, whereas the demand reflects individual decision making. The NCDC is not only a seller of leases, it is also the planning authority and the entrepreneur for investment in infrastructure. Aside from the broad public ends of producing an effective urban environment, the NCDC must cover its expenditures. Normal public services are paid for through rates or local taxation in the usual way. The sale of leases reflects the operation of normal market forces. The virtual abolition of ground rent on the other hand has deprived the NCDC of revenue—but there are countervailing payments by the Commonwealth Government in respect of costs properly attributable to the national capital functions of the city, and to its position as a city-state.

Comparisons in Municipal Approach

The traditional rigidity of leasehold, as established, for example, by the great ducal landowners in 18th-century London, has been gradually broken down and made more flexible. The important thing is that in both Canberra and Amsterdam, the public authority involved retains ultimate control of the land—and that in principle, is the essential point of leasehold, as against freehold. Also, it sets the stage for harmonious collaboration between public and private sectors, in contrast to the "free-for-all" that has been taking place in downtown Montreal, Toronto, and Vancouver for example, with great private profit but dubious public benefit. There are five main pillars of the Canberra system: public land ownership; land tenure; integrated planning, development, and construction; finance; and private sector participation.[11]

The ground rules under this system are clear, and helpful to private enterprise; it is not a crude matter of private versus public. In our "mixed" society, surely the best results can be most effectively achieved where the private and public sectors work together rather than at cross purposes. The assembly of land for large-scale development is clearly not a proper function for private enterprise. Further along in a "Canberra" situation, the framework can be solidly established by the public authority concerned, but the framework can be, and is being filled in by private enterprise. The same sort of situation occurs in Saskatoon, but that does not raise the question of leasehold.

The same sort of fruitful collaboration between private and public enterprise has been evident in two of the most successful examples of bombed-city reconstruction, namely Coventry and Rotterdam. In Coventry, virtually the whole of the damaged central area, or downtown was expropriated in stages. Commercial development has been shared between the city and private enterprise, the point being that since the city had to bear the cost of essential but non-revenue producing public facilities, it saw no reason why private enterprise should have a monopoly of the profitable side of the operation. So the city built some commercial buildings itself. The others were leased to private developers on 99-year leases.[12] On the ground, it is difficult to distinguish between the products of the two sectors; both fit in as parts of a planned composition. It was good for the city, and good business for the developers.

The use of leasehold tenure as a tool for the management of publicly owned land warrants a good deal more attention than has so far been given to it in Canada. It affords a means whereby the market mechanism, operating in the sale of leases, by auction or otherwise, may be harnessed to the public purpose instead of being at odds with it as too often happens at present.

The experience of Stockholm provides a good example of large-scale public ownership of land (since 1904). There is a clear distinction, within the municipal administration, between policy and the mechanics of acquisition. The former is handled by a real estate board, the latter by a municipal company (Strada), operating somewhat outside the normal bureaucratic framework. The real estate board, formed of senior officials, is simply one of a number of different fields within the city administration. It has wide and important responsibilities: 1) approval of land prices as proposed by the real estate division; 2) coordination of housing policy; 3) approval of long-range projects submitted by building companies; 4) supervision of the servicing of raw land, requisite to preparation for building; and 5) organization of financing for land acquisition and servicing. Everything is subject to final ratification by the city council. Stockholm has four ways of getting money to acquire land: 1) normal municipal tax revenues; 2) national government loans; 3) normal commercial bank loans; and 4) long-term bond issues.

In Saskatoon, in 1945, the City Council set up a Real Estate Committee of elected representatives, responsible for land development policies. It was decided at an early stage to sell lots on a lease-option agreement, stipulating that the buyer had to build on the land within a year. Land is sold by the Real Estate Committee, through the City Clerk's office. There is thus no expensive administrative superstructure. The funds originally received from the sale of tax forfeit land were placed in a "Property Development Account" and part of these funds were used for the initial purchase of land in 1955. Since then, the profit from development has formed a revolving fund for the organization of more land. The whole operation involves no burden on the taxpayers. It is good to keep separate accounts for land transactions. In Canberra, by contrast, the profits made by the Crown in city development on cheaply acquired raw land simply disappear into the general revenue fund of the Commonwealth.

Guidelines for Implementation and Operation

It is important that there is competent management of a public "land bank." There is no reason why a public authority should not manage its real estate as efficiently (from a business standpoint) as big property companies. It is essential, therefore, that public authorities embarking on a land acquisition program should have qualified, professional staff organized under a director of real estate. The British call him "city estates surveyor," but the nomenclature is unimportant; the function itself, however, is highly important.

A city may well feel that, in certain cases, there are considerations of general public advantage which may outweigh maximum pecuniary gain. This is of course the whole point of public ownership of land, in essence. The old real estate concept of the "highest and best" use of land, measured purely in terms of the market is not regarded as sacrosanct. To the extent that land, and dealings therein, are transferred from the private to the public sector, public policy in respect of its use may often over-ride market considerations. Even so, it is necessary that public organizations should be "businesslike" in their dealings. The acquisition of land represents capital investment on the part of the authority concerned. Sound business practice therefore, would involve a clear separation between such expenditure and normal expenditure. Likewise, normal revenue may not be the most appropriate source of money for acquisitions. To the extent that land can be acquired out of revenue the community is "saving."

The concept of a capital works budget, distinct from "running" expenditures is well recognized in financial administration. It seems highly desirable to link land acquisition expenditures to the capital works program, if only for the reason that it is part of the community's capital investment. More than that, the process of converting rural land to urban use, or of redevelopment within areas already built up, obviously involves public investment in services. Hence, any land acquisition program must be linked with the budgetary arrangements for capital works. In Saskatoon this was done through close integration between the various departments of the city administration, with the planning department playing a key role.

In regard to land acquisition, expropriation should be a weapon of last resort. Whether it has to be used or not, it is absolutely essential that the price be set independently of the purchasing authority. In Britain, this is satisfactorily achieved. By law, the District Valuer, who is an official of the Board of Inland Revenue, sets prices when local authorities acquire land. He acts according to rules laid down by Act of Parliament, so that there is no possibility of "fiddling." Right of appeal to the Lands Tribunal is a further safeguard. Local authorities are not, in this situation, judge and jury of their own case.

It goes without saying that where expropriation is resorted to, there must be an equitable basis for compensation. This necessarily involves the problem of excess values created by development, or the prospect of development, as against simple "existing use" value. The Law Reform Commission of Canada has recently devoted its attention to expropriation.[13]

Public authorities must act in ways akin to those of private corporations in regard to land ownership. There is no reason why public and private interests cannot work together in harmony, as demonstrated by British and Dutch experience, as well as by Canadian examples such as Saskatoon or Mill Woods (Edmonton). Cooperation between these two sectors for the purposes of achieving adequate and rational use of land should be accompanied by the following guidelines for government authorities:

1. The relationship between different levels of government and different bureaucracies must be as simple as possible. Saskatoon is a better example than the federal/provincial land assemblies.

2. The administrative organization must be businesslike, with clear lines of control.
3. Financing must likewise be businesslike, and a logical distinction drawn between the funds involved, and the general funds of the authority involved.
4. No public authority should ever alienate a square yard of public land; leasehold tenure should become standard practice.

Notes

1. Bosselman, Callies, and Banta, *The Taking Issue* (Washington, D.C.: Council on Environmental Quality, 1973), for example.

2. Michael Dennis and Susan Fish, *Programmes in Search of a Policy* (Toronto: Hakkert, 1972).

3. *Ibid.*, p. 20.

4. D.P. Ravis, *The Saskatoon Experience: Advanced Land Acquisition by Local Government* (Ottawa: Community Planning Association of Canada, 1973).

5. R.W.G. Bryant, *Land, Private Property, Public Control* (Montreal: Harvest House, 1972), pp. 214-15.

6. Ravis, *Saskatoon*, p. 18ff.

7. Dennis and Fish, *Programmes*.

8. See J.J. Costonis, *Space Adrift* (Urbana, Illinois: University of Illinois Press, 1974).

9. William H. Whyte, *The Last Landscape* (New York: Doubleday Anchor, 1968).

10. Director of Public Works, *Town Planning and Ground Exploitation in Amsterdam* (May 1967), p. 32ff.

11. Hans Westerman, "The Role of Private Enterprise in New Towns: Canberra, a Case Study," *The Developer*, 11, no 1 (April 1973). (Record of the Second National Congress of Urban Developers, Canberra, March, 1973.)

12. See Bryant, "The Reconstruction of Coventry," in H. Wentworth Eldredge (ed.), *Taming the Magalopolis* (New York: Doubleday Anchor, 1967).

13. Law Reform Commission of Canada, "Expropriation," *Working Paper 9* (Ottawa: Queen's Printer, 1975).

Public Land Ownership and the Management of Resources

Approaches to Land as a Natural Resource*

Paul Wilkinson
Assistant Professor, Faculty of Environmental Studies, York University

Land is a non-urban as well as an urban resource, and there is a need to examine public ownership of land in relation to non-urban functions such as recreation, agriculture, and resource extraction, and to define the objectives of such ownership. In a legal sense, the term "public" refers to government which, through the democratic process, is ultimately responsible to the general public—that is, to the voting citizen. In a broader sense, however, there is no single element that can be termed *the* public. There are many publics, and their respective concerns and interest alignments change over time, depending on the issues of the moment.[1] One broad definition of a public is any loose association of individuals who are held together by common interests and objectives and by various means of communication.[2] The term "publics" can encompass a wide range of groups, from loosely structured aggregates of individuals who share sets of similar economic, occupational, and social interests, or similar concerns about a common geographic area to highly structured organizations like public-interest groups, government agencies, or industries with specific issue positions and influence strategies.[3]

Therefore, the issue at stake in public ownership should not be ownership by whom—for it is "government" that would own the land—but ownership for whom, on whose behalf, and for what purposes. This principle becomes particularly important when dealing with land as more than space to be occupied or a resource to be developed.

The concept of "ownership" is not common to all cultures. As Beakhust points out (3.5), the native peoples of Northern Canada, for example, do not believe that land can be "owned." Land is part of nature and there for man to use in order to live. A particular person or group may have certain territorial rights or demands on an area of land, but they do not own the land; they merely use it. Similarly, men cannot own the other factors on which survival depends—air, sunlight, water, flora, fauna. This cultural difference has led to numerous conflicts in Northern Canada, such

---

*Introductory paper prepared for this volume. Edited.

as the current controversy over native land claims. In effect, native peoples regarded treaties as "peace treaties," rather than agreements to give government ownership of traditional tribal areas. Only now that native peoples have come to realize that they are under extreme pressure in terms of lifestyle, environmental impact, and indeed survival—not necessarily in a physical sense, but certainly in a cultural sense—have they started to press the argument that they have been cheated.

The need for public ownership of land that has special cultural or physical characteristics is well established. Such lands may have historical, aesthetic, ecological, or physiographic value, which provide special reasons to hold them in public trust. Such a concept is already entrenched in existing legislation. The National Parks Act states that "The parks are largely dedicated to the people of Canada for their benefit, education . . . and . . . shall be maintained and made use of so as to leave them unimpaired for the enjoyment of future generations."[4]

It can also be argued that certain pieces of land must not be used by man for any purpose, except possibly scientific research (e.g. fragile ecological habitats), or only for limited uses (e.g. hazard-zone lands such as floodplains or coastal storm areas). The best way to prevent damaging or dangerous uses is public ownership and regulation. However, little mention is made in this volume of the use of public ownership as a tool to preserve, maintain, or improve ecological systems in general, and the human life support system in particular. In the anthropocentric view, land is regarded as "neutral" until man defines it as a resource to serve a human need. Such a view denies the importance of land in ecological terms. For example, man sees forests as resources for lumbering and recreation, but forests also play a role in climate, erosion control, as animal habitats, etc. Page has pointed out (1.5) that it is not possible to "own" all the elements of the ecological process that affect land; one can only control or have right of use of land. Hare and Andresen also discuss public ownership as a way to preserve land in its natural state for reasons of environmental quality and ecological maintenance (3.1 and 3.2).

In this respect, there is a need for long-term public management of land as a finite and fragile resource. While to a small degree land can be "created" (e.g. by land-fill sites), the major dangers are that it can be destroyed or rendered obsolete for other purposes. Examples of destruction include the poor farm management practices that contributed to widespread erosion in the "dust-bowl" era of the 1930s, or pollution from mining and smelting operations that seriously disrupts ecological systems and results in such barren areas as those near Sudbury. Land can be rendered obsolete for other purposes when options are closed out; for example, urban sprawl means that agriculture is no longer possible in areas which have been encroached upon (see Found 3.3).

Present means of planning and managing non-urban land are ineffective and do not allow for the protection of land of high landscape, historical or recreational quality, agricultural or other resource productivity, or ecological sensitivity. In other words, the present system is based on a traditional economic cost-benefit approach that does not allow for the inclusion of non-monetary and social elements or externalities associated with ecological balance. By making short-term decisions, severe restrictions are placed on the nature of the future. Long-term planning, based on reliable social and physical data, is required. Public land ownership questions often involve meta issues and yet too often decisions are based on insufficient or questionable data. The government has a responsibility to its present and future public to make the best decisions possible. For example, if the Canadian government decides to build the Mackenzie Valley Pipeline—and it probably will—and if one of the major purposes of the pipeline is to meet export commitments, what will Canada do for energy sources in the future? If the James Bay Power Development is completed—and it probably will be—what will be the effects on the climate of much of Canada, on the native peoples displaced by the project, on the economic and political nature of Quebec, and so on?

The papers in this chapter deal with the extent to which public land ownership can be used to assist in the broader management of land as a natural resource. Hare and Andresen consider this question in terms of urban natural environments. Hare concludes that public ownership is in general not necessary to maintain critical elements of the natural environments in cities; exceptions to this are lands associated with environmental hazards. Andresen deals with the management of public land in Ontario municipalities. While being highly critical of the existing environmental management of public land, he nevertheless considers that public ownership is a vital element for the protection of vulnerable urban natural space.

Found (3.3) is concerned with the future of agricultural land in metropolitan regions when faced with a range of demands from urban-oriented users. He is also skeptical of the use of public ownership to solve this class of land use problem; indeed, he suggests that the seriousness of such problems may be highly exaggerated. Wilkinson (3.4) deals with the provision of land for outdoor recreation in metropolitan regions, and forsees the continued growth and demand for recreational space and the need for extended public intervention in potential recreation land.

Beakhust and Cumming (3.5) point out that since land in the North is already predominantly publicly owned, the problem lies in the manner in which ownership is discharged in the light of the interests of native peoples and the fragility of the northern ecology. The authors call for new institutions and improved public education concerning northern development.

The views presented in this chapter differ among themselves and also from opinions expressed at the conference. Public land ownership is not a simple issue that can be easily defined by certain specific goals. It is clear that, in a legal sense, the "public" refers to "government," but questions have been raised concerning whom that government represents, the level and nature of governmental involvement, the direction of the philosophies guiding governmental management and decision making, and the goals (both short and long term) of the ownership. Indeed, the meaning of the term "ownership" has been questioned from both cultural and ecological points of view. Similarly, elsewhere, the meaning of "land" has been questioned, since land is not merely a legally defined area, but one element in human and non-human life-support systems.

A number of instances (e.g. the North, recreational resources, urban natural environments) have been suggested in which public land ownership might be necessary. In other cases like agriculture, public ownership would probably be of assistance in solving some problems, but other methods appear to be more suitable. Finally, it is also suggested that perhaps an equally important mechanism for optimal land management is public land control, that is, the extension of land use zoning and regulation concepts to allow for the integrated management of both public and private land as in the national parks system of Great Britain.

Notes

1. K.P. Warner, *Public Participation in Water Resource Planning* (Ann Arbor: Environmental Simulation Laboratory, School of Natural Resource, University of Michigan, 1971), p. 25.

2. G.N. Jones, "The Multitudinous Publics," in D.L. Anderson, ed., *Municipal Public Relations* (Chicago: International City Managers' Association, 1966), p. 70.

3. Warner, *Public Participation*, p. 25.

4. The National Parks Act, R.S.C. 1952, c. 189 as amended by 1953-54, cc. 4, 6 and 1955, c. 37, act 5.4.

3.1 The Urban Natural Environment*

Kenneth Hare

Director, Institute of Environmental Studies, University of Toronto

A discussion of the relationship between public land ownership and the maintenance of the elements of the urban natural environment.

Is there a significant and specific relationship between public land ownership and the maintenance of an effective urban environment? The built environment is clearly the dominant element in the urban environment. We have designed this built framework in a rather haphazard fashion because of our addiction to "owning" and "using" every single piece of land for human functions. No comprehensive control has been placed on land use, and for that reason urban land use planning has been substantially piecemeal, despite the fact that some kind of planning or design uniformity has been attempted.

Quite apart from this built environment is the natural environment: air, water, parks, ravines, woodlots. The role of maintaining the stability of the elements of this system is of the highest priority. Take, for example, the extensive ravine systems of Toronto. What can one say about their future and their ecological value? To what extent is it possible to intervene rationally in their management, on the basis of what we now know about general principles of forest and woodland ecology? Is there a specific relationship between the concerns we have about the natural environment and public land ownership? I suggest that there are at least five sets of elements that come under the heading of environmental considerations.

First of all, I think we are concerned with quality of the environmental media—air, water, and soil. For example, in regard to air quality, it certainly is silly to have lead-smelting operations downtown. Does the public need to own the land to prevent lead-smelting in this area? The answer is "no," because the area can be zoned in such a way that it is impossible; therefore public ownership is not required in such a case. The quality of water in the city is a more complex case, and it is of considerable interest to public health authorities. It is generally not a question of clean water for consumptive purposes that is the issue, for that can be dealt with by water treatment facilities; it is a question of whether there are large bodies of polluted or contaminated water in the surrounding region. Certainly in some areas, especially in some European cities, it has characteristically been the case that local authorities have attempted to own wetlands, mainly in the interest of public safety and public health; and in most cases, nobody else wants to own these areas anyway. There is

---

*Remarks to conference workshop. Edited.

a possible case for public ownership of land surrounding water bodies or of wetlands. Soil is universal and the public does not have to own the soil to protect it.

The second set of considerations concerns maintenance of the urban ecosystem or at least the biotic part, the urban greenery. Greenery in a city plays an important role because vegetation can filter out contaminants; it has the capacity to purify air; and it certainly can alter the physical characteristics of the city. Obviously land does not have to be owned to guarantee that it remains green or that wildlife can be protected or that things like ragweed can be eliminated. It may be a help to do so, but it is not a necessity.

A third element in which public ownership is essential, however, is land for amenity purposes. In the old world, parks are often not publicly owned; some of the great parks of the earth are privately owned and they are guaranteed to remain parks by the terms of the land ownership. If there is a sufficiently well-established urban culture, there can be private ownership of amenity areas, even public access to private parks and open spaces. But in a new society where there is intense competition for land, such areas should be publicly owned in order to guarantee access to parks, shorelines, lakes, playing fields, sports parks, etc.

Fourth is the aesthetic element that keeps the city worth looking at, preserves vistas, and avoids noise pollution. There is no immediate connection of this element with the ownership of the land. Regulations to maintain the aesthetic quality of the environment will bear just as much on the private owner as upon the public.

Finally there are considerations of public safety, such as wind hazard, shoreline and slope control, and flood control. In some cases, it may be essential, as in conservation areas, to own in order to protect. Certainly the ravines of the city should not be in private ownership, and one of the reasons is public safety. The best way to keep people from drowning on flood plains is to own the land publicly and prohibit the private use of such potentially hazardous areas.

These are cases where ownership may be the key to the kind of environmental control desired. But in general it is necessary to identify the need for effective zoning and regulation rather than to increase public ownership.

3.2 The Management of Urban Vegetation*

John Andresen
Professor of Urban Forestry, University of Toronto

The problems associated with the management of urban vegetation in Ontario.

Toronto's ravine system is under the jurisdiction of the Metropolitan Toronto and Region Conservation Authority (a provincial government agency), but not all ravine land is under public ownership. A great amount is under private ownership, so that even if the Conservation Authority wants to practice the best management concepts, it cannot impose them on contiguous land. Unfortunately, the gap between ideal and real management concepts is widening. The Conservation Authority is not practicing the best management even on its own land because the agency has been diverted somewhat from its original charge to conserve land. It is now more concerned with developing land, especially recreational development, to meet the increasing demands of the urban public.

Recently the University of Toronto conducted a survey of the urban forestry needs of the municipalities of Ontario. There are some 800 municipal jurisdictions in Ontario, including regions, cities, villages, townships, etc. The purpose of the survey was to try to determine how they manage their public land. Out of approximately 450 responses received, there were only about 30 indicating specific by-laws controlling the management of either the vegetation or the public land under a jurisdiction (and this could be anything from a county to a region to a village). This means that in most cases there is no management. Since legislation is minimal, so is monitoring or control. The various departments within the municipalities in charge of the actual maintenance of management usually are low on the totem pole in terms of personnel and budgets, and these usually are the ones to be cut first. Land management activities are going to suffer even more because revenue or returned revenues to municipalities in Ontario are going to be reduced substantially.

The University of Toronto is studying the Ontario Ministry of Transportation and Communication to determine what types of policies and practices they use in managing roadside vegetation. Up to the present time they have had a rather sizeable budget, but it is being curtailed; among the first activities to be eliminated are land management and vegetation management. This may be fortunate because studies here and in the United States indicate that the most economical, ecologically sound, and realistic approach to vegetation is to let nature do the work. If managed

---

*Remarks to conference workshop. Edited.

properly, most of the control of woodlots and vegetation contiguous to roadsides and transportation services corridors is best left to nature. Only minimum management practices, which cost a fraction of present artificial maintenance, are necessary.

We are also doing a study of the policies and practices of the various jurisdictions that control the land along the Metropolitan Toronto shoreline. Some of this land is under the control of the Conservation Authority, but there are at least 80 different jurisdictions involved. Some of these overlap, some superimpose, and some are under private land management; in essence it is a chaotic situation. The goal of the Conservation Authority is to develop a linear park with some type of a cohesive managerial policy. At present, however, policies and practices in most instances are detrimental to the shoreline ecosystem. For example, the ravines that drain into this area are either subverted now or blocked, so that there is no natural marsh vegetation left in Metropolitan Toronto; on either side of the city there is some marshland, but this is beginning to disappear also. By manipulating the environment in response to the needs and demands of a rather affluent public, the ecosystem is suffering quite a bit. Open land in metropolitan areas provides both physiological and psychological amenities (though no hard scientific data is available on this point yet). There is still enough time to come up with some realistic land management policy in the urban sphere to preserve these amenities, and public land ownership will be an important element in that policy because urban land banking is about the only way to control land management effectively.

If there was a responsible citizenry that could, in a long-term, continuous sense, maintain the land through private ownership, public land ownership would not be necessary. Apparently Canada is a nation of migrants now, so there is often a very short tenure of land ownership. Even governments often have short tenure, so their policies, even though they may be good, are not followed through by a subsequent administration. And government agencies, such as the Conservation Authority or the US Army Corps of Engineers, sometimes bend to public will and whim and do not provide adequate protection for the land. It is a dilemma, and one of the alternatives is public land ownership, but it would require a drastically revised land ethic.

3.3 Agricultural Land Use in Metropolitan Regions*

William Found
Professor of Geography, York University

An examination of five problems associated with agricultural land use in North American metropolitan regions, and the role that public land ownership might play in helping overcome them.

The Disappearance of Agricultural Land

A problem that has been identified for at least several decades is the disappearance of agricultural land because of spreading urbanization. It is popularly felt that this process is highly undesirable, particularly in view of concern about food supply in the future, when populations will be larger and land resources may be more scarce.

One should question whether or not the need to preserve land for agriculture is really imperative. In the North American context, one of the great agricultural problems still appears to be over-production rather than under-production. Second, even where land has fairly high capability for agricultural production, it may have an overwhelmingly greater advantage for some other type of use—perhaps even for urban development. If cities are to be built away from areas of good agricultural land, surely it would make good sense to calculate the added costs of urban development in other areas and relate them to the values of future levels of agricultural production in the areas to be preserved. My own view is that there is some sense in preserving core areas of very high agricultural production, such as that portion of the Niagara peninsula near St Catharines, but I would question very seriously any simple rules about always preserving land of reasonably high agricultural productivity. If we are to preserve agricultural land, good land management can be encouraged as much by taxing and zoning measures as by public land ownership. This approach has, of course, the advantage of using private funds for investment in agricultural production.

Derelict Land in the Inner Fringe

This is the ring or belt of land from one to five miles in width that surrounds existing built-up areas. It appears to be land that has been purchased by developers, removed from agricultural production, and is

*Paper prepared for conference workshop. Edited.

awaiting urban development in the very near future. Its existence has been described as extremely unpleasant in an aesthetic sense, as well as a waste of valuable land resources that could be in agriculture or other productive uses.

Although a zone of derelict land use may have characterized North American cities, these zones were particularly prevalent where land use planning and zoning were not in effect. Recent research by the Department of Geography at York University indicates that for the case of Metropolitan Toronto, where planning controls have been in effect for some time, a classical zone of derelict land does not appear to exist. In fact, fairly intensive and productive agricultural land use abuts the frontiers of the city. Current planning practices have to a considerable degree solved the problem of the derelict zone without the need for public land ownership.

Reduction in Agricultural Productivity in the Outer Fringe

Related to the second problem has been evidence of decline in the intensity or extent of agricultural production in lands that extend far beyond the inner derelict zone. It is felt that, due to speculative pressures, uncertainty concerning possible urban development, and the purchase of agricultural land by city persons who are not really farmers, "normal" levels of agricultural production have tended to decline in varying degrees.

Again, research in our department and other centres in Canada suggests that the declines in agricultural production hypothesized for this broad zone surrounding the city are very difficult to substantiate. Admittedly, there are differences in land use management between areas of urban influence and those without urban influence. But the net result does not appear to be a critical reduction in agricultural productivity. Rather, there are switches from livestock to crop farm economies. Again, it appears that this problem has been quite substantially avoided without the use of public land ownership.

Land in Private Estates for an Elite Class

This is an additional problem that has both economic and social dimensions. There has been an apparent tendency for much land on the edge of cities to pass from farmers into the hands of wealthy persons whose incomes are derived from the city, and who could be described as members of a social elite.

Clearly, rural estates, complete with horses and white painted fences, are a significant portion of the landscapes surrounding most North American cities. But research, at least in the local region, suggests that these estates tend not to occur in areas of high agricultural productivity, and that they are often associated with reasonably high levels of agricultural production relative to local capabilities. In regard to the social factor, the maintenance of large rural estates (in Ontario, at least) has been encouraged by laws which prevent severances from large farm properties rather than by invidious social forces. The evidence is very clear that if the rules concerning severances were to be relaxed, much of the rest of the urban population, including working class and middle class, would be permitted (and would take the opportunity) to purchase land in the more aesthetically pleasing portions of the urban fringe. Again, public land ownership appears to be an awkward and unnecessary solution to the problem.

High Land Values Resulting from Speculation

It is felt that the speculative process leads not only to declines in agricultural production, as described above, but also to considerable inflation in the value of land, which is eventually passed on to those who must purchase lots in newly developed areas around the fringes of cities. However, it is difficult to show that the purchase, selling, and re-purchase of land in the rural-urban fringe by persons called speculators has increased the value of land over that which would have obtained without the presence of the speculator. What may be a factor in inflating land values is the extent to which a small group of speculators can collude to effect some kind of monopolistic control. Perhaps the solution is not for public land ownership, but for efforts to break down this form of collusion and reintroduce real competition in the market for land beyond the edge of the city. For example, cities could accept bids from competing developers, complete with the exposure of profit margins, in an attempt to encourage urban development in the least costly fashion. A second factor that has probably had some influence on very high land values has been the severe restriction on the development of new urban land into the countryside. If land is in short supply, then price inelasticity will be demonstrated by very high land values.

At first glance, it may be concluded that public ownership of land in the rural-urban fringe could alleviate some or all of these five problems. Of course, there would be costs associated with public purchase of much of this land; very extensive government funding would be required. Even a quick calculation of the costs that might be incurred for such extensive purchases of land in the rural-urban fringe suggests that governments would be under severe financial pressure in order to make the necessary acquisitions. Associated with the requirements for funds might be the problems of incurring huge public debts, or the temptation for governments to create more money, which leads to additional inflationary pressures. Inflation would also be bound to occur if such large funds were to be injected into the land economy. Another problem associated with land ownership would be the necessity to establish a considerable bureaucracy to decide which lands should be purchased and how they should be used. Before establishing this bureaucracy there would have to be some certainty that the land-related decisions to be made would be superior to those occurring under some loosely constrained, free land market.

Thus, public land ownership could probably be of assistance in solving each of these five land use problems, but other methods may be much more effective. In addition, some of these problems may be grossly exaggerated or may derive from historical circumstances around North American cities that no longer exist.

3.4 Recreational Land in Metropolitan Regions*

Paul Wilkinson
Assistant Professor, Faculty of Environmental Studies, York University

The pressure for additional outdoor recreation space is considered in light of the roles of private and public organizations.

The consumption of and participation in outdoor recreation in North America in general and in Ontario in particular are expanding rapidly. A straight-line projection of attendance at provincial parks in Ontario, for example, would indicate that within 15-20 years, numbers of visitors will reach astronomical proportions. Obviously such projection techniques are highly suspect, but they do point out the magnitude of trends. This growth rate must slow down eventually, but the question is "when?" Factors such as inflation and the energy crisis have had little, if any, effect on non-urban recreation patterns. (Indeed, it could be argued that eventually such factors could increase the demand for outdoor recreation on public land near urban centres because of the lower cost of using these resources as opposed to long-distance travel or the purchase of a second home.) Pressure is increasing on existing non-urban open space and will continue to increase into the foreseeable future.

*Paper prepared for conference workshop. Edited.

In particular, this pressure has been greatest on prime recreational resources, such as lakes suitable for cottages, "wilderness" areas, and skiing hills. The results have been a concomitant increase in land values and speculation, factors which have, for instance, effectively limited the purchase of a cottage within 150 miles of Toronto by anyone except the upper middle class. If recreation is a prime component of "quality of life"—at least in North American terms—then economics may no longer be an appropriate determinant of the ability to participate in outdoor recreation. In social welfare terms, it is therefore the responsibility of government to provide non-urban land for outdoor recreation.

This is not to say, however, that considerable public land resources do not already exist. Ontario, for example, has an extensive system of provincial parks and conservation authority areas. These are recognized by the public and advertised by the government as being "parks," that is, recreational resources. On the other hand, there is much public land that is not considered to be a recreational resource because it is not seen—either by government or public—as serving that function. Examples would include Crown lands (over three-quarters of all of Ontario, in particular northern Ontario, is Crown land), county forests, public utility lands, airport buffer zones, etc. Where possible, these lands should be made available for public recreation purposes. Often this would require only small capital outlays. For example, the Ontario Hydro-Electric Commission has recently changed its policy on electric transmission-corridor rights-of-way. In urban areas, municipalities are being given access to parcels of Hydro land for urban garden allotments; a rental fee is charged to users, resulting in an almost self-sustaining operation. In other areas, Hydro has opened its rights-of-way to hiking and horse-riding.

It is obvious that such lands are often not "prime" recreational resources or resource-based recreation areas. Rather, they are usually intermediate or user-oriented areas. Such is the case, for example, with the county forest system in Ontario, where much of the land is either scrub forest or reforested (former agricultural) land. These areas do, however, have great potential for expanded use, perhaps in innovative and non-traditional ways. For example, a heavily managed county forest could be used as an interpretative centre to teach basics of forest management. Other such areas would be well suited for activities such as snowmobiling, indeed better suited than areas having more fragile ecosystems. Almost all such areas have possibilities for picnicking and perhaps for overnight camping. The potential is there; it just has not been recognized or exploited.

At the other end of the scale is resource-based or prime recreational land. In southern Ontario, the pattern is private ownership and use for a number of reasons, one of which is historical. The trend to private cottages in such areas as Lake Simcoe and the Muskoka Lakes began in the early part of the 20th century, long before public ownership of recreational land became an issue. (For example, there are only seven miles of public beach—excluding road allowances—on Lake Simcoe.) A second factor is the large capital expenditure that is required to develop recreational resources like ski resorts. There is an alarming trend toward transforming privately owned resources (e.g. ski resorts and lodges), which were formerly open to the public, into clubs for the private use of members because of the cost of operation. A third factor is also the result of economic considerations. The government is reluctant to invest in large capital expenditures for recreation, preferring as a matter of policy to leave such developments to the private sector. The problem, however, has been that recreation is often a risky business for the financial community. When combined with government's lack of incentives (e.g. absence of low-interest loans, tax advantages, or development advice), the result has been a general reluctance on the part of the private sector to engage in such ventures. It is argued that government must re-evaluate its policies towards the recreation industry, recognizing its importance to the economy and its peculiar economic characteristics.

One other type of land has, until recently, received little attention. That is land of historical, prehistorical, or physiographic importance. These are unique resources—ones which man cannot create. These lands provide a great recreational-educational opportunity that deserves greater recognition. There is little incentive on the part of the private sector to preserve such resources; therefore, the onus should be on the public sector.

In a certain sense, a seemingly contradictory argument has been presented here. On one hand, it has been argued that, because recreation cannot be dealt with in terms of traditional economics, the public sector must take more responsibility for providing non-urban land for outdoor recreation. On the other hand, it has been argued that government should provide greater incentives to the private sector to develop the recreation industry. These arguments, however, are really each aimed at increasing the stock of land available for outdoor recreation. They merely indicate that both the public and the private sector have a role—albeit quite different—in providing recreational land. Increased cooperation among all parties and more integrated planning for recreation are obviously also needed.

Another possible solution to making more recreational land available is a complete rethinking of the North American concept of private property. In Great Britain, for example, national park areas include land that is owned both privately and publicly. It is the use, not necessarily the ownership, of the land that is publicly controlled. Parts of the park areas are publicly owned as "parks" in the traditional sense. Other parts include urban areas, agricultural land, extractive industries (e.g. gravel pits, forest areas), etc. The use of such land is publicly controlled in the sense that a new housing development cannot be built on land that has been traditionally agricultural without permission. Similarly, a gravel pit or forestry operation cannot be expanded. Provision is also made for the public use of privately owned land by such mechanisms as rights-of-way. (The laws of trespassing, negligence and nuisance do, of course, apply.) Such an approach would be difficult to formulate to fit North America traditions, but not impossible. Meanwhile, there is a great and growing need for public intervention into the provision of non-urban recreational land, since it is unlikely to be provided in any other way.

3.5 Land Claims, Energy, and Northern Development*

Grahame Beakhust
Assistant Professor, Faculty of Environmental Studies, York University

Peter Cumming
Professor, Osgoode Hall Law School, York University

A critical review of federal policies for land and resources in Northern Canada, with special reference to the land rights of native peoples.

Northern Canada (i.e. the Yukon Territory, the Northwest Territories, Arctic Quebec, and Labrador) represents a key national resource from the perspective of energy potential and is one which Canadians have a duty to protect for the present and the future of both northerners and southerners. Such protection is possible only if there is policy, planning, and legislation based on a comprehensive appreciation of the problems involved.

One issue in planning the future of the north is public land ownership, but the crux of the matter is not really public versus private ownership, but rather the nature of public ownership, the way in which lands are disposed of, and the regulation of their subsequent use in the public interest.

The two territories have an area of over 1.3 million square miles with some 60,000 inhabitants, most of them native peoples scattered across almost 100 settlements. This area is a monolithic jurisdiction, with the federal government claiming title to all of the land and adjacent waters, as well as the off-shore and subsurface mineral rights. The area is administered by the Natural Resources and Environment Branch of the Department of Indian and Northern Affairs, with very minor roles played by such

*Paper prepared for conference workshop. Edited.

departments as Environment Canada and the Department of Energy, Mines and Resources. The territorial governments derive their powers from an act of the federal parliament, whereas the provincial governments derive their powers directly from the British North America Act. The territorial commissioners and their deputies are appointed federal public servants and the territorial councils are largely advisory. Lands within communities— "Commissioner's Lands"—have been turned over by the federal government to the territorial governments to permit increasing degrees of local control over municipal affairs. The territorial governments are in the process of turning these lands over to the communities themselves, although they retain considerable powers in Yellowknife and Whitehorse. All other lands and all resources except game remain under the control of the federal government.

It appears that the Northern Program of the Department of Indian and Northern Affairs is guided by a development philosophy inherited from the "Northern Vision" of the fifties—a philosophy of development for its own sake, which usually meant development for the benefit of the corporate sector. The problem with this philosophy in practice is the lack of checks and balances. There are a number of reasons for this:

1 Federal, provincial, and municipal levels of government are largely independent in southern Canada. In the territories there is really only one government—the federal government.
2 The local population is small and scattered, hindered by great distances and poor communications. Many have little or no knowledge of the government system and the mysteries of its operation, and their views are poorly represented in the bureaucratic decision-making process.
3 The rest of the Canadian population is far removed, knows little about the north, and sees it largely as a major source of "much needed" energy resources.
4 The development philosophy of the federal government is coincident with the goals of the energy industry, which has a strong vested interest in the north. One branch of one department (the Natural Resources and Environment Branch of the Department of Indian and Northern Affairs) makes all of the decisions, and its dominant goal is development, despite its name. Moreover, this branch both administers and enforces land use regulations. When the government operates as a developer through state corporations (Panarctic, and now Petrocan)—the "regulated" therefore becomes the "regulator."

This philosophy should be supplanted by development controlled to a much greater extent by native people and regulated in the interests of the physical environment. Since the land is now (subject to native claims) seen as being in some form of public ownership, the main questions are: ownership by which public owner and development in whose public interest?

Fossil fuels are finite resources. If federal policy, as presently stated, is one of eventual energy self-sufficiency, then it is unwise to adopt the short-term development goals of the energy industry, particularly those of meeting export quotas. It seems at this point in time that, no matter what evidence is presented to the Berger Commission[1] and the National Energy Board, the Mackenzie Valley gas pipeline will be built, providing that money for its construction and the reserves for its throughput can be generated and discovered. If construction of a line does proceed, it should be to meet Canadian rather than United States needs, and it is only proper that northerners should receive large benefits from this development. The answer to the question of "development for whom?" is, therefore, Canadians in general and northerners in particular—setting aside for the moment the question of whether gas pipelines *can* bring any significant benefits to northerners.

A major problem transcending ownership issues is the ecological sensitivity of the area. Perhaps even northerners are not always attuned to this fact, but then they have never had the inclination or the means to destroy their environment in the manner of modern industry, both private and public. Hydrocarbon development in the north, and offshore drilling in particular, could well be ecologically disastrous and, therefore, merits strong control and regulation by the public.

The question of "ownership by which public owner?" is also complex. The native peoples' view of the land is that it is there for man to use, but to use wisely. Although recent court decisions are somewhat ambiguous, it can be argued that British and Canadian law clearly recognizes that the native peoples have title to the lands traditionally used and occupied. When native people signed treaties (and some did not, including all the Inuit), they regarded them as peace treaties, not land dispositions. Increasing legal sophistication has now led them to press land claims both in court and with the federal government. The matter is currently under discussion by the federal cabinet and it is likely that many claims will be found to be justified and compensation made. However, the fear is that the government may try to insist that compensation is in the form of money rather than a return of misappropriated lands, which would be retained under federal control. The Inuit emphasize the retention of lands as being the crucial element to settlement.

While the territorial governments in one sense represent northerners more effectively than the remote, southern-controlled federal government, without control over natural resources they remain powerless and financially dependent on Ottawa. At the same time, although native people are well represented on the Council of the Northwest Territories, they are very poorly represented in its administration, particularly at senior levels. The present governments differ very little from the federal position in their development philosophy, and transferring jurisdiction over natural resources to Yellowknife and Whitehorse might well, at the moment, increase the pace of energy-related development and reduce environmental regulation.

With respect to checks and balances, a mechanism is required that will allow the interests of the various "publics"—including native peoples, government, environmentalists, and industry—to be taken into account in the decision-making process. A number of alternatives are available. One would be a gradual transfer of power to the territorial governments as they become more truly representative. A second would be a formal mechanism, similar to the United States Environmental Protection Act, which requires an environmental impact assessment statement before any major development can be undertaken. This is in contrast to the present Canadian system, which employs ad hoc procedures such as the Berger Commission and the in-house review of the James Bay Development Project. The Berger Commission is mostly a response to pressures from native peoples and environmental groups, and it can only make recommendations on actions to ameliorate the impact of the proposed pipeline.

For the James Bay project there was only a post hoc in-house evaluation, none of which was made public. The problem is that crucial development decisions are usually made in a bureaucratic rather than a legislative setting, behind closed doors where debates are conducted at inter- and intra-department meetings of officials, and not in a public forum of elected representatives. In addition many interested parties, and particularly native people, are not given sufficient information on which to base a constructive input to the process.

Another alternative for the control of development would be to put the northern lands controlled by the federal government into an innovative form of trusteeship, rather than into the present form of perceived ownership, which permits Ottawa to act like a private landowner. Under this provision, no major development decisions would be made until mechanisms had developed permitting local people and other public interest viewpoints a major role in decision making.

Another possibility would be the creation of an agency consisting of representatives of the two levels of government, native peoples, and environmentalists, which would advise government on development-related problems and regulatory measures designed to reduce or eliminate them. It could enforce regulations, including imposing development freezes over certain areas. The United States set a precedent when the Secretary of the Interior placed a development freeze on Alaska between 1966 and 1971, established the Land Use Planning Commission, and set aside various lands for native peoples, national parks, federal and state governments, and industry. The situation was relatively satisfactory to all parties, including industry, which then knew and clearly understood the rules to be followed.

Whatever happens in the north, some form of regional decision making seems to be required, perhaps based on major watersheds or social divisions. The area is simply too large to be either centrally or locally planned. Following the Alaskan example, areas should be set aside for different uses, including substantial ones exclusively for native peoples as private owners. The Inuit in the Northwest Territories are proposing a new territory, which would incorporate more effective regional government and local participation.

It is fair to say that in addition to its other problems, there is a lack of information provided by government and media about what is going on in the north, particularly with respect to energy development. Neither northerners nor southerners are presented with future alternatives other than rapid resource development, and northerners are offered a very limited array of choices. There are in fact many options for the north, and these include resource development, but resource development consistent with the ability of the northern environment and peoples to sustain its impact, and consistent with the long-run needs of southern Canadians. Much improved public education, including freedom of access to government information, about these alternatives is a first priority if southerners are not to be stampeded into a program of northern development that is ultimately not in the public interest.

Note

1. Refers to the Mackenzie Valley Pipeline Inquiry held by Mr Justice Thomas Berger of the British Columbia Supreme Court, which was set up in April 1974 to hold hearings into the regional, social, environmental, and economic impact of the proposed Mackenzie Valley natural gas pipeline, and to make recommendations to the Department of Indian and Northern Affairs.

**Part Two:
Case Studies**

The Canadian Experience

The Political Institutionalization of Public Land Ownership

Tools for dealing with land related problems go through a series of stages of development before they come into common usage. How does an idea take shape, build a constituency among "experts" and politicians, and become used in such a way as to pay sufficient political or economic dividends to ensure its durability?

Urban reformers have, since the turn of this century, been developing new concepts and ideas of governmental tools to deal with the problems of the use of land. We are concerned here with how public ownership has been institutionalized in Canada. To understand this process, it is necessary to trace the development of the concept through efforts of reform groups or spokesmen and through the statements of political actors who have had "on line" responsibility for implementing programs or legislative proposals. This chapter will look at the actual results of a series of programs from federal, provincial, and municipal vantage points and will explore what some of the bureaucratic pitfalls may be involved in the process.

It is perhaps important to mention, at the outset, that although Canada has much in common with its neighbour to the south and with other industrialized western democracies, any lessons learned here are not necessarily freely transferable. For one thing, the very expanse of the country and vast government holdings of land have to some extent shaped the official outlook towards government involvement in land ownership. Also, the particular form of Canadian parliamentary democracy and federalism has resulted in a very unique division of land use responsibilities between different levels of government. The federal government is basically the banking institution for housing and land development, but it tends not to retain any actual program control. The ten provinces are the major coordinators for housing and land-related development, and any new programs or policies are usually run through provincial agencies. However, the major workhorses for the local regulation of land use are the municipalities or, in some provinces, the newly emerging regional municipalities; and any new program or policy must be coordinated with these units, which are often jealous of their powers and prerogatives. Some of the more innovative local municipalities have, in fact, started their own land storage programs with municipal and federal monies, involving only provincial sanction and not direct involvement.

In Canada, as in the United States, the problems of how people live on the land, variously described as the "urban crisis" or the "housing crisis," generated a great deal of comment and discussion in the late 1960s. A number of tools were suggested by individuals and by officially sanctioned groups to alleviate the problems. Some tools, like subsidies for lower income families, which could amalgamate support among a wide variety of both consuming groups (neighbourhood groups, tenants' organizations, etc.) and producing groups (national associations of homebuilders, construction unions, etc.), were institutionalized quickly. Others, particularly those with a longer time horizon (and therefore less immediate impact), earned little support from groups in the community and took longer to become viable. The notion of using ownership instead of mere regulation or subsidy is a concept which managed to develop from the definitional to the operational stage in Canada.

It is interesting to compare the initial articulation of the idea of public ownership as a possible tool to deal with various crises in Canada, where the tool has been institutionalized—and in the United States, where it has not been used except in a few scattered and unique circumstances. First, in Canada the process of investigating urban crisis was undertaken by an officially sanctioned commission, the Federal Task Force on Housing and Urban Development, which began meeting in 1968. The mandate of the commission was to "examine housing and urban development in Canada and to report on ways in which the federal government in company with other levels of government and the private sector can help meet the housing needs of all Canadians and contribute to the development of modern, vital cities." The commission made a number of recommendations when it reported in 1969,[1] many of which received little public support, failed to coalesce interest-group support, and disappeared from the public view. Others fared better. In particular the commission recommended that:

Municipalities or regional governments, as a matter of continuing policy, should acquire, service, and sell all or a substantial portion of the land required for urban growth within their boundaries. The federal government should make direct loans to municipalities or regional governments to assist them in assembling and servicing land for urban growth.

This stand was picked up by a number of experts working for groups such as the Community Planning Association of Canada.[2]

This development was mirrored in the United States where a number of similar official groups articulated the position. In 1968 the National Commission on Urban Problems, in its report *Building the American City* 251 (1968) recommended that state governments enact legislation to allow advance land acquisition to enable the timing of growth, the prevention of urban sprawl, and the recapture of government servicing costs. Similarly the President's Committee on Urban Housing voiced such an opinion in its findings, *A Decent Home* (1969), as did the President's Task Force on Suburban Problems (*Final Report* [1968]) and the Advisory Commission on Inter-Governmental Relations (*Urban and Rural America* [1968]). As in the Canadian experience, a number of major urban interest groups also supported the idea. For instance the American Institute of Planners (in its *Policy Statement on New Communities* [1968]), the National Urban Coalition (in *Counter Budget: A Blueprint for Changing National Priorities* [1971]), and the American Institute of Architecture (in the *First Report of the National Policy Task Force* [1972]), all came out in favour of public land ownership as a tool for shaping urban growth.

The next phase of institutionalization is, however, the more interesting one, for it represents the bridging of the gap between mere conceptualization to the more difficult institutionalization of the tool within government programs. In the United States the idea of public land ownership and land assembly has received extensive academic discussion and debate, but there has been very little actual implementation. In the American setting, the public ownership has not received wide support among politicians, although the Congress did pass the Housing and Community Development Act of 1974, which authorized the use of federal funds for land banking. Some communities have toyed with the idea of small-scale land banking programs (e.g. Palo Alto, California, and Boulder, Colorado). However, funds have not yet been forthcoming and no surge of support has forced the issue into the political limelight. There are, of course, numerous reasons for this, but one of the most pressing is the simple fact that the issue is viewed in ideological terms in the United States. It is presented as a threat to other major institutions of society (e.g. to the "free enterprise" system of housing construction). Thus the idea must face not only criticism from the particular groups that would be affected, such as the private land assembly and development companies, but also from groups who equate public land assembly with various political "isms."

In Canada, however, with a tradition of consensus politics, the public ownership was presented as a technical governmental solution to a particular crisis that did not strike at any of the ideological foundations of the society. Viewed as such, the programs could grow without widespread antagonism. It is important to put the development of the concept into an historical perspective and the discussion of the Canadian antecedents mentioned by Dennis (4.7), are quite helpful. In the same way that he could allude to a long Canadian tradition of public ownership and the mere technical nature of this tool, similar political actors could use public ownership schemes to augment other programs of house building, shelter subsidies, and land servicing. Programs in Canada, particularly the federal funding of local programs, could grow substantially without becoming a political issue. In fact, it was often the parties of a conservative bent, such as the Progressive Conservative Party in Ontario, which proposed some of the most wide-ranging public assembly and public ownership programs.

Public land ownership came to be useful in Canada as a public policy tool at all three levels of government—federal, provincial, and municipal. It could be used for different purposes at the various levels, and could be viewed in different time horizons. To make the programs viable, cooperation is necessary between the various levels of government. The review of the federal role in land management (4.1) and the remarks by Ryan (4.2) give an insight into the way the *federal government* views the idea of public land ownership. First of all, it was not meant to destroy the private land assembly business, but merely to augment it, particularly in areas with relatively little serviced land. Second, the idea was primarily to increase housing production throughout the country, and while planning goals are mentioned, they are given relatively small importance. Finally, since the federal government can only serve as a financial institution, the major reliance was on the provinces and the municipalities to develop and manage programs. From the federal standpoint, the advantage of public land assembly was that it facilitated public installation of infrastructure and the construction of major municipal servicing centres such as schools and libraries. Further, being a banker allowed the federal government to have more control over all the inputs into the development process. It tended to assure provincial coordination of agency programs, and of such devices as taxation or subsidy schemes. In a major sense, the provision of land allows the CMHC to meet its national production quotas by making sure that serviced land will be available.

For the second level of government, *the provinces*, programs were not viewed from the long-range focus of the federal government housing banker, whose major interest was housing construction and the national economy, but from the short-term focus of particular provincial political aims.

White (4.3) discusses the rationale behind his government's large-scale entry into the land assembly business. Not only did the provincial government establish a program for small-scale subdivision by the province (the Home Ownership Made Easy plan) and sanction public land assemblies by some municipalities, but it also assembled some $290 million worth of new town sites within the province. White's views represent an interesting elaboration of the Canadian approach. A conservative both by temperment and by political persuasion, White used the tool of public land ownership to take development pressure off a series of medium-sized Ontario towns and transferred that growth to a series of new town sites. Rather than competing with private land developers, the program augmented their efforts by opening up lands that, because of tremendous servicing costs, would not otherwise have been developed. The short piece (4.4) following White's paper represents a distillation of a researcher's critical findings concerning one facet of the Ontario programs.

Rawson (4.5) describes the British Columbia experience, where the central idea was to create as many concrete results as possible before the next provincial election (which took place in November 1975 and resulted in the defeat of the government). In British Columbia, land assembly programs were directed at immediate housing production or immediate permanent conservation and not at any long-term planning or housing programs. Thus, while the idea of land assembly is presented by federal officials as a way to order capital expenditure over time, in British Columbia the tool is viewed much more as a short-term facilitator of immediate development.

Turning to the *local level* of government, we have four papers which approach the municipal role from different angles. The first, by Goldrick (4.6) attempts to relate the private development of land to the development of a viable city unit, and states the case against the private land market in terms of social effect. Goldrick suggests that private ownership of land is central to "finance capitalism," which seeks to appropriate wealth "through the production not only of goods but of new modes of consumption and new social wants and social needs." The primary mechanism to accomplish this are the processes of suburbanization and redevelopment associated with urban growth. These are governed by private land assembly and land speculation activities prior to the social design of new communities and the infrastructures necessary to support them. In this way, Goldrick suggests, "city government . . . [acts] . . . in a support capacity to finance capitalism . . . [to facilitate] . . . the conversion of private property rights into private individual or corporate gain." Goldrick demonstrates this point by citing the Central Area Plan for the City of Toronto, which he believes accommodates the profit-maximizing decisions of speculative developers, despite its emergence from the so-called "reform" council and the incorporation of considerable public land ownership elements.

In exploring the current municipal use of public ownership and setting that development in historical perspective, Dennis (4.7) points out that the problems of large-scale land banking have resulted in a switch in public land ownership activity to city centres—especially Toronto and Vancouver. Public development of sites is possible here because services are already provided and if advantage is taken of obsolete industrial land and of existing publicly owned land, land costs per unit are much lower than at the metropolitan fringe. In contrast with land assembly for new towns, centre-city assembly of land has been directed towards explicit social problems, rather than wider economic growth issues.

Leathem (4.8) then describes the usefulness of municipal ownership in dealing with parkland and servicing problems. Finally, Rumm (4.9) makes a vigorous presentation stating the position of the private developer operating within municipalities. He views public land ownership and other government controls on development as key elements in the increase in price of land and the housing shortage. He places the blame for our urban dilemma on government interference at all levels.

To conclude the chapter there is a short section on the use of ownership dealing with the problems of a national capital region, which must bridge two provinces, numerous municipalities, and the chasms between the federal, provincial, and municipal governments. The National Capital Commission, a Canadian federal government agency, has the responsibility for planning and coordinating development in the Ottawa-Hull region. Public land ownership has been the main tool used by the NCC since its creation in 1958, and at present it owns 125,000 acres in the area. The NCC's land assembly program is evaluated in relation to the effectiveness of the associated comprehensive planning process carried out in Ottawa. The paper by Gallant (4.10), testifies to the uniqueness of the situation. While Ottawa remains a model for the use of public land ownership in conjunction with positive planning controls, in the vital area of housing, at least, there is still what Garland (4.11) calls "the Canadian reality . . . of overlapping jurisdictions." In many ways this example pinpoints some of the most useful aspects of consolidating development power in the hands of one agency. Similarly, however, it highlights some of the difficulties and dangers of such a consolidation of power.

The process of institutionalizing the tool of public ownership begins with the articulation of the idea by various official spokesmen and then proceeds to some sort of official acceptance by political actors. One of the major factors in determining how useful a tool can be is the degree to which it becomes accepted by various groups or becomes associated with various ideological positions. What we do not learn from this process and the positions represented is the longevity of the concept and the means available to evaluate its political or economic effectiveness over time. There is little comment upon the effectiveness of the programs because, although the idea of public land ownership as a tool has been institutionalized, evaluation procedure has not. There is a lack of checks of the efficiency of public ownership in meeting various program goals, whether they be lower housing prices, the recapture of unearned increment, or the attainment of better planning.

Notes

1. *Report of the Task Force on Housing and Urban Development*, Chairman, Paul T. Hellyer (Ottawa: Queen's Printer, January 1969).

2. See, for instance, D.P. Ravis, *The Saskatoon Experience: Advanced Land Acquisition by Local Government* (Ottawa: Community Planning Association of Canada, 1973).

The Federal Perspective

4.1 The Federal Management of Land Development

An evaluation of the Canadian federal government's approach to the control of land development.

The Canadian federal government's stance on public land ownership, and its active role in it, reflects the overview that it is obliged to take because of its particular constitutional position. The tools used by the federal government to manipulate land development are removed from the actual implementation process, since land planning is left to the provinces under Section 91 of the British North America Act (the Canadian "constitution"). Nevertheless, the federal government is a powerful fiscal agency and has used its taxing and spending powers to influence decision making in areas that are not nominally within the jurisdiction of the BNA Act. This has occurred most notably in the areas of health care and education. This capacity could equally be applied to the field of land use planning.

From this "distanced" position, land ownership is seen as part of the process of comprehensive land use management. Federal government officials tend to be critical of Canadian "disrespect" for land and the lack of understanding of its level of tolerance to development, or the long-term consequences of development decisions. At the same time, the federal government has to live with the dominant value that is given to private ownership of land in Canada, and the rights attached to its development.

The use of federal money to assist in the public development of land reflects these general views. It is typically implied that federal government agencies intend to reinforce the principles of more responsible land use by the application of comprehensive planning frameworks. This particularly applies through the requirement of consistent standards for the servicing of land and the housing built on it before projects can receive federal funding. In addition, two other ways in which the federal government can influence urban development are through its role in the stabilization of the economy and in the mitigation of regional disparity.

The actual implementation of federal land policy has always been constrained by the problem of coordinating the three levels of government associated with such activities. As early as 1948, the CMHC (Central Mortgage and Housing Corporation—the federal agency charged with implementing the policy) had power under the National Housing Act's Section 40 to finance joint federal-provincial land assemblies, but until about 1970, the program was little used. Where it was used, it had mixed results, chiefly because there was little coordination between the local municipalities and the upper levels of government, and because the rationale for the program was never articulated. Because the Section 40 projects were in joint partnership, CMHC maintained active federal participation and guidance in the land development process. The provincial governments were apparently not enamoured with the scheme and were not willing to over-ride local municipal council objections to the program. This meant that while the funding was available, it was not used.

In 1969 the Section 40 provisions were augmented by Section 42 of the National Housing Act, which allowed the federal government to finance land assembly on a strictly loan basis, with up to 90% of the funds needed and a three-year moratorium on any repayments—to allow for the sites to be planned and designed. This program was thus more popular with the provinces because, although they were required to repay the loan, they needed less money to initiate a project, and were given free rein to develop the lands as they saw fit. The actual provincial mechanism for land assembly, therefore, can vary from province to province. From the CMHC point of view, the subdivision agreements that a provincial government makes with the municipality in association with its land assembly should reflect unified planning standards. In order to encourage this, CMHC will not provide municipal services of major trunk sewers, etc. after 1976, unless there is a comprehensive plan. There will be no funds for municipal land or for servicing unless the municipality can demonstrate it has some planning rationale. In addition proposed legislation gives additional grants to municipalities providing that they develop medium-density, low-cost housing.

Several papers in this chapter deal with the application of these federal land policies. Ryan (4.2) reviews the objectives of CMHC; John White (4.3) discusses the application of provincial land assembly in Ontario; and Neal Roberts (4.4) provides an evaluation of that program. Michael Dennis (4.7) and William Leathem (4.8) deal with the application of federal monies in the central city of a metropolitan region and a suburban township, respectively. Finally, Rumm (4.9) reflects on the application of these public ownership policies from the standpoint of the land developer.

What seems apparent from this discussion is that the federal government, through its long-distance financing arrangements, has the power to use public ownership to manage and control land use. What is not so clear, however, is how this tool is meant to be directed. It may be focused on the need for planning by various provincial and municipal bodies, but there is no national direction as to what order or priority should be given to various land use goals: social housing, the preservation of agricultural land, balanced urban growth, economical infrastructure, or the recycling of urbanized land. In spite of William Teron's opening statement to the Public Land Ownership Conference as President of the Central Mortgage and Housing Corporation, that "public land ownership is a most important lever in order to manage the land, but not an objective in itself," the concept is being fostered and monies are being spent without a clear commitment to the goals such an undertaking should serve. However, if it can decide on a comprehensive land use planning policy, the federal government has the power to substantially influence the future of the country's urban areas.

4.2 The Central Mortage and Housing Corporation: Public Land Ownership Objectives*

J.P. Ryan
Regional Director for Newfoundland and Labrador, Central Mortgage and Housing Corporation

A discussion of the public land acquisition and development process.

It should be stressed that CMHC believes that wherever private development is doing the job and a stable marketplace exists, there is no need for public intervention in land development. The general program objectives of CMHC are "to promote an orderly and responsible land marketplace, to insure an adequate supply of serviced residential land, to stabilize and where possible reduce serviced land prices, and to promote a high standard of residential development and a satisfactory community environment." Obviously where these standards do not exist there is a real role for the government to become involved in meeting the shortage. Our financial involvement in land assembly is increasing and this year amounts to approximately $265,000,000 (for land development, land acquisition and development, and the provision of infrastructure). To obtain CMHC funding it is necessary for the municipality to adopt the non-profit principle under which profits obtained from serviced lands disposed of are put back into the project for the provision of necessary social and recreational facilities. Starting in 1976, to obtain funding a municipality must have a policy and plan of action to insure a continuing supply of serviced residential land. As well, the municipality must adopt suitable policies for comprehensive land management including an acceptable mix of housing types and income levels.

In our view there is a need for public land acquisition and development for the following reasons:

1 *Economic considerations.* As development continues and citizen demands increase, the level and sophistication of the total social interest structure climbs dramatically. At one time services could have been

*Remarks to the conference.

provided by a municipality without creating an undue financial burden; this is no longer the case. The critical financial situation of a municipality may result in its considering participation in the land development business in an effort to acquire some apparent high returns to augment its financial resources. It seems somewhat incongruous for a municipality to struggle in providing high-cost social infrastructure while at the same time the land development industry is enjoying its largest profits.

2 *Coordination*. Large-scale developments are taking place in major centres in Canada and a number of these involve all levels of government, as well as private industries. The complexity of these projects is such that public ownership of the lands involved can present a solution to a number of development problems.

3 *Land Development Strategy*. There are occasions where an evaluation of a private development indicates something less than the most desirable site for the proposed improvement. In many cases this is the result of the owner having to confine the proposed development to the site available. The criticism of such a site could involve size, shape, and/or location. The solution of such a problem does not always lie in the acquisition of alternative or additional land, as this may be uneconomic or unavailable. There are cases where public acquisition through expropriation would be beneficial to both the proposed development and the municipality. Although such acquisitions would have to be considered most carefully, there are instances where public acquisition would be to the best interest of the general public.

4 *Tenure*. There are practical limits to the amount of land leasing that governments can undertake. In principle, however, there are advantages to this technique that would still apply, notwithstanding the limit of practice. Because of alternative forms of investment, it is unreasonable at this time to expect the private sector to participate as a lessor.

5 *Land Use Control*. There are certain limitations in a municipality's ability to control development. These are usually confined to master planning, zoning, and building by-laws. An additional technique, which can and is being used to control development, is public acquisition of certain key parcels of land. A word of caution about this practice: it could lead to unreasonable action on the part of a municipality. It can just as easily be used to prevent any kind of development, regardless of merit, as it can direct or improve the quality of desirable development.

6 *Political Consideration*. We are all aware of the pressures that are placed on governments at all levels to do something about the increasing cost and inadequate supply of serviced residential land. The clamour leaves the government no choice but to intervene where it is considered that the private market is not doing the job.

Provincial Views

4.3. Ontario's Experience with Public Land Ownership*

John White
Former Treasurer and Minister of Economics and Intergovernmental Affairs, Province of Ontario

An analysis of the evolution of Ontario's public land assembly policies.

We have seen rapidly increasing prices for land and housing, caused in part by a multitude of government regulations, by shortages in supply (some perhaps caused deliberately, and others the consequence of deep-seated economic conditions), and finally, deliberate speculation on the part of our own people and foreigners to acquire land (and lately housing) to be held off the market for sale at a later time at a higher price. One response to this was to tax off all the speculative profit and to deter foreign capital from seeking safe haven in this stable jurisdiction of Ontario. We have had some success as the statistics indicate.

When I assumed ministerial responsibilities several years ago, I was brand new to the field, but I did have some biases induced by several modern "saints." One saint was Lewis Mumford, who says decentralize or perish, which I firmly believe. Another was Ivan Illyich, who says deinstitutionalize or suffer, which I also firmly believe. A third was Jane Jacobs, whose monumental book *The Death and Life of Great American Cities* made an enormous impact on me 10 or 15 years ago. We did attempt to decentralize in several areas, first of all by persuading the federal government to get back to the constitution (The British North America Act), and let the provinces look after those responsibilities given to them. In this matter we were complete and absolute failures. We tried to do it by devolving power and the necessary resources from the provincial level of government to the municipal level; we were reasonably successful to the extent that hundreds of millions of dollars were transferred by way of conditional and unconditional grants. Unconditional grants rose at a more rapid rate than did conditional grants, although not nearly as fast as I had hoped. The municipalities were offered 70 powers embodied in the Statutes which had been the responsibility of the provincial level of government. Certain of these responsibilities were later the planning, official plans, subdivision approvals, and so on.

This attempt to decentralize powers in governmental areas made it doubly important for us to have a device to impose a plan which was beyond the horizon of a single municipality. There are about 75 munici-

*Remarks to the conference. Edited.

palities in the area dealt with in the Court reports. The idea of getting two or three municipalities to agree to a single venture at the same time is very difficult, as the North York Sewer Pipe project indicated. To get 75 municipalities to do something is quite frankly impossible. The Niagara Escarpment covers 4 counties, 4 regions, and heaven only knows how many more municipalities. To get those several dozen municipalities to agree to preserve the Niagara Escarpment, is in my opinion, absolutely impossible, and so I think we were correct in bringing in the Ontario Planning and Development Act (spring 1973). This device allowed us to bring under control 2,300,000 acres in the escarpment. The government intended to buy 20% of that land, and more than that, to control the other 80% by means of a development control system, not used here previously but used with some success in England.

We brought in the Parkway Belt West plan, which once again was difficult, complicated, and innovative—and caused quite a lot of strife and dissention, as we knew it would. It was an attempt to provide an urban separator—which at one and the same time delineated the respective communities and enabled interconnections between those communities to be established—to provide service corridors so we didn't have to buy separate rights-of-way for roadways, hydro lines, sewer pipes, water pipes, and so on, in the rather primitive fashion that had been the case before this scheme was chosen. When we brought that 55,000 acres under control, we announced that we would be acquiring 40% of it.

It's becoming increasingly apparent to me as a retired politician that several forces are working at one and the same time in Ontario. There is a determination growing annually to preserve good farmland, not necessarily on an economic basis, but rather on an ethical basis when so much of the world is starving. During the recent election campaign, there was a great deal of public concern about the loss (at 26 acres per hour) of farmland. The facts may be in doubt, but one did perceive the general emotional direction of people's feelings. There is also a growing desire among many people in existing communities to retain the scale and the style of their communities. Twenty years ago in London, Ontario, I suppose we all aspired to be 2,000,000 people. We wanted to be like Toronto, but now frankly, many of us in London, Ontario don't want to be like Toronto. If our population now is 230,000, we think maybe 250,000 to 300,000 people would be alright for us. This feeling, which is growing over time, leads certain communities (maybe Oakville is an example) to say, I am sorry, we are not going to take a lot of housing, even if the Minister of Housing wants us to do so. As we decentralize certain planning decisions in the hope of expediting housing starts, as we turn these powers back from Queen's Park to the local municipalities to some extent, all the delays that have been blamed quite rightly on Queen's Park are now being experienced at the municipal level. It's tempting to conclude that this is the result of inefficiency or stupidity. I don't think it's that at all. I think the difficulties are due to an intuitive response of citizens in existing communities not to let their communities develop in a way that is going to spoil the environment in which they are raising their youngsters, and so on. There is also a very clearly identified ambition in northern and eastern Ontario to have more industrial development so that youngsters from those small towns can find employment there if they wish rather than migrate to the large cities.

There are a number of ways in which these several urges in society can be met. It would be helpful to have an additional instrument, namely, the capability to create some number of new communities. That became the essence of the Ontario Land Corporation Act. Using my authority, I initiated the purchase of about 14,000 acres west of Dunville on heavy Haldamand clay that the Minister of Agriculture assured me was not worth saving. We acquired something like 14,000 acres, in part by chance, northeast of Jarvis, 40% of which is worth saving and provides an opportunity, I do believe, for a mixed form of community not presently experienced in this part of the country—to preserve good agricultural land and intersperse it with residential development. There is no need, it happens, for important industrial development on the north shore of Lake Erie. We also acquired something like 14,000 acres for a major industrial site with residential facilities near Prescott. This was something of a miracle. It has 401 Highway running east-west through it; it has the big four-lane Highway 416 running north-south; it's at the International Bridge; it's the only deep-water port between Montreal and Toronto; it has the main line of the CNR going through it; the main line of the CPR going through it; and it has several small airports in close proximity to it.

These three large sites have been put in place for a cost of something like $50 million. For that price we have the basis for several large new important communities, which have the prospect of shifting development to the east, preserving good farmlands in the west, taking some of the heat out of Hamilton, and taking some of the pressure off the Niagara Escarpment. All these projects are on the back burner now. I have confidence that the new communities program, using the Statute, will find favour with the public and that it will become a higher priority with the present government.

Since business goes where business is, I think we have to put one or several large industries in eastern Ontario and from that nucleus build a series of manufacturing enterprises in close proximity to the primary plant, to fabricate the product of that primary mill. At the same time it is necessary to establish a hierarchy of industrial parks in eastern Ontario, in which smaller concerns can become the customers of, and suppliers to, the large new industrial park.

I think the next time a big firm like Stelco says we are going to plot a plant in the cornfields of western Ontario, some years from now, the government is going to say no. New industrial development will not be permitted in that part of this province, but as luck would have it, a major industrial park site (like Prescott) can be offered, and cheaply.

I don't disagree with the idea that if a municipality doesn't want to grow, it's not going to buy land for a residential development. I think there are some cities, however, that for whatever reason are prepared to take more population. If their peripheral lands are owned by a small group of developers and the city wants to grow, I think the municipality could find the financial backing to acquire the asset for sale later. I do not think, however, that CMHC and OHC should be in the land assembly business. I know how the game works at Queen's Park and I am quite sure it works the same way in Ottawa. For example, CMHC gets $1.3 billion, intended primarily for housing. By a deadline date in March, there is $100 million left over which must either be turned back to the Treasury (thereby diminishing claims on a subsequent fiscal year) or utilized in the best way possible. I have no proof of this, but it's my hunch that when that happens, $100 million goes into the rapid acquisition of land. Transferring the proposition to the OHC, suppose they are coming to the end of their year and they have underutilized their resources. What do they do? They can't build the housing that everybody wants, so they go out and buy some very expensive land in Malvern.

My intention was to get the OHC completely out of the land business and to make that the exclusive responsibility of the Ontario Land Corporation. If the Ontario Land Corporation was without a provincial guarantee and completely dependent on free market forces and the fierce winds of competition, it would be disciplined in a way that is frankly impossible with CMHC or the OHC.

The question is, how are we going to provide housing for the people who are living in the broad sweep of Metropolitan Toronto now and those who are destined to come here in the next five years or so? At the present time there are about 3.5 million people in this area and the projection a year ago was for 8 million people in the year 2000. My hope was that we might change the projection to 7, or something less than 8. At no time did I believe that government activities emanating from Queen's Park could change 8 million into 3.5 or 4. One of the instruments for reducing these estimates is the idea of establishing some small number (5, 10, 20) of new communities on inferior lands. Insofar as housing people is concerned, I am coming more and more to the opinion that the government should get out of the housing business and get into the automobile business and then we would have a surplus of houses and a small number of Edsels and Bricklins clogging up downtown Toronto! I have an idea that if we use that wonderful device, the tax credit, and got that thousand dollars per family per year spent on housing by government back into the hands of people who are trying to buy a house, it would be a lot more effective than the systems we tried unsuccessfully in the past.

Could we make available some of these lands from new community sites to take the heat out of real estate prices in neighbouring municipalities, e.g., could we start selling lots in the Nanticoke area to take the pressure off prices in Hamilton? I had hoped to do that by having on-site trailers and retail outlets in Hamilton buying some form of debenture from the Ontario Land Corporation which would constitute an option on a lot so that a young couple wouldn't be forced into the Hamilton market in 1975, thereby exacerbating pressure on prices. But I wasn't able to get the OLC going before I left, and the OLC was transformed into a less aggressive instrument, with the board consisting entirely of senior civil servants instead of entrepreneurs.

There were in the past two impediments to a municipality acquiring land if the periphery of their community was owned by a quasi monopoly of one or several developers. Municipalities were unable to acquire land for an industrial subdivision. A couple of years ago, at the request of the Municipal Liaison Committee, I changed the statute to enable municipalities to buy land for housing purposes. We changed the statute to enable municipalities to buy land for development as residential neighbourhoods. It hasn't been acted upon to the best of my knowledge and I think the reason is largely an accounting imperfection. These budgets are on a cash basis, so an expense is created in exactly the same fashion in the books of the province and the books of the municipality. Acquiring land for inventory is like buying neckties for resale. One incurs a debt obligation against which there is an asset. When the municipalities fully understand this accounting deficiency, I suspect that they will establish some kind of corporation, put in a relatively small amount of money, go out and buy the acreage they need (having an asset for collateral), and repay the debt as that asset is leased or sold. They have the statutory power to do so.

4.4 Evaluating Ontario's Land Storage Program*

Neal A. Roberts
Associate Professor, Osgoode Hall Law School, York University

The conclusions from a critical review of public land assembly programs funded through CMHC.

*Extracted and edited from a paper prepared for the conference.

... This study has reached a number of conclusions that might give major decision makers pause to reconsider their programs. The Ontario Home Ownership Made Easy Program (HOME), which is funded through the Central Mortgage and Housing Corporation, Sec. 42 public land assembly system, does not seem to have a clear aim or reason for its existence. It is neither oriented primarily toward planning nor toward the recapture of development gains. Further, evidence seems to indicate that there is no clear proof that the system is in fact stabilizing the market in those communities where it is operating.

The province maintains that the program is influencing the private development market because of the increase of housing supply afforded by it. However, since most of the assemblies were spread so thinly over the province, it would be difficult to establish such a proposition. The opinion of interviewed individuals in the industry and in the local planning offices was that the supply constituted such a small proportion of the market in any given town that such an impact would be negligible. One of the points emerging early in the impact studies of the communities was that where large programs existed, they served as a means for the local, small, house builder and land assembler to get sufficient backing and capital to produce housing. On the one hand this may mean, as Ministry officials would like to believe, that more housing production is actually taking place. This may be the case in those communities with one or two monopoly land developers. On the other hand, it may mean the same group of delivery agencies are simply having to spend less time forming joint ventures and seeking financing from private institutions, and more time talking with the government in order to produce the same amount of housing . . .

The program seemed to be designed not to capitalize on "secret" government capital expenditure plans, for that would be an exercise of "bad faith" by the HOME program. Once more the resources available to gain an advantage over private development were not used. The only major planning advantage the program gave government officials was a future layer of subsidy for certain types of housing programs that were extremely expensive.

While it is premature to reach firm conclusions, some speculative ideas concerning the Sec. 42 programs can be advanced. One mistake seems to have been to sneak up on the existing private-market developers without concentrating programs in particular areas. To have the government as one small developer in any given community may have very little impact. If community surveys are any indication, it would seem that the government must control well in excess of 1/3 of the land coming on the market before there are positive impacts on private pricing and delivery structure. More importantly, the federal and provincial governments seem to have entered the business of land development without determining what they were trying to accomplish, and have evidently failed to achieve dramatic results in any area.

The government as land developer must be prepared to concentrate its energies in given areas even at the expense of alienating particular local private developers. It may have to alienate the particular private local municipality, too, in cases where it is the municipality itself that is causing the housing shortage through exclusionary zoning or development control policies. Unless there is a conscious effort to capitalize on inside government knowledge of public investment decisions and to "gang up" on the private developer, the exercise seems somewhat futile.

4.5 The Implementation of Land Policy in British Columbia*

Mary Rawson
Commissioner, British Columbia Land Commission

A discussion of the use of ownership to augment other governmental land use objectives.

I am speaking from the point of view of a well-informed person and a citizen of the province, and also as someone who is actually involved in carrying out a part of government policy.

The B.C. Government intends to use public land ownership as a tool, but it has not been made a key theme and certainly there has been no coordinated thrust on the issue. There are several provincial agencies that have the right to purchase lands and the British Columbia Land Commission is one of those. Dunhill Developments, an agency responsible for putting housing into place, has carried on an aggressive land assembly policy. It is responsible for looking after acquisition of residential lands in the lower mainland and in the southerly part of Vancouver Island. It has purchased 2,300 acres in the last 16 months. The Department of Housing also has the power to acquire land; it concentrates on purchases for residential use outside the lower mainland and in the upper part of Vancouver Island. It has purchased approximately 3,600 acres of land in over 50 municipal areas. Most of these land purchases are already in the development stage, or at least in the planning stage, and neither Department of Housing nor Dunhill Developments is doing much land banking in the traditional sense, because of the immediate municipal pressures for development of the lands they do acquire.

---

*Remarks to the conference. Edited.

The B.C. Development Corporation, whose interests are in industrial sites, has also made several significant purchases and some controversial ones like the 1973 Tilbury purchase which was 700 acres of land, partly in agricultural use. Another was the reservation of some 300 acres in Surrey as a possible location for a provincial refinery. That has not been settled. I don't have a complete picture of the B.C. Development Corporation's activities, but Kamloops, Prince Rupert, and Merritt have also seen substantial purchases. None of these agencies that I mentioned—Housing Department, Dunhill, or the B.C. Development Corporation—appears to be land-banking beyond a five-year horizon, that is for other than immediate or almost immediate needs. Given a directive for urgent performance (and they did get that directive), long-range land banking would seem not too relevant.

Most of the efforts of the Land Commission to date have been concentrated on getting agricultural zoning into place. We have not yet developed a positive stance on land purchases, and purchases have been made only in response to request. We have not sought out land: few of these purchases have been made at the request of government, but most have been in response to enquiries from private owners. Probably two-thirds to three-quarters of the owners that approach us are asked to go into the open market. The others, we have followed up to some degree. There is first a field inspection by Department of Agriculture personnel; if it looks promising to them, a recommendation from our staff, an appraisal, possibly an offer, and occasionally a purchase is made. Judicious purchase is what we aim for and what so far, I hope, we have achieved. There have only been 18-20 purchases altogether, some very large, some small. The private offers that are typically followed up are bonafide farmers who have come to retirement age or who are ill and unable to continue farming. The commission has tended to act as a buyer of last resort for the retiring farmer, performing a function similar to that of the Land Development Corporation in Prince Edward Island. Like the Land Development Corporation, we also try to make purchases that serve more than one purpose, such as recreation or protection of wildlife habitat, as well as for agricultural interests.

Some examples of Land Commission purchases in response to agencies of government are: for the City of Vernon, a site for disposal of sewage effluent by spray irrigation (about 400 acres). This was a pilot project undertaken over eight years by the city with federal money which has already shown that this method of disposal is feasible. The arid 400 acres to be used will be improved by the irrigation as well as by the application of nutrients. The Department of Agriculture asked us to buy certain lands, for example the Steeples Ranch at Fort Steele (1,400 acres), which was purchased by us last year. It's purpose was to accommodate displaced cattle removed from overgrazed range units, while range improvement projects were carried out on the Crown range by the Department of Agriculture. I suppose it was natural enough that this particular government purchase was received with a certain skepticism by the ranching community, but one year of operation has already proved beneficial, according to the people who have used it—the cattlemen.

The Environment and Land Use Committee (a Cabinet Committee), is another government agency that has asked us to purchase. The purchase of the Langley lands (2,000 acres) was the largest in terms of the dollars that we've spent, and we think in terms of its potential as well, since it is on the edge of the expanding urban population centred on Vancouver. The price of $6.5 million covered the cost of more than 70 parcels of land, 28 dwellings, and some farm buildings. We are preparing a land use plan for this area with the help of staff from the Environment and Land Use Committee's Secretariat, as well as staff from the Department of Agriculture, the Department of Recreation, and others. Our intention is to replot parcel boundaries, create suitable farm units, experiment with recreational use and urban clustering in an agricultural setting, and generally demonstrate compatible multi-purpose use in an area that already was becoming fragmented. The 70 parcels we purchased had already been assembled by a developer.

These purchases have clearly been made with a strongly agricultural bent, but each also is a multiple purpose purchase. In the case of Vernon, this means assisting an urban community with waste disposal, decreasing lake pollution, irrigating, fertilizing, and increasing production of agricultural land. In the case of Fort Steele, improved range land management will benefit both wildlife and grazing for domestic cattle. There are two additional purchases in the southeast area of the province which serve to improve grazing. One also provided a site for supervised activity of the local "bad" boys through their Parole and Corrections Branch. These boys are (among other jobs) restoring a portion of the historic Dewdney Trail which crosses the ranch. So we have a 4 or 5 for 1 buy which benefits wildlife, agriculture, rehabilitation services, and develops an historic site.

The Langley purchase, on the edge of suburban Vancouver, is our biggest challenge so far. There we will be grappling with urban impact. We have suggested solutions to these problems in a variety of ways in other areas. A rural landscape planning study has been done for Spillimacheen in the northerly part of Okanagan; and a computer developed alternative patterns program for Kelowna. But it was decided with the Langley purchase to acquire a significant section of partly urbanized, partly agricultural, partly wilderness land with a view to sorting out the best uses and making a useful demonstration of replotting parcels, incorporating recreational lands and opportunities with agriculture, and so forth.

These purchases have quite frankly been made in the absence of a well thought out, duly-weighted frame of reference. We have yet to develop such a framework, but it is necessary because we want to embark slowly but surely on a coherent and considered policy of land purchase, urban land banking, agricultural, and recreational purchases. A consultant gave us a hand in surveying the planning literature, drafting proposals and a purchase policy for us to consider. His useful analysis confined itself to land banking, which he felt we should avoid for housing for new communities and for industry. He felt we should help the municipalities and leave other types of land banking to agencies and funds that already existed. That struck me as interesting for two reasons, both because of the advice and because most people working in this field do tend to think in terms of land banking, whereas the commission tends to operate within a principle of strategic land purchase. In the absence of a framework, we didn't argue with ourselves whether to buy or not to buy as a philosophical issue. We kept in mind a few simple points, one of which was that the basic purpose of our commission was development of multiple land use. Funds are limited, which is always very much in our conservative minds.

There has been some discussion in British Columbia, not very far advanced, of whether to centralize land purchases in one place. Central control of land buying certainly has some benefits. For one thing, it prevents agencies from unknowingly competing with one another for the same site, and that does sometimes happen. However, it has serious drawbacks too. If I recollect the Prince Edward Island system rightly, it was very hard for various departments of government to get any land bought at all before the advent of the Land Development Corporation, and no doubt the right combination of freedom at the edges and central control still has to be found. In my opinion, however, land purchase is necessary and can be a significant and creative tool of government policy.

I think that all political parties before the 1972 election recognized that there was a problem in respect to disappearance of agricultural land. The right things weren't being done, so the incoming government brought in a freeze, which created an uproar. There is a process of appeal; and a great many activities are permitted in the agricultural land reserve. Some adjustments are being made and agricultural zoning, which was the nub of the uproar, will simply settle into place as an established system and as a respectable and useful tool of planning.

Municipal Experience

4.6 Land Ownership and the Development of a City*

Michael Goldrick
Alderman, City of Toronto, and Professor of Political Science, York University

An examination of the urbanization of the City of Toronto through private land development, and the lack of realization of general community goals.

Growth in the cost and value of land is really an inevitable consequence of the framework of the private land market. Most significant changes that occur in society seem to take place almost unnoticed and such a change, it seems to me, has overtaken the nature of contemporary capitalism. Economists tell us that gradually, but particularly in the last 30 years, we have moved through an era in which industrial capitalism has given way to a new form of capitalism which is sometimes known as finance capitalism. In industrial capitalism, wealth was created primarily through the creation of goods and to some extent the sale of services. In its current form, capitalism seeks to appropriate value through the production not only of goods but of new modes of consumption and new social wants and social needs. This current phenomenon would not concern us in the present context were it not for the fact that it is urbanization that is the primary mechanism through which new modes of consumption and new social wants and needs are produced.

The majority of growth in gross national product in the last 30 years, both absolute and on a per capita basis, is accounted for by urban growth, that is, by the process of suburbanization and redevelopment. This is indeed a phenomenon where urbanization, once acting in a support capacity to industrial capitalism, has evolved to become an integral part of capitalism itself. Of course, private land ownership is central to this new function of urbanization, for when we say that a large proportion of wealth is attributable to the creation of new modes of consumption and new social wants and needs, we are referring essentially to the process of land assembly, speculation, and development that precedes the construction of the highways, the utilities, the schools, shopping centres, and housing which is in the nature of suburbanization and urban redevelopment.

Private land ownership, its exchange, and its development have become the sine qua non of contemporary capitalism. We thus find ourselves
_____
*Remarks to the conference. Edited.

locked into a process in which urban growth and continuous redevelopment are essential for the support and maintenance of our economic system. Obviously this brings with it a form of awful determinism that in my view renders cities virtually ungovernable. Because of the imperatives of urban growth and development, city government becomes an exercise of acting in a support capacity to finance capitalism, that is, as a facilitator of the conversion of private property rights into private individual or corporate gain. As a result, decisions about how land is used in our cities usually reflect the ability of an individual to maximize his or her private profit, rather than to maximize the collective social or functional usefulness of the development to the community.

So long as the development of our cities takes place within the framework of finance capitalism, with its reliance on urbanization structured through a process of private land exploitation, the realization of general community goals will not ever predominate. At one time, the function of cities was to act in a support capacity by providing the infrastructure needed for industry to produce goods, which were sold and which produced the volume of wealth of an economy. Now the exchange of value is represented by the trading and development of land; and land development has become the basis of the growth and development of wealth in our economy. Because of that kind of change and the determinism that it brings with it, there is an imperative behind the whole process that encourages the growth of cities and urbanization. But clearly, because of demand and supply, the scarcity of land, the inability to reproduce it, and an inevitable growth in its value—its cost to consumers also grows.

This phenomenon is reflected very clearly in two instances in the Metropolitan Toronto area. One of the primary issues that the Toronto City Council is grappling with happens to be redevelopment for the central area of Toronto. The volume[1] prepared by the City Planning Department makes specific note of the limitations of public policy making as a result of the constraints of private land ownership. But having acknowledged those constraints, they are accepted as severe limitations upon the decisions that can be made and the directions that can be followed in terms of developing the central area of the city. It is necessary to adhere to the constraints, irrespective of whether or not they reflect rational social decisions. Instead, they are dictated primarily by the imperatives of private land ownership in the private land market. As a result, the formulations and proposals are such that it is questionable whether private citizens should support this kind of plan. The central area plan, since it's following the private market, accommodates individual profit-maximizing decisions at the expense of socially rational objectives, and allows speculator-developers to make enormous profits on land values created primarily by public investment. The plan virtually guarantees that inner-city neighbourhoods will become the exclusive preserve of the wealthy. The plan forces low- and moderate-income people out of the central area. In fact it provides for a net loss of a thousand low-income houses in the next 10 years. The plan accelerates the exclusion of families with children from the central area unless the families happen to be wealthy. It recommends the construction of 30,000 housing units at extremely high densities in the next decade without assuring their occupants minimal open-space recreation or community facilities. This is because of the assumption built into the plan that—in association with a huge growth in office space in the financial district of Toronto—there should be a compensating increase in residential development slightly to the north of it. The plan proposes construction of minor quantities of low- and moderate-income housing on the most expensive land in Canada, requiring enormous subsidies paid primarily from taxes raised from those whom it is intended to house—low- and moderate-income wage earners. The plan condemns almost double the present number of downtown workers to long journeys to work on increasingly congested transportation systems. The proposal is to double the amount of office space that's available in the financial district of Toronto and perpetuate centralization and specialization of development in the central area. It accelerates suburban sprawl at great public and social cost while guaranteeing that speculator-developer monopolies realize enormous profits in suburban land development. The plan encourages some dispersion of office development outside the central core, but in a manner that perpetuates reliance on automobile travel. Finally, the plan permits the development of higher densities in mixed development form (combining residential and commercial or retail development) than have ever before been built in Canada. Would public ownership of land, or at least the reclamation of public rights in land, provide a different set of solutions to a central area problem? I don't know, but it couldn't be very much worse, in my view.

Another problem concerns the development of suburban land in Toronto, where by public fiat a monopoly situation has been produced. The Toronto-Centred Region Plan specifies certain limits on growth in the metropolitan Toronto region. Because of public control over infrastructure, which is the only thing that puts value into land, we've come to the strange position where servicing to the east and north of Metro Toronto has been delayed 8-10 years, due to the collapse of the Pickering scheme. This leaves 21,000 acres or thereabouts for development (primarily to the west of Toronto) in the hands of five property development and ownership companies. I would prefer not to have the future Toronto housing market for the next half dozen years resting in the hands of corporations whose aim in life is to maximize profit. I don't think that socially rational goals are likely to be achieved in that sort of situation as they would be under a system of public ownership of one kind or another.

Would public ownership of land in either of these situations produce a different outcome? Who wins and who loses in these sorts of situations? Is it the private entrepreneurs who have capital, who have acquired rights to property? Are workers gaining, or the people who pay 35-40% of their income for housing? Are those gaining who spend an hour and a half to two hours on congested transportation systems to get to jobs, or who are forced to live in enormously dense areas without recreation facilities, without adequate community facilities? I would guess that the people are not the winners and it seems to me that this is an inevitability of the private land ownership market, which has become functional to finance capitalism itself. So long as capitalism retains that form, and it's certainly bound to do so for a long time to come, the growth of cities is going to be more a function of the imperatives of growth and development of the capitalist system than it ever is of socially rational goals of communities.

Note

1. City of Toronto Planning Board, *Central Area Plan Review, Part 1: General Plan* (Toronto: The Planning Board, October 1975).

4.7 The City of Toronto's Use of Public Land Ownership*

Michael Dennis
Housing Commissioner, City of Toronto

A discussion of the application of public land ownership in Canada, with special reference to programs in the City of Toronto.

Discussion of the arguments concerning public land ownership, or about what difference it makes, seems more related to the late '60s in Canada than to the present. Today a very strong governmental presence in the planning, regulation, and direct development of land is an accepted political fact and a matter of political reality. The issues are those of extent and purpose and the respective roles of the public and private sectors in acquisition and development of land.

Public ownership of land has never been questioned in this country. A hundred years ago the vast majority of land was publicly owned. That

*Remarks to the conference. Edited.

remains the case today in the Province of British Columbia and perhaps in some of the other western provinces. Huge amounts of forest lands remain the domain of the Crown in Ontario. Even in metropolitan centres, from 40% to 50% of all land is publicly owned. That land is used for streets, parks, schools, government buildings, etc. The role of government in providing such services is well established. What was open to question in the past was the nature and extent of the intervention of government in private land markets and the role of government as assembler, owner, and developer of land for the purpose of services which were not within the traditional field of responsibility of government, particularly the ownership and development of land for housing, but also for commercial and industrial use.

The issue of public land ownership of such resources as fuel minerals is similar to the question of the use of ownership as a tool for agricultural preservation, another area where governments are moving to occupy the field. The question in a number of provinces is not so much *whether* they should, as to what *extent* they should.

There have been a number of swings of the political pendulum on the urban development issue since World War II. Faced with drastic shortages and a weak building industry, government simply developed land and built veterans' and wartime housing. In the early '50s a number of large tracts were assembled across the country, many of them in southern Ontario, to insure that land would be available to meet the backlog of housing needs. Much of that land is only being developed today, since the assemblies were at considerable distances from existing centres. Because no institutional vehicle for the development of such new communities was proposed, development had to await the growth and expansion of the cities. That lack of an organizational technique, coupled with opposition from the private development industry (which was beginning to produce substantial amounts of new housing), led to the demise of the first public acquisition and development program.

The next issue to arise was urban renewal. Government turned its attention from the urban fringe to the supposedly decaying city centre. That program, modeled on an American predecessor, was found to be inapt to our circumstances. We soon discovered that large parts of the country had no slums, that slum dwellers did not like being renewed, and that renewal was very expensive. The program was, therefore, shut down.

In the late '60s, concern began to mount about the cost of land and housing, the ability of the country to meet its housing needs, and the role of the developer-speculator as key decision maker in the urban planning process. Based on arguments of cost efficiency, equity, and planning, the Hellyer Task Force, led by a conservative minister of the Crown, recommended that municipalities should acquire and service all or a substantial proportion of the land required for urban growth within their boundaries.

Further recommendations on land assembly were put to the federal government by its Task Force on Low-Income Housing in 1972; and in late 1973 the federal government committed itself to provide $100 million annually for land assembly and servicing for the next five years. In fact, over the last two years, it has been lending money at the rate of $100 million a year. The decision was not accompanied by a clear strategy for the allocation and distribution of the resources involved. In the pattern established by other federal housing programs, it was demand responsive. The federal government was reacting to political pressures from a perceived public desire for increased intervention in the land and housing markets. The pressure was heightened by an election campaign fought in part on the issues of corporate rip-off, monopoly control of land markets, and land speculation. A very strong public reaction against uncontrolled urban growth had emerged, based in part on studies funded by the federal government. The government set up an urban ministry, which proceeded to study the problem of managing growth for the next five years. The task of developing strategies to deal with that growth and (as a component part of the implementation of those strategies) public programs of land acquisition and development fell to the provinces and the municipalities. The pressure to respond to the growth issue and to increasing land costs has come to bear most heavily on them, as can be seen in the range of responses. These include legislation restricting foreign ownership of land, programs aimed at the preservation of cultural lands, the Land Speculation Tax in the Province of Ontario, a broad-scale effort to develop regional development plans, and the establishment of special vehicles for the funding and developing of large assemblies (in Ontario, the Ontario Land Corporation and in British Columbia, the acquisition of a private development company, Dunhill Developments Limited). Not surprisingly, the strongest political responses have come in Ontario and British Columbia, which have experienced the highest rates of migration and immigration, the greatest growth, and the highest housing prices.

The Ontario response came in two stages. From 1970 onward, the province geared up for greatly expanded assisted housing programs and the Ontario Housing Corporation took over the development of existing public assemblies and began an expanded program of land assembly in support of those housing projects. That program took place primarily on the fringes of metropolitan centres with populations from 100,000 to 250,000 people. At the same time, as part of its regional development and population distribution strategy, the province began to assemble land for new towns. The impetus came primarily from the Ministry of Treasury and Intergovernmental Relations as part of its regional economic planning process, rather than from the Housing Ministry in support of housing programs. Four assemblies totalling some 70,000 acres have been announced to date at a cost (my estimate) of $250-$300 million. British Columbia, in 1974 began a similar response by assembling some 5,000 acres for new communities. Its assemblies were primarily within the boundaries of the regions of Vancouver and Victoria rather than by way of new towns. They too will require some time before they are ready for development.

The $100 million per year promised by the federal government does not go very far. Despite federal funding commitments for the Pickering project, all of the $250-$300 million in Ontario has been put up by the province. In order to bring serviced land to market as quickly as possible, Ontario has virtually stopped assembling land for short-term development and has used all of the federal funds it could borrow this year to service existing assemblies. It is running down its existing bank of land. It will have to depend, in the not-too-distant future, on new-town projects for sites for its assisted housing programs. The running down of existing assemblies appears to be having some impact on land prices in the communities in which those assemblies took place.

It is not generally understood that federal funds are available for land assembly and servicing—and as the servicing costs per acre are far greater than the land acquisition costs, limited amounts of land can be acquired. A hundred million dollars per year for land acquisition and development yields less than 10,000 serviced lots per year, at the densities at which those assemblies have normally been developed (that is, about 4% of annual national requirements as estimated by the federal government). The federally funded residential land bank, at the end of 1974, had barely enough land to produce one year's supply of housing for the country, and so it has fallen (particularly in Ontario) to the province to do the job, and it has gotten on with it.

The economics of land development and servicing described above made it possible for centre cities, marching to the beat of their political drummers, to again assume the role of public developer that they had dropped with the demise of urban renewal. Public development was feasible there because servicing costs are minimal (the services being present) and because densities are 10-20 times suburban single-family levels. As a result, land costs per unit are lower in the centre cities, particularly where development takes place on obsolete industrial lands or on publicly owned lands. Toronto and Vancouver were the leaders in centre-city assembly.

A reform council was elected some three years ago in Toronto and had to deal with the same growth issues with which Ontario and indeed British Columbia were attempting to deal in land assembly programs. The city was concerned about wholesale demolition and redevelopment of existing low-rise neighbourhoods, many of which housed working-class people. These neighbourhoods were replaced with rows of highrise towers housing non-family households and in fact barely making up for the low-rise family housing that had been demolished to make way for them. Of greatest concern to council was the availability and affordability of new housing. With increased production and financing costs, and neighbourhood opposition to traditional forms of development, housing starts fell off sharply. Worse yet, low- and moderate-income housing, which constituted roughly half of all housing produced in the city during the period from 1969 to 1971, was no longer being produced; and to the extent that it *was* being produced, it was not properly integrated into existing communities, both in terms of form and in terms of the mix of incomes within the projects.

To deal with these problems, the Toronto Council adopted a comprehensive housing policy and program. It assumed the role of coordinator of all assisted housing programs; it set itself targets for housing approvals to be achieved (4,000 units a year in total, half of them to be assisted, a quarter of them to be family housing). Wholesale demolitions of existing housing were to be stopped and substantial efforts made to upgrade the existing housing stock. The integration of assisted housing projects within existing communities, and of income groups within those projects, was a major goal. Reliance was to be placed on the full range of new federal and provincial housing programs to produce new subsidized housing. To insure that those goals were met, the city itself re-entered the development field as a producer of full recovery non-profit housing. It also provided strong encourangement to private non-profit groups and cooperatives, to Metropolitan Toronto which built senior citizens housing, to the Ontario Housing Corporation, and to private builders operating under government programs. Under all of the rental programs, council stressed the need to integrate both low-income and moderate-income households within given projects.

Like the earlier provincial land assembly programs rather than the new town assembly programs, the city's program of land acquisition and development had as its primary objective provision of sufficient land to insure that its targets for assisted housing production could be met. In support of its various housing programs, council decided to acquire at least $10 million worth of land per year in each of the three years, 1973, 1974, and 1975: that is, it requested 10% of the CMHC annual budget for land assembly. It was assumed this would allow the city to acquire some 50-60 acres of land on which some 5,000 housing units could be built. The stated objectives of the program were 1) to provide suitable, assisted housing sites to avoid repetition of past situations where marginal sites had to be purchased from developers; 2) to redistribute the benefits of public action

134

(the program was intended to help people who might otherwise not have
the opportunity to live in certain parts of the city); 3) to stabilize house
prices for limited-income households because land would be made available over time at cost; and 4) to insure the development of socially viable
neighbourhoods both through the development of large-scale integrated
projects and through the in-filling of new projects in existing neighbourhoods and development of new forms of housing.

Private industry seemed intent simply on repeating its standard-form
highrise building and single-family housing. It now appears that if any
rental housing was to be built, the city would have to take the lead and
would have to provide the land. While it was not an explicitly stated goal
of the program, much of council's policy was predicated on the assumption that, under existing and foreseeable market conditions, the private
sector would not build family rental housing. Another unstated goal was
to provide a model for other municipalities to follow. It was clearly
understood that the City of Toronto acting alone could not solve the
housing problems of southern Ontario; but if a number of municipalities
were to act in similar fashion, then a large-scale program to attack the
price and affordability of housing could be achieved. The city's program
goals were more limited than those at which a national or even provincial
land development program could aim.

The other new development, and a political reality in land assembly, is
the return of the federal government to the field, this time in the role of a
major developer. Previously it had simply funded acquisitions or partici-
pated as a partner in the early days, with the provinces. Now the federal
government in Ottawa is directly developing major projects, for example,
the Woodruff and LeBreton Flats projects. It is optioning golf courses for
development in the Maritimes, considering the possible development of
Downsview Airport as an experimental project in Toronto, and reviewing
sites in a number of other metropolitan centres—all this at a time when it
does not have sufficient funds to meet provincial and municipal land
assembly and development requirements. It is also introducing a new land
lease program under which the federal government will acquire land and
lease it to cooperative and non-profit groups at a rent substantially below
its carrying cost. The purpose of that program is to make land available to
such groups at a reduced cost so that the housing produced can be
afforded by moderate-income households. That same objective could, of
course, be achieved by directly subsidizing non-profit housing programs
and leaving it to the provinces and municipalities to make their assemblies
available to those groups, as they would clearly be prepared to do.
However, there appears to be an iron law of political competition at work
here, so when discussing the political response to land assembly in this
country (and the question of should we be doing it), it's very clear we have

been doing it for a long time and we are doing it. The real issues are where, for what purpose, and how much. It is fairly clear that there is support for public land assembly and direct development in the centre cities, primarily to provide for housing to be built in the short term. Political support is there because the centre cities house a lot of low-income and moderate-income people who can see a direct benefit from the program.

There seem to be few political problems with new-towns programs. They've been far enough out that there has been no organized community to oppose them; and I haven't heard a great deal of development-industry opposition to such programs because it's clear that large-scale funding is required and that there is some measure of risk involved. The government will have to do the planning and servicing in any event.

The one place where the role of the public as developer remains uncertain, and where the roles of public land assembly and development programs remain uncertain, is somewhere between the centre city and the exurban fringe, which is the area where very little activity takes place today. It's not taking place partly because the municipalities don't appear to want it, partly because the cost of land there is much greater than out on the fringe where most of the assemblies have taken place as a result of leapfrogging, and because the one general purpose of a public land development program applicable to centre cities is not involved (i.e. the use of the program to bring the public sector into the development field as a competitor to increase the supply of serviced land and thereby drive down the price).

Suburban municipalities don't want or don't appear to want to see such assembly and development activity, concerned as they are with the protection of their tax base and with possible ratepayer opposition to cheaper housing, and perhaps indeed, subsidized housing in their localities. The other problem is of an organized development industry and its interest in those localities. It appears that the government's chips are not being put on the role of public developer, but on some kind of process of increasing the supply of serviced land in the belief that that will bring land prices down. All the arguments against public development (tax base, ratepayer opposition, and the interest of the industry in keeping prices up) are equally present there and the key question is, what does it take to bring those land prices down? Does just servicing the land do enough? What do you do about the tax base? The federal government, in a welcome initiative, has provided up to $1,000 a unit for medium-density housing in that suburban fringe area. Will that do it? What more has to be done about local opposition?

We have spent or committed approximately $14 million to assemble 45 acres of land right in the heart of Toronto's downtown. We have had a broad range of sites, the smallest one is two houses with room for four units to be built between them, half-acre sites, two- and three-acre sites, and in the St Lawrence district, a major assembly. In almost none of these cases have we been faced with any opposition, partly because of the areas in which we assemble land. It is a real urban renewal program: we are taking out obsolete industries; we are taking out non-conforming dairies; we are going into areas where there is no opposition; we are not moving people out of the areas in which we assemble, except on a very limited scale. When we do, we will re-house them in the interim and then are committed to put them back in the housing that we build, in short order. One of our council's policies is that priority for up to 50% of the units in any given area is for area residents, and so the people in a particular area have a stake in the housing. As far as I am concerned, we are achieving those objectives of innovation of form, integration of people, redistribution of access to housing within the city, and we are achieving it without difficulty. Insofar as the acquisition of land for short-term immediate urban development is concerned, there is very strong public support.

There is an apparent difference between British Columbia and Ontario in terms of the kind of assemblies they are undertaking. The Burke Mountain [B.C.] project is in the premier's home riding, and it is in the developed portion of the Vancouver area. There is some question about what the reaction is going to be to that kind of development in a suburban area. The premier must have some other goodies involved, like bridges, transportation systems, and parks, but he is prepared to take the project on in his own riding. Some earlier assemblies in Ontario are now ripe for development; I'm not clear at all about the policy of the present government. Is it the policy of the Ministry of Housing and of the provincial government to bring the land that it has on the fringes of a number of municipalities into immediate development in such a way as to have impact on land and housing prices, or not? The government clearly does not appear to have a policy of acquiring further land in those areas for immediate development; rather it seems to be servicing what it's got and getting out of the game.

There are problems. How does a municipality that is substantially controlled, as far as its lands are concerned, by three or four major developing companies get started in land banking? This is clearly a question of how much money is available and of an understanding of whether we're talking about land assembly as a competitive device, rather than banking. The point we have tried to make for some time with the federal government is that the difference between a land assembly program and a banking program is interim financing. All of the money that goes into the land ultimately gets taken out by building mortgages, some of which the federal government funds and others of which are privately funded. There is concern about the level of prices being charged and a feeling that land can be "moved" in some fashion. It's going to take a commitment from some level of government to push inducement or punitive taxation to stop people holding land off the market by using some process of selective assessment on the basis of development value. Either you do that, or you assemble the land, or you allow people to continue to charge the prices that they are charging. This would seem to be a logical series of alternatives. Either government puts up the money or it finds another solution.

The province has got a considerable amount of money invested, probably twice what the federal government has, in land assembly. The federal government appears to me to have the resources to tackle the land problem. It takes an initial burst of money set up in a revolving fund. The money comes out of building mortgages and is kept recycled. My recommendation would be that the federal government put up that kind of money as its contribution to solving our growth problems.

4.8 A Township Perspective*

William Leathem
Planner, Nepean Township, Ontario

Discussion of the use of public ownership in Nepean Township, a suburban community bordering Ottawa.

The township of Nepean, with a population of about 80,000 people, is a western suburb of the City of Ottawa; it is the largest township in Ontario. Its growth rate has been astronomical, having grown in little over a decade from 20,000 to 80,000 people. This has posed problems in itself, but in many ways we have overcome these problems, particularly in terms of public land ownership at the municipal level. Within the last three or four years, we have acquired approximately 500 acres for industrial development; our first industrial park of close to 200 acres is at present underway. As a result of a land purchase from the joint partnership of CMHC and OHC, we are now developing our first municipal industrial park with the objective of decreasing the tax burden on a predominantly residential municipality. We have also acquired 200 acres, which is being used as a tree farm to provide trees for parks, streets, etc. In terms of conservation and recreation, we have expropriated two miles of Ottawa River front; we presently have 50 acres of park under development on the Ottawa River; and we also have acquired other lands for conservation and recreation

*Remarks to the conference. Edited.

purposes to make a total of about 200 acres in the last two years. Our requirements for dedication of public land by the developer is 3 acres per 1000 people and we feel we have one of the best parks and recreational systems within the whole region. So we are firmly convinced that public land ownership is right.

We have not, however, gotten into public ownership for the provision of housing. There are several reasons for this; one of them is that we feel the developer is probably the best person to provide land for housing, not the government—in any form. Now, being from the Ottawa area, we have particular problems. The municipal planner is in a very unique city; he is caught right in the middle between the public, the politicians, the developer, the region, the provincial government, and the federal government. The municipal planner, although he may be blamed for a lot of delays, serves a very useful function in bringing all these various groups and agencies together. In Nepean, for example, there has been talk about the lack of supply of serviced land and there is no doubt this lack exists. There is also no doubt that the approval process has been a real problem. It is necessary to go through the bureaucracy of the municipal government, the provincial government, and the federal government. Particularly in dealing with all the various aspects of the provincial government, it has become a real problem to expedite plans quickly and to put serviced land on the market. Nevertheless, within our township we have two OHC projects that have draft approval and are just at the stage of registration for commencement next year. These will accommodate approximately 50,000 people in 14,000 dwelling units. In addition the Woodward Demonstration Project developed by CMHC is within our municipality and will house approximately 14,000 people.

The municipality is often blamed for being a stumbling block in the provision of serviced land. This is very true in many areas; I don't think it is in our municipality. Many municipalities don't want to grow, and in many cases legitimate reasons exist not to. The main reason is financial. For every home that is built in a municipality, it is a financial burden on that municipality, both from the point of view of provision of municipal services and the provision of schooling. My feeling is that to solve the housing problem in Canada, and particularly in Ontario, we have to take a new look at our whole system, and particularly our financing and taxation structure.

The other main problem is one of servicing, especially in the Ottawa area. We have to cross the greenbelt and the problems of putting two miles of services across the greenbelt with no recoverance from those services puts a tremendous financial burden on the municipalities that are trying to supply housing. Within the greenbelt, Ottawa has just about reached saturation; we have to extend beyond it. The municipality does not have the capability to pay for that; we have to look at funding from other areas. I think the crisis is not a crisis of land supply; the land is there. The crisis is how to put it on the market and I think this is the problem to which we should be addressing ourselves.

We hope to experiment with the whole idea that public intervention can perhaps do things in some cases that private industry cannot do, in terms of major land acquisition, and of bringing the major trunks, the road network, and so on, to the site. There are certainly things that private industry does better, and faster, like the installation of ordinary subdivision servicing. What we might hope to see over a period of time would be a gradual combination of these two aspects, with private industry providing subdivision servicing, and a real partnership of public and private interest to produce serviced lots in a controlled situation. In this case we have control of the master planning; we would set the zoning and perhaps a control on the eventual sale price. We feel very strongly that where, for whatever reason, private industry is not producing the land, prices are escalating, and there is a scarcity of land, then it is the government's responsibility to move in and take the initiative, using the cooperation of private industry as much as possible.

4.9 A Developer's View*

Sommer Rumm
President, Ontario Urban Development Institute

A vigorous defence of the private development industry in response to the constraints of government control.

A number of reasons have been presented concerning why CMHC or the government feels that land banking is important. Its objectives are to provide an orderly and adequate supply of land for development and the need to stabilize and if possible reduce prices. Those are exactly the objectives of my company and probably the objectives of most of the people in the industry. We have made many approaches to municipalities offering them land development schemes where we were prepared to limit our profits if they would speed up the development system in order to reduce prices. Our objective under those circumstances is also to create an adequate supply of land in an orderly manner.

In regard to the land development industry enjoying very high profits— last year our company, which is a public company, made some $10

*Remarks to conference workshop. Edited.

million. We paid some $5.3 million in income taxes (federal and provincial); we declared about $1 million dividends, and the recipients of our dividends probably paid $500,000 of that (50%) in income taxes, so that the government got somewhere around $6 million out of our $10 million. Now that left us with $4 million of disposable income to re-invest in our business. In that year we bought about $20 million worth of raw land. The cost of that land two years before was about $12 million—$8 million more than we earned. The net cost was twice as much as the profit we earned. It has to be realized that profits are required by the people of this country so that they can be re-invested in order to produce capacity. If there is any morality to the system under which we work, it is the absolute proof that the housing crisis that we face in this country, unlike that faced in countries like Sweden, or Yugoslavia, or Greece, or Great Britain, is not a crisis of supply; it is a crisis of price. We can supply the market, we have the capacity, but we have been priced out of the market.

It is possible for the private sector to work in conjunction with government. We have carried out pricing projects with the government. In Oakville, for example, the government expropriated land and sold it to us as a private enterprise. We had a contract with the government regarding the amount of profit we could charge. We made a lot of money and we are very proud of the project. It worked out for Oakville and we worked within the limits defined.

There is no need for governments to own land in order to plan. We produce master plans for lands, not only for our own lands but surrounding lands. It is not necessary to own the land to plan it; you do not have to own the land to zone it; you do not have to acquire it to control it. The Province of Ontario in particular is the most over-controlled jurisdiction in the world; we have the least production of land and, in spite of that, we still produce the best housing in the world. The political need to do something about increasing cost is a myth; the way to do something about it is to provide more land. In 1960 we were allowed to produce 4,000 units in the municipality of Pickering (east of Metropolitan Toronto) and we were selling our lots as quickly as we could (at the rate of about 300 a year). Our prices didn't change by more than $300 from 1960 to 1965. But in 1965 that municipality announced that they didn't want to bear the cost and the responsibility, so nobody else could produce any more lots. They got the Ontario Municipal Board to put a stricture on the number of lots produced in the Township of Pickering. Around 1965 they produced about 100 lots per year and that's all that was going to be allowed. What was the net result of that? An instantaneous shortage of land. All of a sudden we could make some money on lots that we hadn't made any money on in the previous five years. So reacted in the normal way. If you bought a house in 1960 and it went up in price and you decided to sell it in 1970 when it was worth $12,000 more, you wouldn't turn down the extra 10 or 12 thousand dollars. That's not the way the market works.

What then is really the problem? It is essentially a growth problem. A lot of people are migrating within Canada or immigrating, and we have the responsibility to provide housing for them. There is a tendency to say "yes, we have to look after them and we have to produce reasonably priced housing, and we have to produce low-cost housing—but not here. Let's move them out to north Pickering." But you know the people in north Pickering say "hold on, not here." Now I don't know where "here" is. There is a social responsibility to accept the needs of the people. The only person in this province, who speaks for those who are disenfranchised, those who don't vote in those municipalities is the private developer.

In regard to the capacity to produce—if we do not make profits we will not have money to invest to build houses. Now those houses that we built are generally speaking for the average person, and we can keep our prices down, and we can meet some pretty rigid price brackets, but we can only do it with the help of the bureacracy. Right now our biggest problem is that there is a whole new group of bureaucrats who say that they can do a better job if the public owns the land. They want to use public money to buy land. We do build smaller projects with government—we are doing 25 OHC houses right now—but what about the fact that in this municipality we have done 2,400 OHC homes over the last two years and we had to have a lottery to give them out. Now we would have done 24,000 if they had let us.

I am told that the government of the City of Saskatoon, with the neighbouring municipality, owns all the land and that all development controls go through very properly; they get the land zoned quickly and they are efficient. The question I want to ask is why in that area where the government owns the land does the city cooperate to make sure there is enough land supply, but where we own the land they won't cooperate to make sure there is enough land supplied? That question has to be answered because, as far as I am concerned, the one thing that is the issue here is the freedom of our society. The road on which we are being placed, that of public land ownership, can only lead in one direction. It can lead to the expropriation of land owned by private individuals whether they be farmers or speculators or in fact you, because when you have gotten through cutting up the 100 acres, and the 10 acres, and the two acres, what about the 50 foot lot? Who is going to own that? I say we can do the job and we can prove it from our past experience. We are being prevented from doing the job by the very groups who are calling for public land ownership.

A Special Case: The National Capital Region

4.10 The Origins of the National Capital Commission*

Edgar Gallant
Chairman, National Capital Commission

A discussion of the problems of coordinating and implementing a land development program in the national capital.

It was about 30 years ago when the government of the day became rather concerned with the haphazard development occurring within the National Capital Region because of the lack of legislative controls over land. At that time zoning and other development controls were weak, or in some areas, virtually non-existent. Accordingly, the government agreed that if the commission's long-term objectives for the national capital were to be achieved, it would be essential to acquire large tracts of land for the major projects of the commission and of the government generally.

It was also recognized that the use of the land acquired had to be of the highest order if it was to make a positive contribution to the development of the capital. Therefore, any land purchased by the federal government (mainly through the NCC), should be disposed of either for purposes of the commission or purposes of the government. If sold or leased to other jurisdictions or to the private sector, it should be done under deed arrangements that guaranteed long-term protection for those lands by dictating certain uses and barring others. After years of management of these lands, which the commission had been selling to private developers, the government decided that the commission should only exchange land or lease it. Our policy now is to lease to private users if we still have parcels of land available in publicly owned industrial parks. Initial resistance encountered has been overcome to a very large extent; and we now have a number of private concerns prepared to lease parcels of land and to build their facilities on such leased land for a reasonably long term. An example is Metropolitan Life, which has leased a parcel of land in an industrial park in Ottawa from the NCC for something like 50 years, and has put its important computer centre there.

The control of land by the NCC has undoubtedly been the most important tool used by the commission for influencing the direction of development in the National Capital Region. It has not been the only tool. Joint arrangements with local municipalities, with regional municipalities, or with the provinces have also been very important, but land control has probably been the most significant and the most important tool at the disposal of the federal government.

---

*Remarks to the conference. Edited.

The commission has therefore supported a policy of acquiring sufficient land to ensure that the major elements of its planning proposals and plans for the national capital could be safeguarded until specific development projects could be undertaken, either directly by the commission, or another government agency, or by another jurisdiction. It was important to have acquired the land in advance of actual needs. Once this land had been acquired, it was sold as well as leased. Present policy, however, is to exchange land with other jurisdictions, or at times with private developers, and to lease land.

In proceeding with land acquisitions in the late fifties and early sixties, the government had initially hoped that more could be achieved through cooperation with local jurisdictions in using zoning powers, for instance, to protect a greenbelt around the urban part of Ottawa. These efforts failed, however, and the government had no alternative but to acquire the land; thus the commission set out on a course of purchasing. After having acquired some 25,000 acres, we no longer could negotiate purchases with the remaining owners and the government then had no recourse but to use the expropriation powers that Parliament had included in the National Capital Act. In the exercise of these powers, obviously many feathers were ruffled, many people's feelings were hurt, and a classic case went before the courts (the Monroe case).

The impact and benefit of the NCC activities in public land ownership in the National Capital Region have enabled the federal government to have land at its disposal in advance of need and therefore, at relatively lower cost. This means that even in rising market conditions, sites are available not only for government buildings, but also for innovative urban developments and for longer term urban infrastructures. The LeBreton Flats project is a very good example of the kind of benefits that can accrue from public land ownership. This area, which was expropriated at the time of the railway relocation program, included some 163 acres and the cost of that expropriation was $18 million; today the value set on those lands is in the order of $80 million. Because it was acquired at lower cost, it is possible for the public authority today to contemplate and plan for the development of a demonstration residential project right in the heart of the city. Without such public land assembly, a project of this kind would have been totally impossible. . .

This program of land ownership and land assembly has also provided the region with extensive open space and enabled a loosening up of the dense urban environment in the built-up area. It has also enabled the government to undertake some innovative projects, pioneering in such simple things as garden plots, ski trails, bicycle paths, and promenades for pedestrians in these linear strips of public land. These projects have been the subject of many enquiries from across the country, and indeed in a number of cities similar projects have been undertaken. Some of these land assemblies, particularly those relating to the railway relocation program, also permitted the removal of undesirable industrial activities from the central part of the city.

In conclusion, considerable (if not determining) influence can be exerted on the direction of growth in an urban area through land ownership. In association with zoning regulations and in cooperation with other jurisdictions, it makes possible not only control of development and the direction in which development could take place, but also creates the prospect for achieving certain giant objectives that have been well defined in advance. I for one, however, would not argue that public land ownership is the answer to all our problems in urban areas. I feel very strongly that, from our experience, a mix of public ownership and effective zoning regulations would have more promise for better urban planning, at least for the National Capital Region.

4.11 A Review of NCC Policy*

Kevin Garland
Planner, A.J. Diamond Associates

A discussion of the effectiveness of the use of public land ownership in the capital area, which illustrates both its strengths and weaknesses.

Nowhere in Canada is there an urban area where public land ownership as a planning tool has been used as extensively as in the national capital of Ottawa-Hull. While the question of public land ownership is only recently emerging in much of the rest of Canada as an issue, the National Capital Commission (NCC) as the agent for the federal government, has been acquiring and developing land on a very large scale in Ottawa-Hull since its creation in 1958.

The act that established the NCC gave it wide powers to acquire land, through expropriation if necessary, and to develop it in accordance with federal objectives for the National Capital Region. The NCC currently owns more than 30% of the urbanized area of the Ottawa-Hull region, with an additional 25,000 acres held by other federal departments or agencies. A recent articulation of the objectives to be achieved by using these holdings states that the region is to be developed as:

1 a fitting symbol of Canada's cultural and linguistic values;
2 an efficient and aesthetically satisfying place in which to carry out the nation's business;

---

*Paper prepared for this volume. Edited.

3 a model of urban planning and development that will benefit other parts of the country and be a source of pride to Canadians.

Why was public land ownership the major implementing tool employed by the NCC? How effective has the use of public land been in achieving NCC objectives?

The answer to the first question lies in the peculiar governmental relationships which make up the National Capital Region. In 1958, the region administered by the NCC took in the cities of Ottawa and Hull and their surrounding rural municipalities. Thus there were two strong provincial governments and a host of small local municipalities (dominated by the City of Ottawa), all of which felt some responsibility for planning in the area. As the political issue of separation grew in Quebec, the use of federal planning power in Hull became less and less acceptable. At the outset, local government was not notably strong. Ottawa and Hull were distinctly separate cities—small, and with little or no comprehensive planning for transportation systems or land use. It was the wish of the federal government to develop a Capital City with some "sense of place"—an attribute woefully lacking in Ottawa in the 1950s. Yet it appeared politically unacceptable to achieve federal control through direct creation of a federally administered city. Constitutionally, Canadian municipalities are firmly within the jurisdiction of the provinces; the annexation of Ottawa and of Hull as a federal district was rejected.

After 1958, large parcels of land were acquired, largely through the relocation of rail lines and adjacent industry. The hope was that in cooperation with local governments, using their powers of development control, federal goals for a more aesthetically pleasing and viable city could be achieved. Thus a master plan was drawn up and federal landholdings were brought to bear to implement the plan. Public land ownership was not deliberately chosen as the best of a number of alternative planning tools. It was quite simply the only avenue open to the NCC to allow it to achieve its plans.

The second question—regarding the effectiveness of the use of public land ownership by the NCC—illustrates both the strengths and weaknesses of this single planning tool. Initially the answer is positive. The NCC's record as a planning agency is nowhere more evident than in the dramatic changes in the visual and environmental quality of Ottawa and Hull in the past decade. A policy of containing urban sprawl and protecting valuable Ottawa Valley farmland has been successfully achieved with the securing of 40,000 acres of land in a greenbelt encircling Ottawa to the south. A magnificent 70,000-acre wilderness area of forest, hills, and lakes (Gatineau Park) has been acquired for public use; it reaches directly into the centre of urban Hull, opposite Parliament Hill. Strips of land acquired in the railway relocation have been used to build scenic parkway drives throughout Ottawa; and such major and necessary arterial connections as the Airport Parkway, the Queensway, and the Portage Bridge have been constructed by the NCC or enabled with the use of federal land at nominal cost. The central core of Hull is being substantially redeveloped with major new federal office employment intended to redress the imbalance of commercial and economic vitality between the two cities. Current planning includes a transit corridor between the two cities. Along this corridor significant new development centres are planned at LeBreton Flats (medium- to high-density residential), at Rideau Centre (united retail-commercial, hotel and office), and at Victoria and Chaudiere Islands (regional recreation). The Wellington streetscape and parliamentary enclave are being visually preserved and enhanced with strategic new buildings, in particular the National Art Gallery, the Ottawa Civic Art Gallery, and the Federal Archives Building. Programs such as the canal skating rink, the urban bikeways and cross-country ski trails, and the construction and subsidization of the National Arts Centre have given the NCC high public visibility and have greatly enhanced the quality of life in the area. The strategic use of public land to guide development patterns in Ottawa-Hull, through both land use and strategic transportation links, and the dramatic change in the environmental quality of the city that the NCC has achieved provide a very clear example of the enormous effectiveness of public land and public investment as planning tools. Public ownership has allowed initiatives to be taken and public benefit to be exploited to an extent which is not possible with the use of development controls alone.

However, this description of the NCC's activities and achievements ignores some critical issues that have also been very evident during the decade, and which are now combining to seriously restrict the effectiveness of NCC's use of its land. Local government in 1958 was strong only in the City of Ottawa. The rural areas and Hull were not active in planning. Customary rural/urban rivalries occurred as Ottawa grew and gradually annexed surrounding townships. The greenbelt, which the NCC had hoped to protect through cooperation with local government, using its powers of zoning and development control, was finally secured only by a long and bitter series of expropriations. Municipalities in which the greenbelt is located continue to view it as an expensive impediment to development rather than a unique rural resource. In January 1969 the Regional Municipality of Ottawa-Carleton (RMOC) was created by the Province of Ontario to act as a regional government with planning jurisdiction for the larger urban and rural area.

The RMOC has prepared an Official Plan that varies in some important ways from the principles of the NCC's master plan. The NCC has been placed in the role of benevolent (and not so benevolent) dictator, using its strategic land holdings to deny local governments the power to implement planning proposals that they feel are important components of their local planning policies. Lack of coordination of planning activity and outright hostility between the NCC and local and provincial planning officials and politicians has become distressingly evident. In the delicate manoeuvering, which has been necessary to achieve federal planning objectives without hurting local sensibilities, the NCC has tended to look like an unresponsive and insensitive "heavy." In spite of recent planning for the Rideau Centre and Le Breton Flats projects, where the NCC has put together consultative planning teams which include representatives of all relevant local government levels, other federal agencies, and citizen or business groups, the planning power of the NCC is gradually being eroded. In 1970 the responsibility for acquiring and managing federal land was shifted to the Department of Public Works (DPW), which now has the sole right to expropriate land on behalf of the federal government. When the few remaining privately owned properties along Wellington were acquired, they were not done so by the NCC to facilitate its urban design concepts for the Wellington streetscape, but by DPW. NCC must now work in cooperation with DPW and attempt to exercise design control, but DPW will develop Wellington West, deciding on building programs and on the hiring of architects. DPW is now developing its own planning expertise and staff, which may undertake yet another level of planning for Ottawa-Hull.

Clearly the NCC has shown that public land ownership backed by the power to invest public money to take development initiatives is a highly effective means of achieving stated public objectives. It has succeeded brilliantly in realizing its own objectives for the Ottawa-Hull area. But equally clear is that it is not politically possible, within the delicate federal/provincial/municipal balance of power in Canada, for one federal agency to single mindedly implement comprehensive planning programs in an urban area that straddles two provinces and has not two, but four, layers of local government. However successful the use of public land has been in Ottawa in practical terms, it is a kind of anachronism. The Canadian urban reality is one of overlapping jurisdictions—of urban versus suburban and local versus provincial rivalries.

Experience in Developing Countries

Public Land Use Issues in the Third World*

Patricia Stamp
Lecturer, Division of Social Science, York University

Any account of public land use issues in developing countries should be prefaced by an outline of the underlying characteristics that distinguish their experience from that of the developed world with regard to such issues. Generally speaking, Third World countries can be characterized by economic weakness and dependency, and political fragility. A growing body of literature describes and analyses this relationship, focusing on the political constraints inherent in nation-states forged by the colonial experience from historically diverse societies, and on the international economic framework that maintains these new nation-states in a clientship with the developed world, as producers of raw materials and consumers of manufactured goods.[1] As a result, any planning activity takes place within a context of political and economic constraints usually more severe than those experienced in developed countries. These constraints must be taken into careful account both in the planning activity, and in evaluation of it.

A second, and more positive difference between the developing and developed worlds relates specifically to public planning. The concept of public control of resources is inherent in the nature of colonial rule. Cities were often colonial creations, or were traditional centres vastly transformed by the colonial presence; urban areas in particular were subject to planning and public ownership. Whether the colonial government instituted this control for the purpose of exploitation of the colony's resources, for the welfare of the inhabitants, or for a combination of the two, is irrelevant in the contemporary context. The fact remains that a tradition of public control was established that could be used by post-independence governments for their own purposes. Indeed, the government's duty to exercise such control as a tool of economic development is probably a universally accepted tenet in the Third World today. The idea of public control of land thus meets with less resistance than in the West; it is in fact usually considered imperative. What was started by the colonial powers for their own expedience has become a

*Introductory paper prepared for this volume.

149

cornerstone of independence policy. Further, public control of land came to be seen as a legitimate tool of new governments for the redress of colonial inequities. For example, much rural land reform in areas of agricultural exploitation has been directed to placing control back in the hands of indigenous inhabitants.

The consideration of public land issues in the Third World involves a third and crucial distinguishing feature: the nature of the traditional societies from which the new nations have been pieced together. They were usually based on ethnic or religious ties, and engaged in subsistence activity. Their social structures were complex and varied, usually involving values and practices quite different from those of the developed world. While these structures are undergoing rapid changes—many of them dictated by population pressure and the urgent need for increased food production—much remains that may be considered of value by the inhabitants. Both in the developing and developed world, modernization and economic growth for their own sake are coming into question. The value of small-scale societies, with more modest aims and with simpler technology than are currently espoused, is being reconsidered in the light of new awareness concerning the earth's limited resources.

Traditional land use is intimately related to social structure and function. In agricultural Africa, for example, land was rarely treated as a commodity of the marketplace, but rather as a function of social relationships. Ownership was vested in the kinship group, and the right to exploit the land derived from one's status in the group. Rights to use of the land might occasionally be bartered: the land itself was inalienable.[2] The instigation of land consolidation, and the introduction of individual title, then, has led to changes in social patterns that are not always beneficial. Women are one group who have suffered; their economic and social status has often been affected through loss of kinship-guaranteed rights to the control of land. Moreover, while traditional land use patterns tended to ensure that a maximum number of people could work the land for their own support, new land practices have tended to concentrate land in fewer hands, forcing peasants from the land or into labour on the land of others. While changes in traditional patterns may well be necessary for the economic well-being of the nation, the formulation or evaluation of land use policy should take greater account of social and grass roots economic impact than has been the case in the past.

Workshop presentations and discussion, drawing on material from Africa, Asia, and Latin America, ranged between three levels of analysis. On the first level, two papers discuss specific instruments of land use policy. One raises questions concerning costs and benefits of a particular type of urban land use, with emphasis on "social cost recovery" (Grimes,

5.1). The other discusses the link between two types of agricultural land policy, "motivational" and "enabling," and economic growth in Kenya (Davis, 5.2). The aim in both of these is to explore the efficacy of certain land use tools without questioning the goals on which overall development policy is premised. In view of the complexity and variety of circumstances within which land use policy must be devised, such studies provide vital assistance in the processes of planning and evaluation being carried out by Third World governments and international agencies.

The second level of analysis takes a step back, as it were, to consider the broader context within which policy is formulated and implemented. Two presentations deal with the conflict between the means and objectives associated with public land use. They share the view that this conflict is a more serious one than in the developed world. Six ingredients (see 2.1) are relevant in this context: 1) comprehensiveness of the program and clarity of its goals and values; 2) adequacy of financial system; 3) integration of the administrative system (including local government structures); 4) a staff that is competent, non-political and well paid; 5) administrative leadership hierarchy; and 6) widely based political backing for the administrative leadership. The studies presented here (and much of the literature evaluating political and administrative performance in the Third World) demonstrate the lack of several or many of these ingredients.

The first presentation relating to evaluation explores the socio-economic environment and the political constraints within which a particular urban land use program in Kenya was attempted, and shows how the policy's implementation was affected by these factors (Stamp, 5.3). The second discusses rural land law reform in Senegal, and raises questions as to whether the development goals of such reform can possibly be achieved given the internal socio-economic structure, and the international economic framework within which Senegal operates (Snyder, 5.4). This presentation, in discussing the feasibility of policy objectives, raises a further, broader question, which relates to the third level of analysis—the question concerning the nature and validity of the goals of land use policy themselves. These goals bear scrutiny, since they are often part of an overall policy of economic development that places priority on growth and increased efficiency of production, rather than on social values and equitable distribution of resources.

Much of the workshop's discussion focused on the question of allocation in the establishment of development priorities. The final presentation here deals with the question of goals. Drawing on the experience of Sri Lanka, it shows how the realistic selection of objectives can lead to genuine and effective economic reform as well as to a more just distribution of the nation's resources (Dawes, 5.5).

Notes

1. Paul Baran is considered one of the founders of the "theory of underdevelopment," as it is called (*The Political Economy of Growth* [New York: Monthly Review Press, 1957]). Other important works include Celso Furtado, *Development and Underdevelopment* (Berkeley: University of California Press, 1971); Andre Gunder Frank, *Underdevelopment in Latin America* (New York: Monthly Review Press, 1966; rev. 1969); Giovanni Arrighi and John Saul, *Essays on the Political Economy of Africa* (New York: Monthly Review Press, 1973).

2. See Paul and Laura Bohannan, *Tiv Economy* (Evanston: Northwestern University Press, 1968) for an empirically based discussion of this thesis.

5.1 Social Cost Recovery in Housing Programs Using Public Land*

Orville F. Grimes, Jr
Development Economics Department, International Bank for Reconstruction and Development (World Bank)

Consideration of the use of public land for low-income housing, the methods of recovering servicing costs, and comparison of social costs and benefits of such activities.

There are several points to be considered in choosing among the potential uses of unimproved land in public ownership. The land is particularly important, since low-cost housing and servicing programs in developing countries are often carried out on government-owned land. Methods of recovering actual project outlays under a typical system of leasehold disposal are also important, but "social cost recovery" is a more meaningful planning criterion, though usually more difficult to realize.

Recoupment of Land Servicing

Plans for using public land for low-income housing, and recovering the cost of service provision, often begin with the premise that ownership should remain with the state. In these instances occupants are given long-term leases (25-50 years is common) and asked to pay ground rents expressed as a percentage of the land's unimproved value. How these rents are actually set depends on the extent to which the government's interest is in receiving the amount that the funds could earn in other uses, or in subsidizing poor families. If financial viability is the prime concern, rental payments will be fixed to produce annual earnings roughly the same as returns on invested funds elsewhere in the economy, given by a relevant market interest rate of, say, 10 per cent. Rental payments will fall short of this amount as subsidies are accorded to preferred tenants. As in Hong Kong, land may be "written down" to a fraction of its market value in reckoning rental charges.

Servicing costs on public land devoted to low-income housing can be recovered mainly because these costs are always lower than the market value of land. Each piece of urban land has a group of site attributes that give it worth. Public services like water, drainage, schools, and markets, to which the land provides access, only begin to portray the locational advantages of a parcel. Tree cover, views, and porosity of soil are natural

*Paper prepared for conference workshop. Edited. The views expressed here are those of the author and do not reflect World Bank opinions or policies.

endowments of land that can affect value. So can the eventual regulatory status—zoning and administrative controls—as well as tenure arrangements.[1] Market prices will include the anticipated rise in value from the finished dwelling. Finally, wholly aside from its use as an input into housing, land is demanded as an asset. It is a springboard to greater financial security for families whose major form of wealth is the land they live on.

For all these reasons, rental payments that approximate market value should result in a budgetary surplus to the public authorities. Low-income families, however, often cannot afford payments of this kind without spending an unreasonable share of their income on shelter. When subsidies are required for these families to purchase land, one frequently used scheme is to sell lots to a wide range of income groups, the highest paying market value for their plots. On occasion, especially attractive features of the housing area—its location, mix of businesses, or potential for future growth—might even imply that high-income families would pay a slight premium over the value of similar sites elsewhere. In any event, families at the lowest end of the income scale are either helped by the surplus from these operations, or whenever possible, are asked to meet the cost of servicing. To make monthly payments easier, families might also be allowed to rent rooms to lodgers. Low-income families in this way build equity in their dwellings more rapidly, have an incentive to finish them quickly, and share more fully in spreading economic benefits over the project area.

Leaseholds can be sold or otherwise transferred, however. To prevent families from selling their plots to richer newcomers, city or national authorities may retain a right of first repurchase for a specified period after initial occupancy. Or they could simply award the plot to the family next on the waiting list at a price that covers existing mortgages and the value of improvements made by the former occupant. And of course, leasehold rights of any tenant delinquent in his monthly payments may be terminated by prescribed procedures.

A further adjustment may be made in gauging recoverable costs. Productive factors, particularly labour, may be induced into housing at less than market prices because of unemployment or bottlenecks in other sectors. The difference between these shadow prices and market factor payments is counted as a benefit of the project, or subtracted from costs. This holds for self-help as well as hired labour: the foregone leisure of families building their own dwellings is generally valued at less than the market wage, and much of this construction is done by persons not ordinarily members of the labour force, or on weekends by employed family members.

A return on public land used for low-income housing of (for example)

15 per cent may emerge from this process. Compared with typical yields on securities or lending rates in other areas of the economy, using the land for this purpose may thereby seem attractive. But it is important to compare this return with what could be obtained from putting the land to other uses (especially close substitutes like middle-income housing), and not to be satisfied that the return by some criterion is "acceptable." Housing is a durable good. New construction represents only about 1-3 per cent, on the average, of the existing housing stock for most countries, developing and developed. With the rapid pace of city growth in the developing world, it is therefore not surprising that housing shortages can produce fabulous rates of return to housing investment. Let us therefore conservatively put at 20 per cent the return a developer could earn if the land were given over to middle-income housing.[2] Here the question of social cost recovery arises. As a first estimate, the full social cost of using public land for low-income housing is this 20 per cent return foregone. And this comparison itself may be altered when the full range of costs and benefits of each type of housing is taken into account.

Recoupment Enlarged: Social Costs

The cost of low-income housing programs in physical terms, is generally an unreliable measure of program effects on the economy as a whole. Although evidence is conflicting, low-income housing may, for example, be more labour-intensive in construction than other types of housing. In one study of Colombia, Mexico, and Venezuela, it was found that about five man-years of work would be generated with $12,000 of annual subsidy given to families earning less than $2,000 per year during 1969-71. If the same amount had been given to families earning more than $7,000, only two man-years' work would have been created.[3] Another study of the Mexican housing industry showed a slightly higher employment creation effect for "minimum cost" single-family dwellings than for luxury single-family or multi-family structures.[4] Other studies have shown the opposite. Yet mobilization of underused labour in economies with labour surpluses is itself an advantage of housing programs of this kind. Low-income housing is generally not a heavy foreign exchange user, but for luxury housing with steel frames and many electrical fixtures, the import content can be substantial.

While rents paid by project participants will nearly always be the largest component of housing benefits, the importance of other factors is increasingly recognized. In Kingston, Jamaica, many public sites used for low-income housing are well located, with good access to central city jobs especially for family members other than the principal earner. Other city residents benefit through reduced transport costs and congestion. Additional benefits could include fewer fires (once the bane of squatter settlements in Hong Kong, Singapore, and elsewhere) and reduced crime.

Finally, social cost recovery takes into account two other features not usually considered in private calculations of gains and losses: the impacts on family behaviour and on the distribution of income. With the scarcity of housing at all income levels, increasing the stock of low-income housing can lower the price of all housing and bring dwellings previously unaffordable within reach of more families than would otherwise be possible. Another way of realizing social gain is by *not* incurring social loss. To the extent that affordable, staged housing construction with secure land tenure replaces the fear and deprivation of life in squatter settlements, families benefit in ways not realizable if the public land had been devoted to another use. Without becoming involved in controversies about whether a dollar's public investment is worth more applied to some households than others, the fact remains that policy makers may wish to give greater emphasis to programs affecting poor families. On these grounds alone there would be extra reason to consider closely the use of public land for low-cost housing.

Public land acquisition programs often focus on the "front end" of the operation: how to acquire land, at what price, for what objective? Questions of social cost, of weighing alternative uses, must be answered as decisions are made. Contemplating purchase of a private tract, policy makers ask themselves if, on balance, it would be more desirable to purchase it for the public or leave it in private hands. Disposition of publicly owned land, however, seems more often to be treated as a problem of efficient public management than one of social choice. A fuller comparison of costs and benefits of prospective uses with those of the best alternatives is one way public land can be used to maximum social advantage.

Notes

1. See Steven Maser, William Riker, and Richard Rosett, "The Effects of Zoning and Externalities on the Prices of Land in Monroe Country, New York," Discussion Paper No. 74-10 (New York: University of Rochester, April 1974); and George E. Peterson, "The Influence of Zoning Regulations on Land and Housing Prices," Working Paper No. 1207-24 (Washington, D.C.: Urban Institute, July 1974).

2. Though this figure may well be an analogue for actual returns, it must be regarded as purely notional in view of the well-known difficulty of obtaining this kind of information in empirical studies.

3. W. Paul Strassmann, "Measuring the Employment Effects of Housing Policies in Developing Countries" (Mimeo, 1974).

4. C. Araud, G. Boon, V. Urguidi, and W.P. Strassmann, *Studies on Employment in the Mexican Housing Industry* (Paris: OECD, 1973).

5.2 Land Policy and Agricultural Development in Kenya*

J. Tait Davis

Professor of Geography, York University; former Field Director, York University Kenya Project

Examination of the implications of general policies of land reform in relation to economic growth in the agricultural sector, and the significance of public land ownership.

The governments of most Third World countries have accepted a responsibility for fostering the development of their territories. In the early stages of coming to grips with this responsibility, they have tended to emphasize economic rather than social dimensions of development in their policies and plans. In doing so they have not been unaware of the importance to development of changes in social and political attitudes and institutions. Rather they appear to have accepted a strategic premise that "the fragile, new nation is best levered into modernity gently and indirectly through its economy."[1] Frontal attacks on existing social and political structures are avoided, partly to minimize the political risk for a new and inexperienced administration, partly because it is recognized that such attacks constitute a bottomless sinkhole for the energies and finances of a basically poor country.

It is ironic that governments anxious to avoid direct assaults on cherished social and political institutions should be confronted in the agricultural sector with the need to radically transform existing systems of land tenure and use. The dilemma is that economic growth in the agriculture sector generally requires a program of land reform. At the same time, complexities of the social and political environment combine to make implementation of a land reform program risky in political terms.

Role of Policy in a Growth Oriented Strategy

In the jargon of development, "policy" is something addressed to the private sector. The government seeks to persuade people to do what they

*Paper prepared for conference workshop. Edited.

otherwise would not do with the factors of production under their control. Low elasticity of supply in traditional agriculture systems is generally regarded as a constraint on overall economic growth.[2] "In other words the traditional cultivator of the soil must either be changed in his whole outlook—which is never easy—or else he must be removed, be it by eviction or emancipation."[3] Most governments will eschew wholesale displacement and eviction as a policy for improving efficiency in agriculture. The alternative must be an effort to change the outlook and behaviour of the traditional cultivator. The dilemma for policy is that the social aim of protecting the economically weak, while it reinforces the political desire to avoid social unrest, conflicts with the economic aim of rationalizing patterns of agricultural production. Policy on land ownership is set in a context of an effort to increase production and cannot be considered in isolation.

It is helpful to consider development policy formulations as belonging to one of two types. The first, motivational policy, embraces all those measures aimed at changing the behaviour of the individual producer. Under obvious assumptions these measures include both incentives and sanctions. The second, enabling policy, incorporates those measures aimed at creating the systems and capacities required if individual producers are to participate in modern economic processes. Policies with respect to land can be related to this typology and evaluated in terms of their prospective contribution to overall economic growth.

Land Policies and Agricultural Development

It has been argued that improvements in land tenure are an essential precondition for the development of agriculture "since an unfavourable tenure situation may stifle the incentive for change."[4] Unfavourable tenure situations include those in which land use options are constrained by social pressures, as well as those in which the rewards of extra effort are confiscated by landlords or governments. Because increases in the productivity of land require investment, security of tenure for the investor is considered to be a precondition to the making of such investments. In Kenya, for example, the principal policies addressing the issue of tenure in land are the Land Adjudication Program and Land Registration.[5] The Adjudication Program basically makes a transition from customary law to statute law and from communal to individual ownership. Subsequent to adjudication the confirmed rights in land are registered under the provisions of the Registered Land Act (1963) and customary law ceases to be applicable. Between 1954 and 1972, 2,577,894 hectares of land were adjudicated and registered in Kenya. Overall cost of the program was about K£10 million. It is difficult to assess the impact of this program on agricultural production in the small-farm sector. Most evidence is circumstantial. What can be noted is that between 1954 and 1974 gross marketed production from small farmers rose from less than 20 per cent of the total to more than half. In per capita terms, crop sales rose from less than 25 shillings to more than 105 in the same period. In regional distribution terms it can be noted that the greatest increases in production for market have been associated with areas adjudicated and registered.

A second facet of Kenya's experience with motivational policy concerning land relates to sanctions for unsatisfactory land management. Wide controls over agricultural land are given to the minister by the Agricultural Act. One important consequence of land adjudication and registration has been to facilitate the application of sanctions for improper use and mismanagement. The registration of title to land has an enabling effect as well. Commercial, and some government-administered credit programs require proof of title as a condition or security for an advance. In the case of Kenya, agricultural credit from commercial sources is significant. In registered small-farm areas (Trust Lands) commercial bank loans for all purposes totalled K£1.7 million in 1970; government loans totalled K£1.0 million in that year. Without a registered title to land it is fair to conclude that commercial credit on this scale would not have been available.

Public Land Ownership and Agricultural Development

In some respects the question of land ownership is both academic and irrelevant. There are so many possible gradations between absolute private and absolute public ownership. All private property rights are conditional, not absolute. The state may at any time abolish or abridge any or all of the privileges of private property. For a government dedicated to economic growth there is, however, a touchstone for determining in specific cases an appropriate division on the ownership question. This touchstone relates policy to production and productivity through land use. At this point the question of ownership and the locus of responsibility for use is neither academic nor irrelevant.

Some examples are 1) situations where an activity necessary to the development of agriculture is best performed by the public sector; 2) situations where the use judged "best" in the public interest yields financial returns to the private owner that are an insufficient inducement; and 3) situations where the public sector is the agency best able to assume the risk associated with a particular development scheme.

Among the functions essential to the development of agriculture in a developing country, agricultural research may be mentioned as an illustration of the first situation. The manpower required, the relevance of this work throughout the agricultural sector, and the need for consistency over long periods of time combine to place agricultural research among the responsibilities of the public sector. It follows that the facilities and land required for this activity should also be in public ownership.

The second situation is more complex. It does, however, incorporate the rationalization for the largest areas commonly held in public ownership in a developing country. There will be situations where public interest requires a pattern of land utilization that cannot yield an adequate financial return to a private owner. A common example would be forest areas required for the preservation of surface and subsurface water levels. In a cost-benefit analysis the situation is characterized by a high social benefit, but a low financial return.

In most developing countries situations will arise in which only the public sector is able to undertake particular projects or programs. This may be because of government monopoly of necessary expertise, because of access to foreign aid, or because the risks attached to a particular venture make it undesirable from the point of view of a private investor. Whether or not the public sector will become involved in a specific project is, of course, at the discretion of government decision makers.

In a very general sense land policy, and the question of public land ownership, is considered in a developing country as only one element in an overall effort to achieve development. To the extent that development is associated with economic growth, all policy will be expected to reflect this bias, and the other consequences and impacts will be given less attention.[6]

The transition from customary to statutory rights in land and from communal to individual tenure has been accompanied in Kenya by strict government controls. Although land may be granted with freehold or absolute ownership, this amounts to little more than that the owner does not have to pay rent to the government for the land and that there are no express development conditions attached to the grant of absolute ownership. By and large this approach has been acceptable politically and socially. A system of individual ownership of production units coupled with comprehensive powers to regulate and intervene on the part of government has the appearance of a workable solution to the problem of increasing agricultural production and productivity.

A grey area for policy has only been touched upon in this paper. That is the merit of an association between responsibility, use, and ownership. How permanent should be the allocations of responsibility and ownership between the public and the private sectors? By what criteria is the allocation to be altered? How inconsistent will be the allocations derived from an economic growth bias when emphasis shifts to social concerns for equity in the distribution of things?

A second grey area relates to the definition of "public interest" as a justification for public land ownership. When is an interest "public" enough to merit an investment of public resources? More important, how far into the future should a government attempt to anticipate a "public interest"? It might be better to leave a substantial fuzziness around the question of public land ownership to be interpreted at a time and in a fashion suited to the manner in which the question emerges.

Notes

1. Ronald Robinson, "Practical Politics of Economic Development," in Robinson, ed., *Developing the Third World: The Experience of the Nineteen Sixties* (Cambridge: The University Press, 1971), p. 1.

2. For a discussion of this point in the context of the Rostow conception of the take-off, see Mogens Boserup, "Agrarian Structure and Take-Off" in W.W. Rostow, ed., *The Economics of Take-off into Sustained Growth* (New York: St Martin's Press, 1963), pp. 201-24.

3. Boserup, "Agrarian Structure," p. 206.

4. Bruce F. Johnston and John W. Mellow, "The Role of Agriculture in Economic Development," *The American Economic Review* (September 1961):582.

5. Tudor Jackson, *The Law of Kenya: An Introduction* (Nairobi: East African Literature Bureau, 1970). Chapter 9, "Land Law," contains a review of legislation and its development in Kenya.

6. The nature of emerging and polarizing inequalities is explored at length in *Employment, Incomes and Equality*, Report of an Interagency Team financed by the United Nations Development Program and organized by the International Labor Office (Geneva, 1972).

5.3 Political Implications of Low-Cost Housing in Kenya*

Patricia Stamp
Lecturer, Division of Social Science, York University

A case-study of low-cost housing in Thika, Kenya in which the implementation of the scheme is not in the interests of the low-income group for which it was designed.

*Paper prepared for conference workshop. Edited. Research for this study was conducted during the summers of 1973 and 1974. While I received information and advice from a number of people in Kenya, I am particularly grateful to the officers and councillors of the Thika Municipal Council.

In Kenya, a great deal of effort with regard to housing has been focused on a type of scheme entitled "Site and Service." In the scheme, plots would be laid out and provided with basic services such as sanitation, electricity, and roads, and then allocated to people for building their own dwelling, using temporary materials to do so, in accordance with administrative specifications regarding certain minimum standards of construction and materials. The rationale behind site and service schemes was summarized in the Report of the United Nations Mission to Kenya on Housing, 1965.[1] In the conditions of rapid urbanization that are currently occurring in Africa, there is an urgent need for low-cost housing, but usually insufficient capital resources, either public or private, to develop such housing. Site and service schemes are designed to overcome this handicap by involving the occupant in a partnership to construct his own housing, using cheap materials chosen by the occupant. In Kenya, a ceiling was set on income allowable to a plot holder; an annual income of $700 or less was the eligibility requirement. The value of the completed house was to be no more than $1,200.

Thika, which is a rapidly growing industrial town of around 30,000 inhabitants located 25 miles north of Nairobi, was selected to be the location of eight site and service schemes, involving several thousand plots. A Danish planning team was established in the municipality to produce plans and specifications for the plots. In 1971 the Town Clerk remarked to the press: "Thika hopes to set an example to other towns on how to cope with urban problems through planned housing policy." But by 1973 the program was in a shambles: the development scheme was considerably behind schedule; the few plots that had been developed had expensive houses, built with permanent materials such as brick; and finally, almost all were in the hands of middle-class people with incomes of well over $700 per year. What had happened? The following is the main sequence of events.

The Town Planning and Development Committee of the Municipal Council of Thika struck a Plot Allocation Subcommittee and allocated the first three schemes to individuals in the town. In 1971 the Town Clerk complained to the Commissioner of Lands in the Ministry of Lands and Settlement[2] that mis-allocation was taking place. Relatives of the councillors, the councillors themselves, and those who could provide them with some sort of political support were receiving these plots. When the next set of schemes came up for allocation, the Town Clerk rejected the Subcommittee's list. As a result of this, he was given a vote of no confidence in a council meeting, and a more amenable Town Clerk was appointed in his place. The Commissioner of Lands, on his part, sought to regulate plot allocation by attaching to the Letters of Allocation for the plots (required to be signed by the Municipal Council for the formal transfer of Crown land to the municipality) a proviso forbidding the subletting or transfer of plots. When the councillors failed to ratify these Letters of Allocation in order to render the transfer binding, the commissioner used the opportunity as legal grounds for withdrawing the plots from the council's jurisdiction, and for setting up a new procedure for their allocation to citizens. A district-level Plot Allocation Committee reviewed the applicants selected by the Council Subcommittee, and reallocated plots according to the outcome of this review.

The outcome was not dramatic, however. Of about 600 plots, 450 were left in the hands of those who had originally been allocated land. This was justified through the raising of the income ceiling for applicants. The political hazard of enforcing the initial regulations and depriving those first allocated plots was too great. But although the reallocation did not succeed in its purpose, the councillors were shocked by what they perceived as a usurpation of their jurisdiction; moreover, they had lost their most important source of patronage and they became extremely unpopular in the town. The measure of this was seen in the municipal elections of 1974, when only two out of the eight who ran were re-elected. Within the council itself, legislative functions practically ceased following the allocation debacle. The Danish planning team's contract was not renewed and neither were local experts brought in to continue the development schemes. Morale among the administrative officers plunged. The central government, for its part, strengthened its hand with regard to the municipal authority through intervention in the crisis, enhancing the tendency in recent years for ministries to arrogate local authority functions. Thus, the consequences of the attempt at a low-cost housing program were two-fold: the goals of the policy were deflected on the one hand, and the political structure was weakened on the other hand.

In explaining this, one can draw on two sets of factors that impinge on policy implementation. The first concerns the general socio-economic constraints, which in their general outline are applicable to much of Africa. The tendency for low-income housing to end up in the hands of middle-income people has been documented by the Housing Research and Development Unit of the University of Nairobi.[3] Paradoxically, the people who need the housing, and who are the target of the housing policy, do not meet the financial criteria for plot allocation and are denied plots on this basis. Even if they do succeed in obtaining a plot, they are likely to sell it, as the market value of such plots is high enough to warrant the trade-off of reasonable housing for financial gain. Another general constraint is the gap between subsidized housing (in whatever form) and the market rental value, a gap which may be as high as 200%.[4] As a result, subletting is a widespread phenomenon, and the basic dwelling unit is the room, not the house. A final constraint is the tendency for government officials and politicians to view low-cost housing schemes with suspicion, in that cheap housing has colonial connotations, and is not considered worthy of development efforts (this tendency is well-documented in the Kenyan press).

The second factor involves those special circumstances—political, economic, and social—that pertain to Thika itself.

The heart of the problem lies in the nature of Thika's municipal government. A development plan presupposes an effective instrument for its implementation; Thika's low-cost housing program presupposed a functioning system of local government. Kenya's municipal government structure is based upon the British model, characterized by "decentralization, legislative dominance, co-optation through the committee system, multi-purpose activity, and voluntary citizen participation."[5] While there are serious problems inherent in measuring performance against this model (even in Britain), three criteria for effective functioning may be identified. First, the idea of municipal citizenship should be widely accepted, and a local resource base, both human and financial, should exist to fuel the system. Second, the actors in municipal government should have a commitment to the system, and the skills necessary to run it. Third, the idea of local autonomy and responsible citizen participation should be accepted in the country as a whole, particularly among the central governing elite in the ministries, who have the power to withhold resources from local authorities or to initiate and guide legislation that may alter local government jurisdiction.

None of these criteria are met in Thika. With regard to municipal citizenship, there is no coherent community able to place effective demands upon the municipality. Thika is a town where employees come to work in largely foreign-owned companies, residing "only temporarily" no matter how long they stay. Large numbers of residents return to the countryside on weekends, to participate in the social and political life of their rural community. As a result, there is a political and economic vacuum in the town, as loyalties and cash flow outwards. Those who do consider themselves to be Thikans, without other loyalties, tend to be groups who are disenfranchised in one way or another—members of ethnic groups other than the Kikuyu (in whose territory Thika lies), the remaining Asian population, and single women with illegitimate children who have fled the traditional social system of the countryside to find work in the city.

There are problems with both administrative and political leadership at the municipal level. The councillors were by and large politicians who were put forward in the 1968 elections as uncontested candidates by the Kenya African National Union as a reward for their participation in the Mau Mau rebellion (which is now viewed as a part of the independence struggle).

Their responsibility thus lay toward the party hierarchy above them, rather than downwards to an electorate. The administrators, while they had a higher level of education than the councillors, tended nevertheless to be of a lower calibre than administrators either in the central government or in the Nairobi City Council. This is the result of an internal "brain drain," where administrators of merit find greater financial and personal rewards in a career at the centre or in private industry—in the national rather than a local context. Beyond the limitations of the actors themselves, there are a series of tensions within the Municipal Council that hinder effective functioning. Tensions exist between the two sub-ethnic groups that are represented in the council; councillors view administrators with some hostility out of resentment for the better education the latter have gained, while the administrators view the councillors as a hindrance to effective government and are wary of the political influence they can bring to bear in their own interests. The combination of tensions leads to a fairly weak municipal government with an ad hoc decision-making process. The central government is called on—or sees fit—to intervene in municipal affairs on a routine basis.

This last point relates to the third criterion for effective municipal government: acceptance of local government in principle. The central government is extremely wary of the idea of local autonomy for historical reasons. The cumbersome, ineffective decentralized administrative system that was Britain's legacy to Kenya at independence had been seen as a neo-colonial technique for "divide and rule," and was rejected as such. While the idea of autonomous local government was not discarded, there was a strong ideological commitment to centralized government as a tool of development. The trend toward centralization thus arose from the need to strengthen government credibility, and the belief that central government was better equipped to deal with problems of development. Centralization occurred through ad hoc decisions on the part of bureaucrats in the ministries, of the kind that took place during the site and service scheme debacle. It also occurred through formal policy in the form of Amendments to the Local Government Regulations of 1963, which whittled away at the local authorities' power and autonomy.

This analysis does not presume to provide prescriptions for effective policy with regard to public land use. It is clear, however, the planners must engage in this kind of exercise, taking into account the social, political, and economic realities of the planning environment, if their activities are to have any hope of achieving their aim.

Notes

1. Report prepared by Laurence H. Bloomberg and Charles Abrams for the Government of Kenya (Nairobi: Government Printer, 1965).

2. The Central Government Administrative Officer responsible for all public land transactions.

3. P. Houlberg, N.O. Jorgensen, and R. Steele, *Site and Service Schemes: Analysis and Report*, HRDU, University of Nairobi (1971).

4. Jorgensen, "On the Problem of Subletting," Interim Report No. 3, HRDU (September 1968).

5. H.F. Alderfer, *Local Government in Developing Countries* (New York: McGraw Hill, 1964), p. 10.

5.4 Land Reform and Public Land Ownership in Senegal*

Francis G. Snyder
Associate Professor, Osgoode Hall Law School and Division of Social Science, York University

A description of some aspects of public land policy, which evaluates goals, examines the benefits, and questions whether "development" is possible within the existing international economic system.

In June 1964 Senegal passed the Law on the National Domain, which has been supplemented by numerous implementing decrees and most recently modified by legislation on administrative reorganization. According to government documents, the basic purposes were to simplify and clarify the land law, to end customary rents and tithes, to supply a legal basis for reorganizing rural areas in order to permit planning and improvement of agricultural productivity, and to stop land speculation. About 95-98% of the Senegalese land area was vested in the state by allocating to it responsibility for a newly created legal entity called the National Domain. This measure was in fact a vesting of development rights. Following generally a "land-to-the-tiller" philosophy, the legislation permitted persons actually working and living on land to continue to do so for the time being, thus cutting off interests of absentee landlords, non-cultivators, and others not working and living on the land in question. National Domain land was divided into four categories: urban, reserve, pioneer settlement, and village land (*zone de terroir*); here I refer only to the last. Transfers of village land were banned except by the state after a declaration of public utility and consequent registration of title to land in the name of the state. Controls on inheritance were provided to guard against fragmentation of holdings. The legislation foresaw the establishment of rural communities

---

*Paper prepared for conference workshop. Edited. Because of the summary nature of this paper, there are no footnotes. References are available on request.

to cover all of the national area, each community to be managed by a rural council composed of members elected (according to subsequent legislation) from among the peasants—two-thirds by universal suffrage and one-third by a general assembly of the cooperatives in the area. The council is to operate under the general tutelage of the subprefect.

Official strategy for the implementation of the law provided for three phases, overlapping yet distinguishable. The first, or legal, phase comprised enactment of the legislation which replaced pre-existing "customary law" with comprehensive national legislation. The second, administrative phase was to comprise the establishment of new administrative structures, including rural councils, which were essential to the realization of the announced economic goals of the law, and in their own right a crucial element of government reform of rural life. A final, economic phase was to entail allocation of land by the rural councils, its redistribution if necessary, and the improvement of agricultural methods. The government forecast a time span varying from 10 to 25 years for implementation of the law (that is, completion of the three phases). This time horizon lengthened with increasing administrative experience in attempting to implement the reforms.

From 1964 to the present the government has followed two different strategies of implementation. In the mid-1960s, following enactment of the Law on the National Domain, the administration chose pilot projects located in the different regions of the country and, taking the nation as a whole as the relevant unit, planned subsequently to implement each phase of the law sequentially. For various reasons this strategy was abandoned around 1970, and it was determined that all three phases should be completely implemented in a given region before proceeding in turn to the other regions in an order of priority established by the administration.

Within the framework of this strategy, application of the law is only beginning in the Casamance Region. As of the summer of 1975, official communication of the law by the administration to peasants was underway, but the administrative phase had not yet begun. Field research in 1970 and 1973 indicated that while some peasants were aware of the existence of the legal reforms at that time, most peasants in the area studied did not become aware of the contents of the law until 1975, when the national administration exercised development rights with respect to land situated there. In order to illustrate the manner and some consequences of implementation, let us consider two types of actors in this drama, first the government administration, and second the peasants, bearing in mind that each category includes numerous individuals and groups which are lumped together here for the sake of brevity and convenience.

The manner in which the administrative bureaucracy in the Casamance dealt with the law changed substantially from 1965 to 1975. In the years immediately following enactment, bureaucratic confusion about the meaning of the new and complex legislation led higher levels of the administration to curtail diffusion of information concerning the law to local administration and to ban completely its communication to peasants. By 1971, however, certain consequences of the law began to be felt, as the jurisdiction over land disputes was transferred from the courts to the administration. By 1975 the administration was using the law as the legal basis for acquiring land for projects such as a tourist site and an agricultural training centre. By this time local administrative officials were well aware of the contents and some of the likely consequences of the law, as they were engaged in attempts to communicate it to peasants directly affected by the government's exercise of development rights.

Peasants, on the other hand, were substantially less well informed about the meaning of the law, since communication of the law to them by the administration was limited to those whose land was the target for particular projects requiring the exercise of development rights. Even this communication was restricted to a period immediately prior to government attempts to acquire the land. This represented, nonetheless, a considerable change from 1970, when peasants had little if any knowledge of the law. By 1975 residents of villages affected by the exercise of development rights under the law demonstrated a detailed and exact knowledge of many aspects of the law. Peasants in neighbouring villages still had little direct information from the administration concerning the law, and in these villages rumours (some obviously ill-founded) concerning government policies were circulating. These differences in peasant levels of understanding were less a function of population or of geographical area than of official control over communication and rural social organization, as they existed within a fairly small area comprising nine or ten villages of a total population of less then 5,000.

In addition to a disparity in levels of information, official communication of the law, together with the content and manner of its application, aroused latent political tensions in rural villages and refocused factional and other political activity around this issue. Peasants with different economic interests were (or were likely to be) differently affected by the law. Peasant perceptions and reactions to this brought to light two types of contradictions. One involved the contradictory interests of peasants and the government bureaucracy. It was manifested in rumours of bribes paid to peasant leaders and village chiefs, increased mobilization of village and intervillage factions, and increased intergenerational conflicts (as links among older and younger peasants, young urban migrants of rural origin, and administrative officials were mobilized). It also gave rise to widespread beliefs on the part of peasants that local bureaucrats were manipulating legal complexities in their own interest, convincing peasants, for example, to entrust them with fallow rural land in order to avoid its being taken by the state without peasants realizing that, under the law, such land would be deemed to belong to the bureaucrats and not be restorable to the original owners.

The second contradiction involved the peasants themselves. As a result of the administration's exercise of development rights, certain peasants inevitably lost land in which they, their kin, and their ancestors had interests recognized by local "customary law." These interests were not acknowledged by the National Domain legislation which had doctrinally superseded "customary law," even though peasants continued to orient their behaviour to it. Any administrative safeguards provided by the law to protect peasant interests in such cases were nullified by the fact that rural councils had not yet been established in the area. Peasants became increasingly unwilling to improve land and, more importantly, hesitated to engage in land transfers which, despite being formally prohibited by the National Domain law, were the basis of rural social and economic organization, and had been so for centuries. These and other factors contributed to an increasing differentiation among categories of peasants which has been underway for at least several decades. On the one hand, the tendency by the administration to identify development as entailing the growth of rural capitalism has meant that wealthier peasants have been considered as the most progressive. They have the means to employ wage-labour and to adopt new technology more readily, and the fact that their land holdings tend to be concentrated rather than fragmented facilitates more effective use of their superior resources. On the other hand, the legal reforms have brought into more prominence alliances between these peasants and the local administration, partly because in many cases rural wealth is related to having children in government employment.

Any definitive assessment of the implementation and consequences of the Senegalese experience of public land ownership would be premature at this time. However, the evidence suggests several points which may be raised. First, the principal beneficiaries of the reform may be the incumbents of the state apparatus rather than the mass of the people. Especially in the short term, prior to the establishment of operative rural councils, the National Domain Law greatly extends the discretionary power of the government bureaucracy. Other studies suggest that an increase in government power may well be the long-run result as well. In addition, the law enhances the economic trends currently under way in many areas of rural Senegal toward increased economic differentiation, embryonic class development, and further dependence of rural villages upon remote economic forces rather than on strengthening their capacity for self-reliance and improving their living conditions.

Second, the Senegalese case presents certain similarities to Latin American land reforms. These are characterized as "counter-reform" in the literature. Legislation gives the government authority to acquire land with minimal accounting to peasants and with the possibility of manipulating complex laws written in a language which most peasants are unable to read, even if they had access to the texts. The scope of government discretion is especially great in the period before rural councils are established. Further, the time horizon for application of reform measures is long, thereby allowing an opposition with knowledge of the law to organize in order to influence its application in their favour or to subvert its application entirely. Finally, the administrative agency most closely associated with planning the application of the law (in Senegal the Land Use Planning Office [*Direction de L'Aménagement du Territoire*]) has only advisory rather than executive status.

Third, it appears that in assessing the National Domain Law and its eventual effects one must be careful not to equate law reform with land reform. Inherent in land reform are the goals of increased equality and the improvement of peasant living conditions. An increasing scope of administrative power and the potential for solidification of a rural base for a bureaucratic class appear to be associated with the Senegalese reform. These necessarily draw into question the purposes and indeed the technique of public land ownership as a means of achieving land reform in the Senegalese context.

The context of underdevelopment itself raises the question of whether genuinely redistributive land reform, through public land ownership or otherwise, is possible in a poor, dependent country which has chosen an outward-looking development strategy. Reform of land laws is only one of many issues to be considered. For example, the continued existence of rights in land provides the sole form of social security for many urban poor, unemployed, or those in the informal sector. Reform of land law must therefore take account of employment, among other issues, if it is to be effective. A fruitful assessment of public land ownership, as of any other legal technique, requires that it be considered in a specific historical context, involving specific economic, social, and political conditions.

5.5 Land Policy in Sri Lanka*

Fred W.H. Dawes
Canadian International Development Agency

Examination of public land ownership policy in the light of the recent political and economic history of Sri Lanka.

Over the past 10-15 years Sri Lanka (Ceylon) has embarked upon a major program of state control of natural resources, particularly land and water use, through public land ownership. Like the rest of Asia, Sri Lanka has suffered greatly from considerable population increases coupled with a lowering of the real value of its main exports of tea, rubber, and coconut, and the current tremendous increases in the price of fuel oil. The major challenge in recent times, however, involves that of transforming a colonially controlled economy to that of a politically free one. Throughout the developing world, during the past 15 years in particular, former colonial peoples have fought to assume the responsibility of conducting their own political and economic affairs. This change has been traumatic and often has resulted in great tragedy. Many countries of the developing world have had to resort to dictatorial forms of government in order to maintain civil order compatible with development. Sri Lanka has been able to develop a socialistic form of democracy based upon a strongly supported British tradition. Although economic development has been slow, the democratic process has probably been strengthened during these early, formative years.

Older traditions than those established by the British are now influencing development in Sri Lanka. Over 1500 years ago, extensive irrigation systems were developed for the growing of rice. These systems are in use, and are being rehabilitated and expanded today. The British, through the control of malaria, were able to open up wet zone lands little used before, for the growing of tea and rubber. Many of the older dry zone lands, during the British period, were abandoned in favour of higher production in the export market. Now, the dry zone lands are again being developed for domestic food production.

Recent economic events throughout the world have forced Sri Lanka, like other developing countries, to tighten its belt and set more stringent priorities. Current programs should be viewed in relation to some of the following statistics: Sri Lanka's population is 14 million, living at a density of 200 per square kilometre, or 3,030 per square kilometre of arable land, in a total area of 16 million acres. The GNP was $110 in 1972; 5 million acres are under cultivation in 1.5 million land holdings. Rural unemploy-

---

*Paper prepared for conference workshop. Edited.

ment stands at 16%; urban unemployment at 25%. Forty-three per cent of all households have incomes of less than US $400 per year; there are considerable nutritional deficiencies; and calorie and protein intake dropped somewhat between 1970 and 1973. The value of exports in tea, rubber, and coconut dropped from $200 million in 1960 to $60 million in 1974. Between 1962 and 1974, 560,000 acres were nationalized.

With this background it is not hard to appreciate that the Sri Lankan government has placed top priority on increased domestic food production, and on increased employment. Specifically, the following measures have been initiated. First, rice prices have been supported to world market levels and credits have been provided to the farmers for food crop production. Second, agricultural productivity centres have been established to improve extension services, credit, input supply, and marketing services. Third, the Agricultural Lands Law (1973) provides security to tenants and controls rents. Fourth, the Land Reform Law reduces private rice paddy ownership to a maximum of 25 acres, and other land to 50 acres. Fifth, the Tea Control Act (1974) enforces minimum production standards. These measures clearly indicate that the Sri Lanka government relates increased food production and increased employment to government control over land ownership and land use. Public ownership of land does not appear to be a disagreeable concept to eastern peoples. On the contrary, such a concept is likely much closer to local traditions than was the colonially imposed concept of private land ownership.

In Sri Lanka, government policy with regard to public ownership of land is related to the much older tradition of central control over irrigation and irrigated lands. As in many such situations, the status quo enjoyed by the small wealthy class who benefitted directly from colonial rule had to be destroyed. This process has been lengthy and costly in developmental terms because capital resources fled the country, and the climate for new investment is thought to be unhealthy.

If it is true that private capital for development is hard to come by for the above reasons, it is equally true that IBRD (World Bank) capital, and other forms of bilateral capital including capital from Canada, is increasingly being made available because such agencies are finding that the objectives of the Sri Lanka Government are reasonable and just, and because the Sri Lanka Government is making more capital available for the local cost component of developmental projects. Typically, Canada supports any kind of government, whether politically left or right, as long as that government's policies help to bring about economic and social justice for the majority of people.

The Sri Lanka Government is currently implementing a large irrigation system in the Mahaweli River valley which will bring over 200,000 acres of land into rice and field crop production. External financing is being made available from the World Bank, Canada, the USA, and other donors. All this land is government owned and will be distributed to farmers according to the principles stated above. Canada will be supporting other agricultural programs in the dry land areas, where it is anticipated that dry land farming methods developed in Canada will be adapted to Sri Lanka soil and climatic conditions. Again, food production and employment are both expected to increase significantly under a system of rural land ownership by the government. Careful assessment of such programs by a number of international donors leaves little doubt that they can succeed in an economy that is not based on the western concept of private land ownership. However, Third World programs of development, particularly in the agricultural sector and including overall rural development, are being planned with the active participation of the developed world. This is an odd phenomenon. Canada likes to give the appearance of being laissez-faire, of supporting a free economy where most resources come under private ownership. Land particularly is cherished as the right of the individual to own and use to his own profit. We support the principle of a free market economy, although we are painfully aware that we are increasingly unable to control the violent upward and downward swing of the economy. Our industrialists insist that the vicissitudes of the market make it impossible for them to plan much more than two years in advance.

Yet in the developing world, almost every country produces a five-year development plan under the strong tutelage of governments from the developed world. Such planned economies are often much more socialistic than our own. Many of them are based on public (or tribal) land ownership in various forms. Social and political upheaval results more from the high expectations introduced into the country by the developed world, with the support of the local elite, rather than because of measures of land reform introduced by governments such as Sri Lanka. More havoc will result from higher energy costs and lower food prices than from any other causes. Sri Lanka, no more than Canada, can forecast what will happen to its economy if inflationary factors are not kept under control.

A poor developing country like Sri Lanka, however, serves to illustrate what a country can do to control the use of its resources for the common good, and in the face of the grave domestic problems of food shortages and massive unemployment. The Sri Lanka example suggests that certain considerations regarding land use be highlighted in the context of these problems. First, how extensive should public land ownership be to control land use for the maximum public good? Second, when all the facts are considered, will public land ownership stifle development, or conversely, have we outgrown the free-enterprise, private ownership concept of natural resources? Third, to what degree can productivity be raised (if at all) through cooperation rather than competition? Fourth, is the private ownership of natural resources, particularly land, conducive to healthy economic growth in the long run, or is it only an aberration, found to be necessary during a country's early history when new lands are being opened up? Finally, can leadership in the private sector really be expected to come to grips with these issues, or must they be faced and solved by government?

5.6 A Discussion of Public Land in the Third World

Patricia Stamp
Lecturer, Division of Social Science, York University

This is a synthesis of conference workshop discussion on public land use and ownership. There was general consensus among discussants that planning policy—including land use policy—is a profoundly political issue, and that the political forces shaping it or affecting its implementation should not be ignored (as has often been the case among planners and scholars in the past). Specifically, feedback to planners and administrators from programs underway needs to be provided in more formal and rigorous ways. Further, the social justice of development policies was a matter for deep consideration. Drawing on these concerns, discussants highlighted three related themes from the presentations: 1) the nature and purposes of land reform, 2) the issue of production versus distribution in development planning, and 3) the constraints imposed by the international economic system on socially-oriented policy.

With regard to the first, Griffith Cunningham (a York University social scientist who spent 10 years in socialist planning in Tanzania) raised the question of whether the expression "land reform" is appropriate in the Kenyan context. Using as a reference point the Tanzanian experience, where major restructuring of land use patterns is taking place, he argued that Kenyan land policy merely took "the Kikuyu land which the British had stolen, and hand[ed] it back to the Kikuyu . . . That is just the end of colonialism—a changing of the guard." Secondly, it gave peasants legal title to areas that were communally owned or insufficiently controlled or occupied. Inequities with regard to land use are perpetrated; the landless remain so, by and large, and the position of rural land labourers remains the same as under British colonialism. Land reform is the term that should be applied to the correction of these inequities.[1]

While it was stressed that the land transfer program in Kenya is a separate issue, and that the example brought to the workshop involved the transition from customary to statutory terms of land ownership, this point regarding the connotation of land reform as a redistributive process was reiterated. It was suggested that the transfer from unwritten customary law to statutory law was an interesting legal and political issue, but one that deflected attention from the serious questions of redistribution. Further, concern was expressed regarding the priority placed by the Kenyan government and those of other Third World nations on productivity and the expense of reallocation of resources. It was mentioned that the World Bank has contributed to the selection of this priority by favouring productive investment aimed at international financial viability rather than a "non-productive, distributive kind of investment." William Doebele commented that "history tends to show that any country that has gone the route of increasing productivity, thinking it can deal with distribution later, gets locked into a series of social and economic institutions which make distribution almost impossible at a later time."

Finally, the presence of an international economic system based on the capitalist mode was discussed as a determining factor critical in shaping development policy. The constraints and opportunities inherent in this system tend to lead to policies oriented toward production and export, and inimical to the interests of the masses. Against this it was argued that export considerations need not be directly linked to the internal economic structure, nor shape the decisions regarding land use. Japan, "the greatest exporting country in the world," and a country with very successful land reform, was cited as the demonstration of this point. Internal elitist political interests are seen in this view as the cause of inequitable land development policy. However, an error in applicability of the Japanese example was pointed out by another discussant: clearly, Japan as an exporter of manufactured goods does not stand in the same relation to the international economic system as the raw material producers of the Third World. In Senegal, the spokesmen for land policy are members of the government who have interests in maintaining an economy oriented toward export, one that causes peasants to migrate from villages to provide cheap labour for foreign capital industries. In other words, the interests of neither the influential capital enterprises nor their elite clients in the developing countries are served by policy oriented to keeping a maximum number of peasants on the more fairly-distributed, but relatively less productive, land.

The discussions and presentations revealed the essential conundrum facing development planning, and found its most critical expression in land use policy. This problem may best be expressed in Colin Leys' words concerning the "contradiction of neo-colonialism,"

in its essential meaning of a system of domination of the mass of the population of a country by foreign capital, by means other than direct colonial rule. By its nature such dominance requires the development of domestic class interests which are allied to those of foreign capital, and which uphold their joint interests in economic policy and enforce their dominance politically. This system is however unstable. The underdevelopment which begins with colonialism (if not before) and continues under neo-colonialism implies limits to growth and a growing polarization of classes as the exploitation of the masses become more apparent. To avert this, foreign capital seeks a redistribution of income internally . . . so as to expand domestic markets and hence production and wage employment. But any substantial redistribution of income is at the expense of the owners of domestic, mainly small-scale capital—i.e. the domestic allies of foreign capital.[2]

Callisto Madavo, a representative of the World Bank, in drawing together some of the key themes of the workshop and of the conference as a whole, acknowledged the complexity and intractability of the problems of development, particularly that of inequities in allocation. He suggested that nevertheless certain specific aspects of land development could—and should—be tackled. Referring to Jane Jacobs' characterization of large-scale enterprise as dehumanizing and ultimately inefficient, he argued that local authorities, as small-scale organizations close to the people and processes that are targets of development, should play a more important role in development. Effort should be directed towards strengthening them and overcoming problems inherent in their functioning. Secondly, he stated that the conference had demonstrated that there are effective criteria against which the efficacy of an implementation agency or mechanism (technical styles and financial methods, for example) can be measured; it is time that these criteria be brought into play. Finally, there should be constant attention to the question of priorities in land use planning.

Leys ends his study with a bleak statement that students of land use policy in the Third World should note:

Academic studies can contribute little to the effort to achieve new strategies of development grounded in the interests of the mass of those who are currently the victims of underdevelopment. Perhaps the most such studies can do is to try not to obscure the structures of exploitation and oppression which underdevelopment produces, and which in turn sustain it.[3]

Planners, for their part, should ask the question as to whether *they* can contribute to the effort to achieve such strategies, and if this is not the case, should be aware of the limitations.

Notes

1. Colin Leys argues a similar point, stating that agricultural policy following independence was largely directed towards bringing peasant

production from a subsistence mode into the capitalist mode created by the settler farmers. The question, he suggests, "is not whether the policies were a success in terms of the rate of growth (4.5% per annum between 1964 and 1969) or total output ... [but] what significance the agricultural policies of the 1960s had for the long-run character structure of Kenyan society as a whole" (*Underdevelopment in Kenya* [London: Heinemann, 1975], pp. 114-15).

2. *Ibid.*, pp. 271-2.

3. *Ibid.*, p. 275.

5.7 The Chartwell Notebooks: Two Cautionary Tales on Public Land Ownership in Developing Countries*

William A. Doebele
Professor of Advanced Environmental Studies in the Field of Implementation, Graduate School of Design, Harvard University

An examination of the implications of alternative public land policies through events in two "not-so-mythical" developing countries.

[Special Note: Through a time-warp which temporarily existed in the western Pacific due to extraordinary sun-spot activity in 1985, certain documents mailed to me in May of that year were in fact delivered in October 1975. They appear to be the notebooks of a British journalist, one Cecil K. Chartwell, written at a Conference on the Public Ownership of Land in Developing Countries held in Hobart, Tasmania 10 years hence. The covering letter indicates that he was sending them to me for comment prior to writing an article. While I am obviously not able to respond to him directly (since I have ascertained that he is now only 13 years old), I though that excerpts from this curious document might be worth printing in this volume. My comments on them appear at the end of the excerpts. W.D.]

Excerpts from Notes Taken on the Presentation of the Delegate of the Republic of A-landia, Describing that Country's Experience with Large-Scale Public Ownership of Land ("Urban Land Banking")

As is well known, conditions in A-landia in 1975 were not greatly different from those in many other developing countries. National wealth was controlled by a small minority, which was also the traditional landowning class. This class owned most of the land around major cities, and, as urban populations rapidly expanded, augmented its wealth by subdivision and development. Frustrated by the lack of sites on the market for building a

---

*Paper prepared for this volume.

home, the urban poor frequently turned to invading sections of the city which eventually came to be dominated by them, especially in the larger centres.

Many persons in A-landia had argued that extensive public owner-ship of peripheral land (land banking on a large scale) would lower land prices, and permit a more orderly pattern of urban development. These arguments came to very little until a series of misjudgments by the ruling conservative government created the conditions for a bloodless coup, the leaders of which promised "a new era of social justice." Determined to break the sources of wealth of the old elite, the incoming government declared that it would expropriate all undeveloped urban-peripheral land holdings of more than 10 hectares, and found that the proposal had strong public support.

In order to observe the constitutional guarantees of compensation without bankrupting the country, the expropriation was paid for by means of 20-year bonds. Carrying out of the "10-hectare rule" suddenly put the state in control of approximately one half of all peripheral lands. A special authority was set up in each city to deal with this sudden new public asset. This report deals only with the experiences of the authority established in the capital, a city of some three million at the time.

The most pressing problem faced by the Capital City Land Authority (CCLA) was that of invasion. The governmental takeover was, of course, widely reported in the newspapers, together with maps of the newly publicly owned areas. The poor of the capital city, who had long regarded the large landowners as their exploiters, interpreted government ownership to mean free public access, and widespread squatting followed immedi-ately. This put the new government in the highly unpopular position of using armed force to protect its property from the very poor it declared it wished to benefit, and the cry was raised at once that its behaviour was little different from the old landlords. In fact, however, it was in a very difficult position. The "invaders" almost inevitably chose the most accessible locations for their shanties—prime land at highway intersections, etc., which was ideal for industrial or other types of productive develop-ment. Moreover, the uncontrolled settlements were laid out in such a way that it would be almost impossible to introduce proper urban services later without high cost and the demolition of many houses.

The CCLA responded by attempting to create "site and service" areas on a large scale. That is, areas deemed to be suitable for low-income residence in a hastily prepared metropolitan plan were subdivided and "basic services" (paved roads, one water tap per lot, pit latrines, elec-tricity, and sites for future schools and playgrounds) were provided. The CCLA set charges to 1) cover the costs of installing the services, and 2) pay off 50% of the amortization of the bonds owing on that land to its original owners. (The remaining 50% of bond costs were absorbed as a subsidy.) Access to the program was limited to exclude those of middle and high incomes.

It was hoped that these site and service projects would provide alternatives to invasions. Regularly employed persons, who could meet the monthly payments (which even though relatively low required a steady income), found them attractive. On the other hand, their locations were more distant than previous invasion areas, so the lowest economic strata of the city (who could not afford any regular monthly charges, and who also needed extremely easy access to central locations to survive) continued to invade. Since the CCLA's holdings were so extensive, adequate defence at all points and all times was difficult and unpopular. Moreover, a number of persons who bought into the site and service projects were unable to meet their payments after the worldwide recession of 1977-78, and their numbers were large enough that they successfully defied CCLA's efforts to evict them. (The fact that some invaders were still getting government land free strengthened their psychological resistance.)

Nor was this the end of it. Need for low-income housing from urban migration, natural increase, and undoubling of the extremely high densities in the central areas, came to some 20,000 serviced lots annually in the Capital City. CCLA, appreciating its own administrative limitations, decided to accommodate only half of this potential, but even this came to the production and allocation of 40 serviced lots every working day.

As in many developing countries, the various urban services were divided among several governmental agencies, with some being organized as semi-autonomous public authorities ("so they could have the efficiency of private enterprise within the framework of government"). The Ministry of Public Works (which provided the ground preparation, and roads) was at odds with the Ministry of Health (which had to approve all pit latrines) because of a long-standing dispute over budgets, and the personalities of the Ministers concerned. The Water and Sewer Authority was in principle cooperative, but had exhausted its financial resources in building a new reservoir, and had very little available capital. The Electricity Company was less helpful, arguing that world copper prices were declining and it would be wise to delay all new systems as much as possible.

The CCLA was thus faced with a lack of bureaucratic coordination which finally the President himself had to resolve. This action, however, did not improve CCLA's basic cash-flow problems. Site and service lots were being sold on 25 year level-payment plans, so that only small annual sums were available (even before the defaults of 1977-78) to pay the high "front-end" costs of the initial installations. A World Bank loan was negotiated to cover about 60% of the program, but the Bank was reluctant to go further until the CCLA had established a reasonable "track record."

Thus, the whole program was considerably smaller than total demand, and fell behind schedule even on this reduced basis. This bitterly disappointed a wide spectrum of the working class, which had been led to believe that public land ownership and the site and service program would go far toward solving their housing problems.

In the meanwhile, since one half of the land supply was in CCLA's "land bank," speculation on the remainder rapidly increased. Capital City was growing, and the middle and upper classes, as well as industry, commerce, and institutions competed for sites, increasing prices substantially in the whole "private" area. CCLA did, of course, prepare two industrial parks for industry, which were quite successful (although they greatly increased invasion problems in the nearby areas planned for future industrial expansion).

Inflation in A-landia continued at 10-15% per year, rapidly eroding the value of the bonds paid in compensation, and bringing about continual litigation for readjustment. At the same time, the CCLA was forced to raise prices on its newest site and service lots, causing resentment against those who had been awarded them earlier under more favourable terms. Queuing problems arose, since everyone wanted to get an allocation as quickly as he could, whether or not the lot was immediately needed, in order to "beat" the next escalation in prices. (Attempts were made to readjust upward the terms of the older sites and services agreements, but the original buyers argued that since *their* services were installed at a time when costs to the CCLA itself were lower, they should not have to pay more. This argument, plus the political reality that many thousands of families were involved, forced the CCLA to limit itself to very nominal increases.) As prices were raised on later sales, there was hoarding; speculation in serviced lots, although technically prohibited, became almost impossible to control. (Although the government could block legal transfers of title without its permission, there was an active market in "rights of possession.") As frictions increased on many issues, some of the entrepreneurs who had previously organized invasions now turned their talents to organizing unions of site and service occupants to resist CCLA controls and higher prices, and demand more and more services.

[At this point, the notes of the observer at the Tasmanian conference state simply, "more of the same for 15 minutes." They then pick up again, apparently at the end of the delegate from A-landia's remarks.]

As a result of all of these difficulties, the Government of A-landia and CCLA found themselves increasingly in the uncomfortable position of creating dissatisfaction in some group no matter what policy they adopted. The A-landia experiment with broad public ownership had alienated the lowest economic classes by putting the government in the position of a selfish landlord using armed force to defend the rights of property against "the rights of people." It alienated the working class by raising expectations about site and service lots which it was unable to fulfil and being forced to use differential pricing. It alienated the middle class, who found it must either buy a housing site at a much higher price in the constricted privately held sectors, or engage in illegal transactions to acquire rights of possession in a site and service area. It of course alienated the richer classes, both those whose land was taken, and those who disliked government competition in the land market. And it alienated the intellectuals, who felt that land was a prime factor in productivity, and that CCLA's centralized and heavy-handed management was slowing economic development and the growth of the GNP.

Thus, like many colonial powers, the government one day in 1980 simply gave the whole thing up in disgust. Land still vacant was returned to its original owners (together with an approrpiate adjustment of bond obligations). Some site and service projects were turned over to the unions of occupants (like a landlord turning over an apartment house to a tenant union), while others were continued, but on a greatly reduced scale of operations. Two industrial parks in process of construction were completed and sold as quickly as the market would permit.

The delegate from A-landia then concluded by saying that although he was not himself disillusioned with the concept of land banking, nor its applicability in specific situations, he did wish to bring to the attention of all developing nations the many pitfalls it contains, given the economic, political, and social dynamics of many countries. He stated that he did not believe any of the difficulties encountered in his nation were necessarily insoluable, but he felt that any future country moving in this direction should prepare itself carefully to cope with issues of this sort before launching into massive commitments.

Excerpts from Notes Taken on the Presentation of the Delegate of the Republic of B-landia, Describing that Country's Experience with Capital Gains Taxation of Urban Land

Recognizing the difficulties of large-scale public ownership of land exemplified by the A-landia experience, B-landia pursued a more cautious course. In 1975 its position had been not greatly different from A-landia: land in the urban peripheries was largely held by a small wealthy hierarchy, prices were high and constantly rising, and there were strong political resistances to change. Due to a series of political events it is not necessary to recount here, the power of the landowners in the Parliament and ministries (including the Prime Minister) was greatly weakened in the 1976 elections, and reforms became possible.

With respect to land, the new regime felt that there were two problems:

1) controlling speculation and reducing prices, and 2) assuring orderly urban growth. While land ownership by the public is often presented as an ideal solution to both, it was thought that the two objectives could be contradictory, and it would be a more cautious and sound policy to approach them separately.

Speculation and high prices were attacked by imposing an "anti-speculation capital gains tax," which was 80% levy on the net gains from sales of real property.[1] These percentages were aimed at draining off the exhorbitant profitability of speculation, while assuring an active market. In addition, to avoid antagonizing the middle class, which regarded their house as their main economic asset in life, homes were completely exempted from the tax if another home were purchased within a year.[2]

All real estate transactions were required to state the market price of the purchase before they could be recorded; to assure that the prices declared were honest, it was provided that the government could expropriate any property at the value so stated.[3] The Ministry of Finance set up a special revolving fund equivalent to one million dollars, and at the beginning of each month all the parcels transferred in the previous four weeks were put into a lottery. Six parcels, representing about 2% of total sales, would be selected at random, and expropriated at the purchase price as declared by the parties, plus 5%. Within one week they would then be publicly auctioned, with the Ministry recycling the proceeds into the next month's expropriation.

In the case of sales declared at market value, the owner expropriated would in principle be able to buy it back at the auction, using his 5% overpayment to outbid the market. If the value had been underdeclared, the original buyer would, of course, have to use his own funds to outbid the market and recover his property.[4] If the transaction price had been overdeclared, the expropriated owner could buy back at the auction at a lower price and pocket the difference from his excessive compensation. However, in this case, he would have paid 80% tax on this excess, since his overdeclaration would have increased the capital gains tax due on the transaction. Thus, for example if the market value of a property was $10,000, and it was recorded as passing for $12,000, or 20% above market, an unnecessary tax of 80% times $2,000, or $1,600 would have been paid. If this transaction were one of the 2% chosen by lot for expropriation, the government would pay 105% of $12,000, or $12,600. The expropriated owner would buy back at the auction at something a bit more than market value, perhaps $10,200. He would pocket the difference between $10,200 and the $12,600 awarded, or $2,400. However, he had already paid an unnecessary tax of $1,600, so his net profit would be only $800, or 8% on the capital values involved. From the government's point of view, it was pleased to take an 8% loss occasionally to assure that the whole system worked well. Since it was only "monitoring" a 2% random sample, most overvaluations would simply result in the collection of more taxes than would have been "necessary." These extra collections were judged to offset by a generous amount the occasional "losses" from examples like that just given.

The general effect of the system, was, of course, to give everyone strong incentives to declare prices as close to market as possible. It did have the effect of delaying construction for a maximum of five weeks, since no title could be secure until the next month's lottery. The real estate business, however, quickly adjusted to this, and most transactions were recorded a day or two before the deadline, so that the results of the lottery would be known within a few days (with, of course, no effect in 98% of the cases.)

The immediate impact of the "anti-speculation capital gains tax" was to lower land prices.[5] Before the tax, wise investment in the periphery could easily yield gains of 25-33% per year, or 75-100% after a three-year holding. Net losses were almost impossible, since land values in a growing city virtually never decreased. Thus, land purchases were one of the most popular forms of investment in the country, not only for the rich, but for the middle class and even the poor, by means of "syndicates" which bought land and sold fractional "shares" at low sums that many regularly employed persons (such as taxi drivers or shopkeepers) could afford.

Once profitability was set at 20%, no matter what the length of holding, there was reduced advantage in keeping land out of the market. If, for example, an owner calculated that a property that he had bought for $5,000 was now worth $10,000, and would be worth $15,000 in two more years, he would gain 20% of $5,000, or $1,000, by waiting the two years. He would, however, have $10,000 "tied up" in the land. If he sold at once, there were many opportunities in B-landia to invest $10,000 with reasonable security and receive more than 4.9% interest (which is the rate to produce $1,000 on $10,000 in two years, compounded). His advantage, therefore, was to sell at once. This decision generalized put a downward pressure throughout the market, and only those persons holding open urban land for specific purposes, such as building a future home or starting a factory or store in a desirable location, retained it for extended periods.

With the speculative profit in land removed, other forms of investment became more attractive. Savings, both large and small, which had flowed into land now flowed into commercial and industrial ventures, and even savings accounts and the stock market, which had long been moribound, began to revive. This money was, of course, much more readily converted into the capitalization of productive activity than the profits from land, which frequently in the past had been simply cycled into further land speculation, or, in some cases, foreign bank accounts. More importantly, the effect of lowered land costs was, of course, immediately reflected in lowered total costs of housing for all income classes, and significantly reduced the expense of starting many types of industrial and commercial enterprises. It did, of course, reduce the amount of municipal revenues based on assessed values, but in B-landia, unlike the United States, these never represented more than a small percentage of the municipal budget, and the Ministry of Finance simply used a part of the proceeds from the anti-speculation tax to increase subventions to municipalities in the same amount as they had lost.

Another interesting phenomenon occurred. The anti-speculation law had provided that the tax should actually take effect one year after its passage by the Parliament. This meant that for 12 months persons could transfer free of the tax, and resulted in a rush to sell in almost all segments of the market. So much land so quickly became available that prices dropped sharply (in some cases even below the values at which they finally stabilized after the tax came into effect). Fortunately, the government had anticipated this possibility, and had authorized the newly-organized Section of Advance Land Acquisitions in the Ministry of Public Works to engage in "selective land acquisition to promote more orderly urban development and promote the general public welfare." A sum of $15 million was allocated for this purpose, and the Section was thus able to take advantage of the very favourable prices which existed during the year-long "grace" period.

Some families, who had almost all of their wealth tied up in urban land, and various real estate companies in the same position, saw the value of their assets reduced to a fraction of their former worth, and protested vigorously. Even though individual homes were exempted from the tax, the general weakening of the market tended to depress the value of homes as well. Thus, many home-owners (but chiefly in the middle and upper classes) grumbled as they saw their hope of profitable sales dwindle and, in some cases, the market value of their homes even decrease. For most, however, future sale was a somewhat remote possibility, and many calculated that if their present house was now worth less, so also would be the next house which they would purchase from its proceeds. As noted above, the main effect of the tax was on undeveloped land. An overwhelming proportion of the urban population regarded this as a great benefit, lending the government strong political support to counter dissent from the sources just mentioned.

Thus, B-landia was reasonably successful in its land price reduction policies, through taxation. These policies did not, however, touch directly on the issue of more orderly urban development, although the tax, by drastically reducing the amount of land held out of the market for speculation, tended to encourage a more continuous pattern of peripheral growth and virtually eliminated the old pattern of "leapfrogged" urbanization.

B-landia had the usual types of negative land-use controls: zoning, subdivision regulation, building codes, and the like. The new regime felt, however, that more positive interventions were needed. Unlike A-landia, it did have a metropolitan plan for its capital, which was based on the idea of creating major subcentres of employment and commerce, to decongest the overconcentration in the old central business district. At the same time these new subcentres were to be well-connected with each other by mass transit so that cross-commuting among them could be rapid and cheap. Thus, a lower income wage-earner would have the choice of seeking work within his subcentre at little or no transportation costs, or canvassing all of four major centres (the old one plus three proposed new ones) at a somewhat higher cost (but not much greater than journey to work expenses when much employment tended to be concentrated in a single centre).

Accepting this as a reasonable strategy, the new Advance Acquisitions Section of the Ministry of Public works attempted to use the period of rapidly declining land prices occurring in the "one year interim" to assemble land in the three proposed subcentre areas. This, however, was largely unsuccessful in two of the three desired locations. In spite of the general weakening of the market, owners on these sites held out for very high prices—not for later speculative profits based on general market conditions, but because they had come into possession of the metropolitan plan, which they realized would make the proposed new centres ideal sites for high densities, intensive commercial facilities, and other income-producing uses. This possibility still had high value in the market.

According to the expropriation laws of B-landia, private property could be taken at market values prevailing *prior* to the announcement of a governmental action affecting those values, and it was suggested that the Advance Acquisitions Section could expropriate, rolling back prices to 15 April 1976, the day the Capital City Metropolitan Plan, with its designated three subcentres was released to the public. This, however, proved to be a false hope. While the plan was announced on 15 April, it employed a technical staff of 45 persons, and as long as nine months before, there were numerous "leaks" of the exact proposed new subcentres. Well-financed companies quickly moved to buy in these locations, and by the announcement date the market was already heavily inflated.

In the case of the third subcentre, expensive new public capital investments were required. (A major new rail rapid transit extension, for example. The two other subcentres were to be serviced by relatively inexpensive renovation of existing rail lines.) Private investors doubted the commitment and capability of the government, and therefore prices remained relatively low. This site was assembled into the ownership of the Advanced Acquisitions Section.

Attempts of the Section to develop it into a major commercial centre, were, however, at first unsuccessful. In spite of the section's being in the Ministry of Public Works, the problems of financing and coordinating infrastructure were enormous. The new rail line required the cooperation of the Ministry of Transportation, and a necessary new trunk sewer required heavy investment by the semi-autonomous Water and Sewer Authority. Moreover, the section soon found that there were few government officials with the sophisticated understanding and technical skills needed to orchestrate the development of such a complex enterprise. The project had strong presidential support, however, and eventually the necessary fiscal, managerial, and administrative resources were mobilized to make it succeed, and it is today a major focus for a considerable portion of the city.

The Advance Acquisitions Section had also used the weakened land market to acquire six large parcels (each over 200 hectares) from peripheral owners who feared the consequences of the new tax, and sold at very reasonable prices. Two of these large parcels have been transferred to the City Department of Recreation, which has converted them into badly needed metropolitan regional parks. The remaining four have been sold at cost to the Ministry of Housing, which is using them for a staged site and service program.

Like A-landia, there have been difficulties in defending large peripheral parcels known to be in public ownership from invasions. However, the four properties have been much more defendable than the enormous holdings acquired by the CCLA in A-landia. Site and service have also had the usual problems of administration and coordination among agencies, as in A-landia. However, unlike A-landia, low-income families in B-landia were not led to expect that serviced lots would be available to all comers. The new B-landia regime has emphasized its position that since land costs are one of the largest (if not *the* largest) element in low-income housing, its attack on land speculation was, in fact, one of the most beneficial of all possible strategies for helping the poor obtain housing—an assistance which applies "across-the-board," as it were, and without any bureaucracy (aside from the anti-speculation tax collection administration) to allocate its benefits. While it is hoped to rapidly expand the site and service program, it is, in a certain sense, icing on the cake of the more substantial benefits arising from lowered land prices.

An interesting phenomenon occurred in this respect in the year following the new tax policies: the 20% limit still permitted a nice profit on land transactions which could be turned over in one year. The quickest way to do this was by the subdivision of existing larger properties into individual lots. To move rapidly, these would have to be aimed at a mass market. There therefore arose, almost overnight, a large group of entrepreneurs who purchased on credit from existing landowners, subdivided and sold lots, using the down payments to repay their own obligations to the original owners, and making a full 20% profit on the increases, generally within less than a year. (A system very similar to the "barrio pirata" system in Bogotá, which furnishes lots aimed at a low-income market on a large scale.) Thus the poorer classes of B-landia's capital city had greater access to lots than ever before. They were getting secure title (after completing their installment payments of several years) to parcels suitable for building at prices much lower than in almost any other developing country.

One very basic problem remained, however. The lots being sold had no services, and neither the city nor the semi-autonomous enterprises which furnish services were financially or administratively prepared for the sudden new demand which had been thrust upon them. The new B-landia regime responded to this with national legislation which required all agencies furnishing urban infrastructure to publish price lists for the construction of all types of facilities (including trunk lines) and from such lists to compute a total price for servicing any neighbourhood which requested this information. In addition, it was required that the costs attributable to unskilled labour be itemized separately, so that any neighbourhood group might know how much each service would cost in cash, or in a combination of cash and contributed labour. Any neighbourhood which could produce 50% of the required total and demonstrate a well-organized and feasible program for collecting the remaining 50% (plus an interest element) within 18 months, was entitled to be listed for construction of the necessary facilities to its area as soon as possible, according to the priority of its qualifying compared to other neighbourhoods.

The result of this legislation was an avalanche of applications for the construction of infrastructure to each of the responsible agencies. Prior to the new regime, the price of urban lots in the capital of B-landia had been very high, and low-income families who did not wish to suffer all of the insecurities of invasion had been forced to scrimp and save for years to purchase. In spite of the difficulties, most of the low-income families in the city which had at least one regularly-employed wage earner had been slowly building resources for the all-important step of buying their own piece of land and the economic and social security it would bring. Now, with lowered land prices, many found that they could assemble enough money both to buy land, with enough left over to participate in a neighbourhood plan for services. Since any neighbourhood could buy any combination of services in any order it wished, those with the poorest residents would select only to purchase common water taps—the most essential of all services. The next step would be electricity, then individual water service, then perhaps better street paving, then sewage, etc. (Individual neighbourhoods varied a great deal in their preferred sequences.)

Information feedbacks of course occurred, and families would purchase lots in neighbourhoods whose requests for utilities most matched their family resources. Purchasers of newly subdivided land began requesting information on service costs from the subdividers before they would purchase, and these entrepreneurs thus found it to their advantage to solicit cost listings from each agency for their particular sites. The next step was the entrepreneurs "packaging" the land sales with various combinations of services options, and helping to form neighbourhood organizations to get them. Competition created better organization and differentiation in the market, and soon a wide variety of choices was open to families suitable to many levels of their available resources. To be frank, this development was quite unanticipated by the B-landia regime, but since it was immensely popular, the government did not hesitate to take credit for it.

After the initial confusion, the various agencies "staffed up" to meet the new demands. (The legislation has wisely provided that an item of 30% could be included as "general administrative expenses" in making the price lists, and this proved to be somewhat more than enough to cover the actual costs of expanding the office staff to cover the new demands as they occurred.) Since every project was self-financing within 18 months (at interest), there were no budgetary limits on what could be done. All of this, however, resulted in producing thousands of urban lots with services, individually owned. The problem of the actual construction of the house remained. Following its usual cautious course, the B-landia government decided to meet this by the deliberate encouragement of "autonomous" housing. A national building code was passed, providing absolute minimum norms for safety and sanitation, but avoiding other specifications. Young architectural and engineering students were employed during vacations to set up "autonomous construction advisory centres" in the main low-income areas. At first these were a disaster, since the students saw them as a vehicle for persuading low-income families to build to middle-class standards, advice which was irrelevant and wasteful to many of their clients. As contact and understanding increased, however, the students began to understand their clients needs, and offered valuable services, often working long hours without pay. Simple manuals and booklets were prepared. Most interesting was the fact that later, when older bureaucrats attempted to subvert the effect of the National Minimum Building Code by adding restrictive regulations "interpreting" it, the students were invaluable allies in successful resistance.

Of course, none of these programs provided housing for the very poorest classes of the capital—individuals and families without any regular employment. These had to be dealt with by various subsidy programs—the details of which are beyond this discussion. Even in these cases, however, there were some beneficial spillovers. It turned out that when families obtained tenure in a serviced lot, they invested rapidly in housing, increasing space as quickly as their resources permitted. One common use of this space was for rental rooms, which, since they have relatively low capital costs, can be marketed at low prices. The stock of such rental space in B-landia expanded rapidly, providing minimal accommodations for many poorer persons (albeit never for those totally without incomes.)

The world-wide recession of 1977-78 did its damage in B-landia as elsewhere, and defaults occurred on many of the negotiations described above. However, since most of the systems operated on rather short commitment spans, the damage was dampened, and the market revived fairly quickly when conditions improved in 1979.

Disaster only overcame B-landia in 1981. In that year a less cautious reformist administration was elected in January. In April, it was revealed that even the 20% limit had permitted several large landowners to make over $1 million profits on the subdivision of their immense agricultural holdings near the capital city. The government thereupon decided that 20% was too liberal a profit to permit, and the tax was increased from 80 to 95%. This effectively killed the whole subdivision process, and generally "froze" the entire real estate market. To stimulate activity, the government felt obliged to take over large amounts of peripheral land (at its now very depressed prices), and shortly found itself in the same position as A-landia, whose story has already been told.

Notes

1. The law provided that for "inflation indexing," that is, that all prices could be adjusted according to official indices available for every year. Thus, if a property had been purchased in 1920, its owner could adjust his "base" for capital gains by compounding the indices for each year from 1920 to 1975, so that both his purchase price and sales price would be in constant dollars. In all the figures given in this report, this adjustment is assumed to have been made.

2. Certain types of gifts and transfers within the immediate family, gifts to charities, and other limited special cases were also exempted from the tax.

3. Normally, this would be the actual price as determined by the transaction. However, the law only required that the market value be declared, not the amount actually passing hands. Thus, if one sold a piece of real estate to a close friend at less than fair market value, one would receive less money, but still be taxed on the full "market gain." Similarly, if one drove a hard bargain and sold at a higher than market price, the tax would only apply to the "market gain," not the higher actual profit.

4. There were occasional properties sufficiently unique that only one, two or three buyers would be interested. In such cases, it was possible to understate the price and risk the auction, since if it occurred, it would be relatively easy to "rig" the bidding so that it would not be truly competitive. The government considered this problem, and decided to accept the possible tax losses on such situations rather than incurring the costs and possible abuses of a mechanism to prevent them.

5. Its effect was somewhat differential. Speculation in undeveloped land had been much more pronounced than in developed real estate. Reducing the profitability of speculation therefore tended to have a greater impact in the undeveloped land market.

Commentary by Mr. Doebele

While many of the developments described in Mr Chartwell's notebook have no direct analogies in experience as of 1975 (indeed, if it were not for their unusual origin, one would be forced to characterize them as purely speculative), many other things he touches upon do relate to phenomena already observable. To take some of his major points *seriatm*:

A-landia Report. It has been observed in many developing countries that publicly owned land, particularly in large parcels is difficult to defend from invasion and squatting, for a complex of psychological, physical, and political reasons.

While site and service programs are relatively recent and it is difficult to make generalized evaluations, it does appear true that difficulties increase with the scale of the projects undertaken, and that the coordination of inputs from various agencies is frequently a serious problem, particularly if programs are attempted on a "crash" basis.

While there are some indications that inflation will cause pricing problems in site and service projects, the larger political and economic ramifications described by Chartwell do not have analogies in experience in 1975. Public housing projects (which have a much longer history) have, however, encountered somewhat similar problems in inflationary situations.

B-landia Report. There is apparently no developing country that has imposed an anti-speculation tax on real estate of sufficient magnitude and effective administration to bring about the situation Chartwell describes. The Swedish capital gains tax on real estate announced in 1967 and effective in 1968 was almost as heavy as that used B-landia. (Sweden taxed 100% of capital gains from real estate held for less than two years, and

75% of gains on longer holdings. The rate of the tax on the gains varied from about 31 to 78%, depending on the taxpayer's other income.) Land prices did drop substantially in Sweden in 1967, permitting many municipalities to enlarge their land reserves. Speculation in undeveloped land has, since 1968, been at a very low level, but this may be as much a result of the extremely strict system of development permits as from the capital gains tax. Developed real estate is still considered a good investment against inflation, and the 75% cutoff still makes capital gains profits less heavily taxed than earned income. Chartwell's account does not tell us whether B-landia simultaneously tightened its development controls (although he does mention it began to implement its metropolitan plan more seriously). If substantially increased capital gains taxation was in fact combined in B-landia with strong development control measures, the effects described by Chartwell become much more plausible.

The concept of policing a capital gains tax by means of an auction test of randomly sampled transactions appears to have no precedents and must be the invention of some imaginative B-landia civil servant. It is worth noting that the public auctioning of land in newly developed areas is a central point in the South Korean system of land use controls (called "Land Readjustment"), and seems to work reasonably well in conjunction with a basically private market.

The metropolitan plan described, based on creating three additional major centres, seems to draw heavily on *The Structure Plan for Bogotá* (Llewelyn-Davies, Weeks, Forestier-Walker and Bor, Consultécnicos, Ltda., and Departamento Administrativo de Planeación Distrital, Bogotá, 1974). Chartwell's account of how the preparation of the plan itself tended to stimulate speculation which will make its own implementation more difficult would also seem to have precedents in the Bogotá experience. Indeed, it is one of the hazards of the urban planning process generally.

As the representative of B-landia himself mentions in the text, the land disposal system which evolved in B-landia had certain parallels with the so-called "barrio pirata" system in Bogotá. (For the best description of this system, see George Vernaz, *Bogotá's Pirate Settlements: An Opportunity for Metropolitan Development*, Dissertation, University of California, Berkeley, June 1973).

The concept of the "price listing" and "optional packaging" of infrastructure services again appears to be an indigenuous B-landia invention. It does, however, have a rough analogy in the so-called Local Paving program, begun in Bogotá in 1963. This provides that when a neighbourhood *Junta de Acción Comunal* raises 30% of the cost of a project for paving local streets or sidewalks, the responsible agency must give priority to that project. (The remaining 70% is paid in installments over 30 months, with no interest if payments are prompt.) It has proved to be a popular program.

The idea of using university students to provide technical assistance in housing has been attempted in a number of developing countries.

The B-landia experience of lower-income families, who have relatively secure tenure, building rented rooms to increase their income is consistent with known experience in Bogotá, where as many as one-third of families in pirate settlements have such rooms, and it is estimated that about one-half of all rental accommodations in the city are provided in this way (see Vernaz, pp. 30 and 104).

The final "freezing" of the land market that occurred in B-landia in 1981 with the increase of capital gains taxation on real estate to 95% is confirmed by the history of the United Kingdom from 1947-52, in which the nationalization of land development rights came close, in its effect, to a 100% tax on entrepreneurial profit from land, and did substantially dampen real estate activity.

I thus conclude that, while much of A-landia and B-landia's experiences (as reported at the Tasmanian conference) cannot be confirmed by what we know at the end of 1975, neither can it be said that any of the developments summarized by Chartwell will be totally unexpected, and may well be about to transpire in A-landia and B-landia in the manner he has described.

Conclusion

Conclusion

A Review of Idea and Debate: The Social Implications of Public Land Ownership

There is no consensus among the views represented in this volume concerning the significance of public land ownership in tackling the problems associated with urban growth and development. Contrasting values, political objectives, evaluations of current practices, and settings in which these are experienced, abound. Canadians are less fearful of public ownership of land than Americans; the British and Swedes have gone much further in experimenting with such programs without notable success; in the developing world, critical social and economic problems swamp the ready acceptance of state control of land. Everywhere there is relative dissatisfaction with the human environments we create. The ever-present future impact of the decay of the physical environment provides an uneasy backcloth to our short-term attempts at marginal solutions to these problems. However, it is this last activity that dominates when those concerned with the management of land debate the issue of public ownership.

So, the positions established in this book deal almost exclusively with the implementation of alternative forms of public land ownership and an evaluation of these in terms of their financial, political, and general planning objectives. Public land ownership is viewed as a given fact; a tool to be used in conjunction with other planning techniques to augment the private land market and the associated urban development process. Public ownership efforts are aimed at limiting the negative effect of the private market, but not changing the principles on which it works.

The major debate of the book is the consideration of whether public land ownership, in association with other planning controls, is an effective means of moving toward the goals defined for a land management policy. These are either specific, middle-range objectives, which assume away the basic values and goals implicit in them, or highly generalized objectives, which are seldom challenged and typically decorate the "objectives" sections of planning reports—the preservation of agricultural land; the conservation of natural resources; the maintenance of open space; the protection of special cultural or physical environments; the protection of natural ecosystems; and the maintenance of individual and community rights and opportunities. In fact, the use of public land ownership with reference to these general objectives is questioned by several authors in this volume, who suggest that existing planning regulations provide sufficient control if they are used effectively.

The more specific land management objectives are tied directly to alternative styles of public involvement in land ownership. The basic intent is to control the supply of serviced land available for development, to determine its location in order to prevent urban sprawl, and to create viable new communities without playing into the hands of private land speculators. In addition, social objectives of public land ownership policies are defined, such as the control of housing costs, provision of access for underprivileged groups to the housing market, provision of land for public uses and maintenance of residential environments through the application of housing standards.

There is no clear agreement regarding the likelihood that public land ownership can achieve these objectives. Opinions vary as to which strategy should be used. There is clearly an ideological basis for this disagreement. Betterment taxation or site value taxation are criticized on one side because they are steps on an inevitable path to full-scale nationalization of land, and on the other because they are unwieldy, costly, and ineffective in obtaining for the public that wealth derived from land as a result of public action. The experienced land manager says it is impossible to use public land ownership to manipulate the urban development process to support ideological stances; there are no simple doctrinal solutions to the problems of urban growth and community development. This argues for the application of a value-free professionalism in relation to the selection of land policies and their implementation.

However, land use *is* an ideological issue and the maintenance of the private land market and of individual freehold titles to land lies at the heart of the debate presented in this book. Public land ownership, seen merely as a land management tool to be used in conjunction with the existing market system, is criticized as an instrument of marginal change, protecting the principle of private land without effectively attacking the problems it produces. Freehold title, which confers on the owner the right to profit from public actions in which he has played no part, is undermined to some extent by all the controls discussed in the book. The right to *own* land is incorporated in our constitutional rights, but land as a commodity to be bought and sold, especially when it is concentrated in the hands of a corporate real estate industry, is seen as an abuse of the rights of private property. Speculation and manipulation of the land market, which reinforces concentration of wealth, is not generally viewed as a legitimate return from the risk of capital implicit in the ownership of private land. Without some strong government involvement in land development, the initiative is in the hands of the private developer, and community access to land is limited.

Such basic issues regarding the ownership of land are raised frequently in the volume, but are not resolved. There is underlying uncertainty about the capacity of government to manage land in any more effective fashion than the private market. More planning does not necessarily mean better planning, and replacing a corporate elite by a government bureaucracy does not necessarily improve community access. In the view of some, the government as developer takes on many of the values of the private developer. This uncertainty in public ownership seems to be based, first, on the almost sacred belief regarding private ownership. We seem unable to connect the private land market directly with major urban problems, and so we do not compare the costs of current efforts at problem solution, or the future costs arising from inaction, with the positive benefits that might accrue if we achieved "fiscal equity and good planning" through public land ownership. The second source of lack of confidence in public ownership comes from concern about the costly and confusing legal and bureaucratic tangle that could develop if urban and peri-urban land was entirely public.

An alternative view is that when government makes a *full* commitment to the principle of public ownership, creative and efficient means can be worked out to develop land privately while maintaining public control. Much of the uncertainty and ambivalence on this issue is related to the lack of clear values and objectives on which to base policies aimed at substantial innovation in controlling the ownership and use of land. Two issues of immediate significance emerge from the book in this respect. The first deals with land as a public trust, and implies a return to the concept of communal land. This idea reappears, most interestingly, in the discussion of land policies in developing countries. Public control is an historical tradition in this case; land is not a marketplace commodity, and "ownership" is a function of membership in a social group. It implies the right to *use* land, not to alienate its development.

The second issue relates to the use of public land ownership as a part of a process of social redistribution of wealth. This implies ensuring for all citizens the right of access to land, and the encouragement of community participation in decisions. It challenges fundamentally the rights of private ownership. This returns the argument to the issues developed at the beginning of the book, which emphasized the generally unstated, but inherent, objectives of public land ownership: the maintenance of individual human dignity through the provision of one of the basic rights of life (the occupance of individual personal space), and the provision of land for the support and maintenance of human communities.

From this viewpoint of the potential social impact of public land ownership policies, another set of largely unanswered questions emerges. When judged on the basis of a *human* scale of values, how effective is public land ownership in tackling the basic social problems associated with the use of land? Can public land ownership increase the equality of access to personal living space, especially for low-income groups? How is the supply of critical social support services improved through the public ownership of land? To what extent are communities that are affected by public ownership given a sense of control over their environment? Is there an increase in citizen access to the process of planning and management associated with public land ownership?

In relation to these questions, the ultimate measure of the effectiveness of public ownership is determined by the quality of the lives of those who occupy public land, and of the environments in which they live. But we have to be careful in setting levels of expectation. The effects of an increase in the amount of land owned publicly must be set against the interconnected "meta problems" that society faces. Problems at the global scale (population growth, resource depletion, environmental decay, social disorder, starvation, and poverty) are translated at the local level into overcrowded housing, inadequate water supplies, high levels of air pollution, widespread crime, traffic congestion, excessive density, and other threats to personal space. The level of individual pressure may vary from Bangladesh to Metropolitan Canada, but a sense of the undermining of individual rights and dignity is universally felt.

The extent to which public land ownership *can* become a major instrument to ameliorate these social conditions therefore becomes the key question. The expectations of the contributors to the volume are not high. Their belief in the effectiveness of the increased planning control that goes with public land ownership is not strong. Perhaps, however, social evaluation should not be carried out purely from the standpoint of North American land developers, planners, politicians, and academics whose views are mainly represented here. In simple and direct terms Enrique Penalosa (1.1) states that land is "the basic resource not only of human settlements but of life itself." He sees this issue as a fundamental one in relation to private rights and community needs. Land, he suggested, "must be viewed as a public trust and its use must embody principles of social needs, environmental safeguards, and environments for future generations . . . public acquisition of private land holdings is a fundamental right of the community . . . municipalities must have the legal ability to take over land . . . at prices within their means."

The human needs associated with a public land ownership policy can be broadly divided into individual and community access to land. The nature of *individual access to land* implies consideration of the opportunities open to an individual to occupy sufficient space in which to live at the standard at which he expects (this includes the question of supply and price of land); security of that occupance (tenure, individual rights, and control); and the quality of that space, and the shelter it contains (including the degree of privacy, location, and surrounds, as well as physical structure). From these conditions can come an assessment of the quality of personal space: how the world is viewed from the position of the individual in his/her personal space—the human scale of housing development. The importance of land as a symbolic expression of personal success is as vital an element as the relationship between the quality of life and the quality of the living environment. What are the measures of satisfaction we should use and how may standards be derived from these elements?

The second human needs element, *community access to land*, may be taken to include the provision of space for essential community support services (schools, roads, parks, hospitals, etc.); community security from disruption (introduction of non-complementary land uses, impact of traffic flow, contamination of air or water, etc.); and the encouragement of a sense of control over community space, implying greater community access to the planning process. Public ownership of land can be the basis for more direct public involvement in the development process, but only if the political intent, access structures, and resources to support citizen efforts are also present. Since urban government bodies can be just as unresponsive as private corporations, considerable restructuring of public agencies would have to be involved in such a major transition. We do not know what can be done, because we have not seriously tried.

The question as to whether or not social problems can be attacked explicitly through public land ownership schemes is not answered directly by the contributors, though several alternative means of creating such a link are suggested. These include: 1) the use of the greater planning control that comes with public land ownership—gearing it towards innovative social design; 2) channelling public funds into social services intended to ameliorate problems and using the advantages of public land ownership to select sites and locations; 3) providing greater access for the poor and dispossessed to protect their personal space; and 4) encouraging greater public participation in urban growth and development associated with public land. But there is obviously skepticism about the ability of government agencies to carry out such subtle human engineering with the sensitivity necessary for it to be effective at the scale of the individual, the household, and the local community.

In the longer run, the success of such social policies, whether they are implemented through public land ownership or other means, must depend on the desire to change. It is pointed out that essentially we are talking about the redistribution of wealth through the control of "finance capitalism" and its process of land allocation. It is asserted that such a critical *social* process cannot be carried out in the open marketplace; that there has to be public intervention. For some this means that if existing planning controls are effectively implemented, the social objectives of public land ownership can be attained. But this seems to be an expression of the ambivalence on this issue that is frequently voiced. There is dissatisfaction with existing processes and their outcome. It is sensed that we need "substantial change" to handle the macro socio-environmental problems that face us. However there is a drawing back from so significant a change as is implied by public land ownership on a large scale. Chevalier and Burns (1.3), who face this need for innovative response to our current dilemmas most directly, are equally ambivalent: "free enterprise in the development and use of land and in the ownership of improvements, is not at issue in the present discussions, either in an ideological or operational sense." It clearly *is* an issue. We deplore the results of private enterprise development, are skeptical of the ability of governments to intervene and effect change—and then propose solutions that can only repeat the outcomes of past policy. For, as it is presently applied, public land ownership is indeed a tool of finance capitalism; it ends up subsidizing private development in order to obtain marginal social benefits.

In this sense, land is only a symbol for access to the other wider and essential elements of social support. Ownership itself is clearly less important than access to affordable and secure "shelter," and this is not possible for a significant segment of the population (even in Canada) under a private market process. The critical question then becomes, what is the nature of the mixed private/public system that can move us towards basic social goals? In the West it tends to be the middle-class value position that determines the nature of our response to such questions. A population with overwhelmingly middle-class ownership objectives will end up supporting the private enterprise system, if it feels it has a chance at access to the privileges accorded to the affluent in such a society.

The final outcome of a private/public land allocation system under these circumstances seems inevitably to lead to a reinforcement of existing inequalities. Hall, in a seminar given immediately prior to the conference, was asked what difference 30 years of active public intervention in land allocation has made in the United Kingdom. He suggested that the outcome fitted almost exactly the model that might have been designed by an enthusiastic, conservative free-enterpriser! The rich are living in semi-rural "greenbelt" communities or in high environmental quality inner-urban enclaves. The middle class are absorbed in improving their residential settings and in ownership. They are competing for high-priced residential properties in suburbs and settlements beyond greenbelts. The employed working class are settled in public housing of varied quality (provided largely on a mass-production basis), while the lowest income and unemployable group (with little hope of upward mobility) have no access to decent housing and are competing for high-priced rental accommodation in decaying inner-city areas.

Will current land ownership and development policies be any more successful in North America? It seems unlikely, although much depends on the learning capacity of what is inherently a more flexible society than that in Britain. Chevalier suggests ways in which a new perspective on land ownership and the means of achieving "goods" for individual communities might be attained through the restructuring of public organizations, the reorientation of professional knowledge, and the extension of public information (and presumably participation). This is "substantial innovation" achieved through taking advantage of the learning capacities of the existing system. The possibility of its success is perhaps supported by the fact that there has been a change in the way in which people view public ownership of land. Values have shifted to the extent that public involvement in the provision of space for parks, schools, and other public services is now taken for granted. Whether this process can extend to include an acceptance of a public development base for housing is less certain. A major re-thinking of the core values behind private land ownership, and the reorganization of the societal institutions that structure action in regard to those values cannot be avoided.

One final issue concerns the problem of "scale" in land development and its significance in determining the nature of social impact. The dilemma is that while *individuals* can express their needs (and only they can fully evaluate the way in which these are supplied), the demands on society to answer them, when multiplied many million times, become large scale. The scale of the problem determines the scale of the response. How can such a response be *delivered* at a human scale? The implication of Jacobs' remarks are that we must recognize that provision of social support to the individual does have significantly beneficial community-wide effects. This is a cumulative *social* process, analogous to the cumulative regional economic outcomes associated with "growth poles"—a process from which *all* gain, not just the direct beneficiaries of public aid. The recognition of this principle could give public-based land development a chance. This assumes that the private enterprise organizations that control the present system do not take advantage of society's inevitable need for their help and threaten to withdraw their services from such public enterprise. Which brings us back to the inevitable challenge of the *status quo* implicit in any attempt made through public land ownership to affect social change.

Index

Index

Agricultural land 14, 36, 42, 85, 91-4, 117
  private rural estates 92-3
  urban fringe 70, 11-2
  zoning 91, 123, 125
  See also Public land ownership, land as a resource
Alaska 100-1
American Law Institute, Model Land Development Code 39, 66-8
Amsterdam 40, 74-5, 77
Andreson, John 84, 85
Arctic Quebec 97
Australia, land policy 40, 55
  Canberra, Australian Capital Territory 73, 75-7, 78, 79
  Federal Capital Commission 76
  National Capital Development Commission 77

Beakhust, Grahame and Cumming, Peter 6, 83, 85
Berger Commission 99, 100, 101
Betterment 37, 47-8, 49-50, 53, 58, 70
Blumenfeld, Hans xiii, 39
Bosselman, Fred 36, 39
British Columbia, land policy 30, 109, 122-5, 130, 132
  B.C. Development Corporation 123
  B.C. Land Commission, 1973 70, 122-5
  Dept of Agriculture 123
  Environment and Land Use Committee 124
  Langley land assembly 124, 131
British North America Act 98, 112, 116
Bryant, R.W.G. xiii, 4, 40, 62
  Land: Private Property Public Control 62
Burns, Thomas. *See under* Chevalier and Burns

Canada, land policy 14, 15, 37, 40, 71-4, 105, 106-10, 112-14, 134

Federal land policy 105, 108, 110, 112-14, 137; Central Mortgage & Housing Corporation (CMHC) 15, 71, 112-13, 114-15, 119, 121, 133, 137, 138; National Capital Commission (NCC) 110, 142-7; National Housing Act, 1949 71, 112-13; Task Force on Housing & Urban Development, 1968 (Hellyer Report) 70, 106, 130-1; Task Force on Low-Income Housing, 1972 131
Municipal land policy 71-2, 105, 109-10, 113, 116-17, 120, 129-37, 135, 138. *See also under* Halifax, Nova Scotia; Ottawa-Hull; Saskatoon, Alberta; Toronto; Vancouver
Provincial land policy 15, 105, 108, 113. *See also* British Columbia; Ontario; Prince Edward Island
Public land ownership xiv, 14, 35, 37, 61, 105, 107-10, 112-14, 129
Canadian National Railways 74
Canberra 75-7, 78, 79. *See also* Australia, land policy
Central Mortgage & Housing Corporation (CMHC). *See under* Canada, land policy, Federal land policy
Chevalier, Michel and Burns, Thomas xiii, 5, 200, 201
Communal land ownership xiv, 3, 5, 20, 21-2, 36, 83-4, 197
  developing countries 150, 174
  New England 36
  New York 36
  Northern Canada 83-4
Community Planning Association of Canada 106
Cumming, Peter. *See under* Beakhust and Cumming
Cunningham, Griffith 174

Davis, Tait 151
Dawes, Fred 151

Dennis, Michael 107-8, 109, 113
Dennis Report 71
Developing countries xiv, 149-92
  agricultural development
    157-61
  communal land ownership 150,
    174
  international economic system
    175
  private ownership 160
  public land ownership xiv, 149,
    150, 151, 160, 172, 177-92
  public planning 149
  rural settlement 12
Developing countries, cities 10, 12
  colonial origins 149
Developing countries, housing pro-
    grams 153-6, 162-5
  social cost 155-6
Developing countries, land reform
    13, 150, 157, 166-70, 174-5
  servicing costs 153
Development Land Tax (DLT). See
    under United Kingdom, land
    policy
Doebele, William xiv, 175
Dunham, Allison 66

Edmonton, Alberta 72
Energy 85, 97, 99, 100
  National Energy Board (Canada)
    99
Environment Canada 98
Environmental Protection Act
  (US) 100
Europe, public land policies 40

Food production 29
Forest management 84, 87, 95
Forestry. See under Forest manage-
    ment; Public land ownership,
    land as a resource; Urban natu-
    ral environments
Found, William 84, 85

Gallant, Edgar 110
Garland, Kevin 110
George, Henry 35
Goldrick, Michael 109
Government intervention, land
  banking/assembly 31, 32, 39,
    53-4, 57, 65, 66-8, 70-1, 73, 80,

    110, 112-14, 118, 122-5, 130,
    131, 137, 139, 143
  Boulder, Colo. 107
  Connecticut 68
  garden cities 53
  Maryland 68
  Palo Alto 107
  Rotterdam 18
  Suffolk county, NY 68
Government intervention, land
  categories, rehabilitation 37,
    42, 44
  redevelopment/renewal 37, 44,
    130
  to be developed 37, 43, 118,
    130
  undeveloped 37, 43
Government intervention in land
  market 3, 4, 5-6, 35-40, 43-5,
    62, 68-9, 122-5, 130, 131, 132-
    5, 136, 137
  administrative complexity 6
  as developer 122, 134
  comparative municipal ap-
    proaches 77-9
  expropriation 11, 39, 80
  regulatory/legislative complexity
    5, 7
Government of Canada
  Central Mortgage & Housing Cor-
    poration (CMHC). See under
    Canada, land policy
  Dept of Energy, Mines & Re-
    sources 98
  Environment Canada 98
  Ministry of State for Urban Af-
    fairs 15
Grimes, Orville 150-1

Halifax, Nova Scotia 70-1
Hall, Peter xiii, 5, 37-8, 57, 200
Hamilton, Stanley xiii, 32, 38-9
Hare, Kenneth 84, 85
Hartman, Chester xiii, 6
Housing. See under Human settle-
  ments
Howard, Ebenezer 53
Human settlements
  community 4, 7, 9, 35, 41, 199
  local government 6, 39, 67, 69,
    138
  neighbourhoods 26

Human settlements, housing
 highrise 31, 42
 low-income 10, 41, 133, 134
 medium-density 31
 public 41
Human settlements, land use control 9, 10
 cf North American and British systems 38, 46-7, 52, 105
 land management 5, 11, 14, 15, 35-6, 124

Illyich, Ivan 116
Individual rights 4, 5, 29
Industrial location, impact 11
Institutionalization of public land ownership 110
 in Canada 105
 in United States 107
International Bank for Reconstruction & Development (World Bank) 175, 176
International Union of Local Authorities 11

Jacobs, Jane xiii, 6, 24, 32, 66, 116, 176, 201
 The Death and Life of Great American Cities 6, 116
James Bay Power Project, Quebec 85, 100
Japan, 41, 175

Kenya 151, 157-61, 162-5, 174
 agricultural development 157-71; land adjudication and registration programs 158-9
 municipal government structure 164-5
 Thika low-cost housing scheme 162-5

Labrador 97
Lake Erie 118
Lake Ontario 29
Lake Simcoe 95-6
Land as a natural resource. *See under* Public land ownership
Land assembly. *See under* Government intervention, land banking/assembly
Land banking. *See under* Government intervention, land banking/assembly
Land development. *See under* Urban growth/development
Land management. *See under* Human settlements
Land policy, general objectives 48
Land use. *See under* Human settlements
Land values/prices 3, 10, 11, 15, 48, 63, 93-4
 controls 11, 58
 speculation 4, 10, 11, 48, 59-60, 92, 109, 196-7
Latin America 13
 Bogota 187, 191, 192
Leasehold systems 74-9
Leathem, William 110, 113
Leys, Colin 175-6
 Underdevelopment in Kenya 175-6, 177
Lichfield, Nathaniel 56
Life support systems 27, 29-30, 84
Local government. *See under* Human settlements
Logue, Edward xiii, 24, 36, 37

Mackenzie Valley pipeline. *See under* Northern Canada
Madavo, Callisto 176
Marginal change 5, 16, 195
Montreal 47, 74
Mumford, Lewis 116
Muskoka Lakes 95-6

National Capital Commission (NCC), Canada. *See under* Ottawa-Hull
National Capital Region 142-7
National Housing Act, 1949 (Canada). *See under* Canada, land policy, Federal land policy
National Parks Act (Canada). *See under* Recreation: public land ownership
Native peoples. *See under* Northern Canada
Neighbourhoods. *See under* Human settlements
Network organizations 17-18
 National Economic Development Organization 17

Network organizations *(cont.)*
  Norwegian hydro industrial
    democracy project 17
  Tennessee Valley Authority 17
Northern Canada 83-4, 97-101
  communal land ownership 83-4
  ecological sensitivity 99
  energy potential 97, 99, 100
  Mackenzie Valley pipeline 85,
    99, 101
  Native peoples 6, 83, 85, 98-
    100, 101
  Panarctic (Petrocan) 98
  public land ownership 98, 99
  territorial governments 98, 99-
    100
Northern Canada, Natural Re-
    sources & Energy Branch (De-
    partment of Indian & Northern
    Affairs) 97-8
  development philosophy 98
  northern program 98
Northern Canada, Northwest Terri-
    tories 97, 101
  Yellowknife 98, 100
Northern Canada, Yukon Terri-
    tory 97
  Whitehorse 98, 100
Nuder, Ants xiii, 5, 7

Ontario, land policy 15, 108-9,
    116-20, 121-2, 131, 140
  eastern Ontario, industrial loca-
    tion 118
  Home Ownership Made Easy
    (HOME) 108, 121
  land banking 116-20, 121-2,
    128, 131, 132
  land survey 28
  Ontario Housing Corporation
    (OHC) 119, 131, 133, 137
  Ontario Planning and Develop-
    ment Act, 1973 117
  Ministry of Housing 136
  Ministry of Transport and Com-
    munications 89
  Ministry of Treasury, Economics
    & Intergovernmental Affairs
    (TEIGA) 131-2
  National Capital Region 142-7
  Niagara Escarpment 29, 91, 117,
    118

Oakville 117, 139
outdoor recreation 94-7
Pickering 128, 132, 140-1
Prescott land assembly 118
Ontario Land Corporation Act
    118, 119, 120; new towns pro-
    gram 118, 135
Ottawa-Hull 110, 134, 137-8,
    142-7
  LeBreton Flats Project 134,
    143, 146, 147
  National Capital Commission
    110, 142-7
  Neapean Township 137-9
  Regional Municipality of Ottawa-
    Carleton (RMOC) 146
  Woodruff Project 134

Page, John xiii, 6, 84
Penalosa, Enrique xiii, 4, 7, 198
Planning 10, 11-12, 13, 24, 46,
    47, 59, 63, 127
  biocentric approach 29
  constituency-based 17
  land policy 46-56
  large-scale 30-3, 39, 44, 66
  neighbourhood 26
  new communities 118, 135
  non-urban land 85, 91-4
  public participation 24-7
  urban renewal 32, 135-6
  zoning 6, 9, 47
Prince Edward Island, land policy
    15, 125
  Land Development Corporation
    125
Private developer 12, 128, 134,
    136, 139-41
Private land
  as a commodity 6, 9, 10, 11, 64,
    196
  values 3, 10, 11, 126
Private land market
  critique 4, 9, 68, 197
  finance capitalism 109, 126,
    127, 199-200
  impoverishment of poor 4, 9, 10
  inequitable distribution of bene-
    fits 10, 35, 48
  management practices 35-6
  social/community costs 3, 5, 9,
    10-11, 48, 128

speculation   10, 11, 43, 48, 59-
  60, 109, 196-7
unearned income   3-4, 5, 7, 10,
  35, 38, 48, 64
urban problems   4, 9, 42, 129
Private land ownership   4, 5, 14,
  15, 112
constitutional support   9
freehold rights   73
government regulation   3, 4, 62
government support   14, 109,
  200
ideology/values   3, 16, 29, 36,
  112, 196
land and citizenship   3, 13
land development   12, 139
public planning   47-8, 63-4
urban growth   126-7
Public land ownership, Canada
  xiv, 14, 35, 37, 61, 105, 107-
  10, 112-14, 129
Public land ownership, developing
  countries. *See under* Developing
  countries
Public land ownership, evaluation
  and assessment   14, 37-40, 56,
  57-62, 79-81, 120-2, 195-201
Public land ownership, implementation techniques   xii, xiii, 5-6,
  38, 45, 49-55, 79-81, 195, 196
betterment tax   37, 47-8, 49-50,
  52, 53, 58, 70
city purchase   53
fee simple interest   57
leasehold/unification of reversion   38, 40, 54-5, 57-8, 59,
  61, 74-5
nationalization   6, 55, 57, 58
pooling/reallocation   51
Public land assembly   31, 32, 39,
  53-4, 57, 65, 66-8, 70-1, 73, 80,
  110, 112-14, 118, 122-5, 130,
  131, 137, 139, 143
purchase development land   53
site value tax   39, 50-1, 65
transfer/unification of development rights   40, 49, 51, 57-8,
  73-4
zoning   6, 9, 47
Public land ownership, land as a
  resource   xiii, 8, 27-30, 83-6,
  87-8, 89-90. *See also* Urban

natural environments
agricultural land   36, 42, 68, 85,
  91-4, 117, 118, 123, 125
biocentric planning   29
ecological fragility   6, 36, 84, 99
ecosystems   84, 90, 99
forest   84, 95
historical/cultural landscapes   36,
  84, 96
life support systems   27, 29-30,
  84
recreational space   36, 42, 74,
  85, 88, 94-7, 117
water supplies   27-8, 87-8
wildlife habitat   88
Public land ownership, meta problems   85
energy consumption   85, 97, 99,
  100
environmental decay   84-5, 99
food production   8, 29
landscape quality   85
population growth   9, 42
urban problems/urbanization   8, 9
Public land ownership, objectives/
  values   xi, 4, 7, 37, 42, 45, 46,
  56, 58, 114-15, 195-6
as a planning tool   5, 35, 42, 43,
  195
betterment levy   58, 60
distribution of benefits/equal-
  ity   37
land as human right   4, 5, 12, 43
land as ideological issue   36, 37
land management   4, 37, 40, 79,
  86, 129, 196
land as public trust   4, 10
land use/planning benefits   xi,
  37, 38-9, 59, 61, 63-4, 113,
  117, 197
price control   11, 58, 59-60, 64
redistribution of wealth/social
  justice   xi, 4, 5, 196, 197
Public land ownership, public participation   6, 24-7, 45, 199
Public land ownership, social impact   197-9
Public land pooling/reallocation
  51
Lex Adickes (Germany)   51
Parliamentary Enclosure Acts
  (UK)   51

Public service infrastructure 9, 62-3

Quebec 85

Rawson, Mary 109
Recreation, public land ownership 94-7
  British national park system 86, 96-7
  National Parks Act (Canada) 84
  Niagara Escarpment 29, 91, 117
  Ontario Hydro Electric Commission 95
  recreation cottages 95
  recreation demand 94-5
  "wilderness" areas 95
Red Deer, Alberta 72
Roberts, Neal 113
Rumm, Sommer 110, 113
Rural/urban fringe 91-4
Ryan, J.P. 108, 113

Saskatoon, Alberta 40, 71, 72-3, 79, 80, 141
Senegal 151, 166-70, 175
  Law On National Domain 166-70
Small-scale: communities (Ontario) 17
  development 31, 117, 201
  ownership 32
Snyder, Francis 151
Soviet Union, state planning 41
  Moscow 41
Speculation. See under Land values/prices; Private land market: critique
Sri Lanka, land policy 151, 171-4
  economy 171-2
Stamp, Patricia xiv
Strong, Ann Louise 36
Substantial innovation 5, 16-17, 18, 200, 201
Sweden/land policy 5, 7, 19-23
  absolute ownership, impact 222
  building rights 20
  communal land ownership 5, 20, 21-2
  corrective legislation 22-3, 190-1
  freehold purchase 21
  ground rents 20-1

mining rights 20, 22
Stockholm 44, 53, 78-9

Tanzania 174
Teron, William 113
Third World 149-92. See also under Developing countries
Toronto-Centred Region 28, 128
  Central Ontario Lakeshore Urban Complex (COLUC) 29
  parkway belt 29-30, 117
Toronto, City of 109, 126-9, 132
  Central Area Plan 109, 127-8
  housing policy 128, 132-5
  urban renewal 135-6
Toronto, metropolitan area 44, 47, 78, 95, 117, 126-9
  fringe planning control 91-2
  land banking 132-5
  Metro Toronto and Regional Conservation Authority 89
  ravine management 87, 89-91
  shoreline management 90

United Kingdom, land policy 33, 43, 46-7, 49-56, 200
  Central Land Board 69
  Community Land Act, 1975 46, 53, 54-5, 56
  Conservative government 52-3, 70
  Development Gains Tax, 1974 49
  Development Land Tax (DLT), 1976 49, 54, 70
  green belt 47, 52, 53
  Labour government 52-3, 54-5
  Land Commission Act, 1967 37, 49, 69-70
  Land Compensation Act, 1973 50
  London 43, 78
  new towns 41-2
  Town and Country Planning Act, 1947 49, 51-2, 53, 54, 69, 73
  Uthwatt Report, 1942 40, 49, 51, 73
  White Paper on "Land," 1974 69
United Nations, Conference on Human Settlements (Habitat), 1976 xii, 8, 13
  Seminar on Land Use, Madrid, 1971 8, 10-11

United States, land policy   31, 40,
    42, 55, 66-8, 107
Environmental Protection Act
    100
Housing & Community Develop-
    ment Act, 1974   107
Public land ownership   36-7;
    Advisory Commission on Inter-
    governmental Relations, 1968
    107; institutionalization   107;
    National Commission on Urban
    Problems, 1968   107; Presi-
    dent's Committee on Urban
    Housing, 1969   107; Presi-
    dent's Task Force on Suburban
    Problems, 1968   107; support
    for   107
Urban growth/development   xi,
    4, 7, 9, 12, 14, 24, 31-2, 41, 63,
    66, 126, 131, 139
Cleveland   31
Moscow   41
Urban natural environments   85,
    87-8, 89-90

air quality   87
forestry needs   89
management   89
public safety   88
ravines   87, 89
recreation space   88
vegetation   87, 88, 89
water quality   87-8
wildlife   88
Uthwatt Report, 1942 (UK). *See
    under* United Kingdom, land
    policy

Vancouver, B.C.   32, 61, 72, 78,
    109, 132

Water   27-8, 87-8
White, John   108-9, 113
Wilkinson, Paul   xiii, 85

York University Public Land Own-
    ership Conference, 1975   xii

About the Editors

Dalton Kehoe is an Associate Professor of Social Science at York University and is coordinator of Canada's largest undergraduate program of urban studies. He is an urban sociologist with interests in citizen participation at various levels of urban decision making, and in the development of local community in large urban areas. Professor Kehoe is an Associate of the Institute of Environmental Research which is currently introducing comprehensive social planning into the development of a large downtown residential project in Canada's capital city. He is just completing an introductory sociology text and working as a co-author of several papers on the process and problems of community-centred social planning.

David Morley is an urban geographer who, after serving in university departments in Australia, England, and Canada, joined the new transdisciplinary Faculty of Environmental Studies at York University, where he is an Associate Professor. This led to his involvement in a variety of projects dealing with the management of human environments and its policy implications. Recent work has included the study of alternative transportation environments, social environmental impact studies, the environmental implication of "limits to growth" policies, and the study of neighbourhood change. Professor Morley is interested in public policy innovation through the adaptation of institutions associated with planning urban and regional environments.

Stuart B. Proudfoot is an Assistant Professor in the Faculty of Administrative Studies at York University and a Ph.D. candidate in Political Science at the University of Michigan. He has been a research assistant for the private Planning Association of Canada (now the C.D. Howe Research Institute) in Montreal and a consultant to the Canadian Institute for Development Aid. He teaches urban politics, with special interest in the politics of urban planning and development and public policy analysis. Professor Proudfoot's current research is focused on how the urban zoning process reflects values. In particular, he has been investigating how urban planning has been altered by the politicization of the development process in Toronto.

Neal A. Roberts is an Associate Professor at the Osgoode Hall Law School of York University and is also cross-appointed to the Faculty of Environmental Studies. His graduate work was in both the disciplines of law and political science and he has taught at law schools in England and Canada. He is the author of *The Reform of Planning Law* (1976), a study of the legal, political, and administrative reform of the British Land Use Planning System. Professor Roberts is currently engaged in a study of the government land development programs of seven industrialized countries, and the fruits of that work will appear in the future as a Lexington Books publication.